JUDGES AND THEIR AUDIENCES

JUDGES AND THEIR AUDIENCES

A Perspective on Judicial Behavior

Lawrence Baum

PRINCETON UNIVERSITY PRESS

PRINCETON AND OXFORD

Copyright © 2006 by Princeton University Press
Published by Princeton University Press, 41 William Street, Princeton, New Jersey 08540
In the United Kingdom: Princeton University Press, 6 Oxford Street, Woodstock,
Oxfordshire OX20 1TW

Third printing, and first paperback printing, 2008
Paperback ISBN: 978-0-691-13827-5

The Library of Congress has cataloged the cloth edition of this book as follows

Baum, Lawrence
Judges and their audiences : a perspective on judicial behavior / Lawrence Baum.
p.   cm.
Includes bibliographical references and index.
ISBN-13: 978-0-691-12493-3 (cloth : alk. paper)
ISBN-10: 0-691-12493-0 (cloth : alk. paper)
1. Judges—United States. 2. Judicial process—United States.
3. Law—Psychological aspects.
KF8775.B378 2006
347.73'14—dc22   2005054514

British Library Cataloging-in-Publication Data is available

This book has been composed in Sabon

Printed on acid-free paper. ∞

press.princeton.edu

Printed in the United States of America

3   5   7   9   10   8   6   4

To Carol

CONTENTS

TABLES

PREFACE

PEOPLE ARE COMPLICATED. We try to achieve a lot of things, and those things often conflict with each other. Our actions flow from both logic and emotion. Because of these complexities, it can be difficult to understand the behavior of other people or even our own behavior.

Political scientists who study judicial behavior generally rely on a few models of behavior that have much in common with each other. In the models that dominate the field, judges are not very complicated. As depicted in these models, judges on many courts want only one thing, good legal policy as they define it. They act in a logical, unemotional way to pursue that goal. Thus these models rule out of consideration a great deal—all of judges' emotions and most of the goals they seek to achieve.

All models of human behavior simplify reality, and even highly simplified models can be very useful. Indeed, such models facilitate the study of behavior by making analysis more manageable. The simplified models that scholars employ to study judges have done much to help us understand judicial decision making, and our understanding continues to grow.

And yet these models are not entirely satisfying, primarily because they rule out so much. It is possible that what they leave aside is not very important to judging. Perhaps most of judges' goals and all their emotions affect only their lives outside court, not their work in court. But that seems unlikely: the line between those two segments of judges' lives could hardly be that sharp. Besides, some of the judicial behavior that we observe does not fit comfortably within the simplified models that scholars employ.

For these reasons it seems worthwhile to step outside the standard models and consider judges' behavior from other vantage points. Several years ago I began to think about what I call judges' personal audiences. These are the people whose esteem judges want for its own sake, not because that esteem might help them make good legal policy or achieve some other end. In thinking about personal audiences, I focused on two questions. First, what kinds of audiences are likely to be most important to judges? Second, how might judges' interest in approval from those audiences affect their behavior as judges?

Thinking about those questions led me to a perspective on judicial behavior that is based on judges' relationships with their audiences. Not everything about judicial behavior can be understood from that perspective, but these relationships illuminate a good deal about what judges do. Consideration of judges' concern with what their audiences think of them helps in understanding some aspects of judicial behavior that the dominant models in their current forms do not encompass. It also suggests new ways to understand familiar patterns of judicial behavior.

This book presents the perspective that resulted from my thinking about judges and their audiences. I begin in chapter 1 by discussing what I see as the limitations of the dominant models of judicial behavior. In chapter 2, I draw on the scholarship in social psychology to develop a conception of judging as self-presentation to a judge's audiences.

The three chapters that follow examine a range of audiences that might be important to judges. Chapter 3 applies the conception of judging developed in chapter 2 to judicial audiences that scholars often take into account—court colleagues, the general public, and the other branches of government. The analyses of these audiences lead to conclusions about the extent and form of their influence on judges, and some of these conclusions differ considerably from the depictions of these audiences in the dominant models. Chapters 4 and 5 consider personal audiences to which scholars give little attention, such as social and political groups with which judges identify. I argue that these audiences can have fundamental effects on judges' choices, effects that need to be taken into account to achieve a more comprehensive explanation of judicial behavior.

Chapter 6 pulls together the implications of the book's explorations of judicial audiences. The chapter suggests several ways that a perspective based on judges' relationships with their audiences can be used in the study of judicial behavior. This perspective strengthens the motivational bases for the dominant models of judicial behavior, helps in adjudicating disagreements among these models, and identifies ways in which they could usefully be modified. This perspective also points to new lines of inquiry into the bases for judges' choices.

In these ways, I argue, the vantage point of audience can enhance our capacity to explain those choices. In turn, my hope is that this book's use of that vantage point contributes to our collective efforts to gain a better understanding of judicial behavior.

ACKNOWLEDGMENTS

IN WRITING THIS BOOK I benefited from a great deal of help, and it is a pleasure to acknowledge those who provided assistance.

I received very good help in compiling information from Brett Curry, Joe Lyons, and Karen Swenson. Their work provided much of the raw material that I use, and that material also helped me in developing the lines of argument that are presented here.

The book incorporates research I have done in collaboration with Corey Ditslear on the selection of Supreme Court clerks and with Lori Hausegger on the relationship between the Supreme Court and Congress. I appreciate their allowing me to use that research, and I also appreciate the insights I gained from working with them. Brandon Bartels shared with me the data he collected on salient Supreme Court cases, data used in some analyses in chapter 5.

A number of professional colleagues provided ideas, reactions, and sources on topics. They include Brandon Bartels, Brad Canon, Howard Gillman, Mark Graber, Clarissa Hayward, Randy Hodson, Ted Hopf, Kent Jennings, Jon Keller, Dean Lacy, Tom Nelson, John Parrish, Jim Pfiffner, Kira Sanbonmatsu, Jeff Segal, Don Sylvan, and Herb Weisberg. Lew Bateman gave me useful ideas and encouragement for development of the book. Roy Flemming and Lynn Mather each offered a number of helpful ideas about issues that I address. Mike MacKuen and Randy Schweller made very helpful suggestions for empirical inquiries that I then pursued. I presented parts of the book's arguments and evidence in seminars at Texas Tech University, the University of New Orleans, the University of North Carolina at Chapel Hill, and the University of North Texas. Comments and suggestions at those seminars were quite useful.

Jim Brudney and Bob Arkin read and commented on parts of the manuscript on which they have special expertise. Lori Hausegger and David Klein read each chapter and provided long lists of helpful ideas. I appreciate their very substantial contributions. The anonymous reviewers of the manuscript for Princeton University Press made insightful comments that improved the book considerably.

I received valuable assistance from the people I worked with at the Press. I appreciate all the help that Mark Bellis, Jennifer Nippins, and Richard Isomaki gave me. Chuck Myers did a great deal to make this book possible, and I am very glad that I have had the opportunity to work with him.

I have already thanked a number of colleagues at Ohio State University for their contributions. I owe more general thanks to my colleagues for what I have learned from them over the years, a good deal of which has worked its way into this study. I am especially indebted to Greg Caldeira and Elliot Slotnick for that assistance. I appreciate the leave provided by Ohio State, which made it possible to focus on completion of the book. During most of the period that I worked on it Paul Beck was chair of the political science department, and in a number of ways he helped me to do the work that resulted in the book.

The argument incorporates Carol Mock's comments on a number of specific matters. Even more important are the perspectives on theoretical issues that I have gained from talking with her over the years.

Those who provided this help do not necessarily agree with what I have to say, and they should not be held responsible for it. Nor, of course, are they responsible for any limitations that remain. Whatever those limitations may be, the book has benefited a great deal from all the help I received.

JUDGES AND THEIR AUDIENCES

Chapter 1

THINKING ABOUT JUDICIAL BEHAVIOR

In 1989, Cincinnati Reds manager Pete Rose faced an investigation of his alleged gambling activities by major league baseball. Rose's attorneys filed suit to block the investigation, and they steered the case to a Cincinnati judge who faced re-election in 1990. That judge, Norbert Nadel, allowed his announcement of a decision to be televised. When he "started the hearing with a microphone check," according to one writer, "you knew Pete Rose had the home-court advantage" (*Cleveland Plain Dealer* 1989). Indeed, the ruling gave Rose what he wanted. (*Cincinnati Enquirer* 1989)

As George W. Bush ran for president in 2000, commentators speculated about possible candidates for Bush appointments to the Supreme Court. J. Harvie Wilkinson and J. Michael Luttig, two subjects of the speculation, sat on the federal court of appeals for the Fourth Circuit in Virginia. In two cases decided in June 2000, Luttig wrote opinions attacking relatively liberal positions that Wilkinson was taking. In an environmental case Luttig linked Wilkinson's position with that of two liberal Supreme Court justices. In a freedom of speech case Luttig used Wilkinson's name more than fifty times, with four of the mentions coming in a paragraph that described sexually explicit material related to the case. (*Urofsky v. Gilmore* 2000; *Gibbs v. Babbitt* 2000)

On the day in 1992 that the Supreme Court announced its decision in *Planned Parenthood v. Casey*, Justice Anthony Kennedy talked with a legal reporter in his chambers before the announcement. Looking through his window at the crowd of demonstrators on both sides of the abortion issue, Kennedy referred to the impending decision in which he coauthored the decisive opinion. "Sometimes you don't know if you're Caesar about to cross the Rubicon or Captain Queeg cutting your own tow line." Shortly before taking the bench, Kennedy asked to be alone. "I need to brood," he explained. "I generally brood, as all of us do on the bench, just before we go on. It's a moment of quiet around here to search your soul and your conscience." (T. Carter 1992 39–40, 103)

A few weeks earlier, Justice Harry Blackmun spoke for an hour at a luncheon meeting of the Legal Aid Society in San Francisco. During his talk Blackmun read some of the fan mail he received from the public. He also expressed his disappointment about the Supreme Court's growing conservatism on civil liberties issues. "It seems to get a little lonely. If I had more sense, I suppose I would turn in my suit." According to a reporter, this statement elicited "a chorus of 'No!' " Blackmun responded that he would "stay there for the moment." (Holding 1992)

Justice Antonin Scalia frequently speaks in public about his views on legal matters. In these talks he sometimes discusses issues that the Supreme Court addresses, such as capital punishment and the church-state relationship. In a 2003 speech, for example, Scalia criticized a federal court of appeals ruling that inclusion of "under God" in the Pledge of Allegiance violated the First Amendment (Salmon 2003). Nine months later, when the Supreme Court voted to review that ruling in *Elk Grove v. Newdow*, Scalia acceded to the plaintiff's request that he recuse himself from the case. (Lane 2003)

THE FIVE EPISODES just described are diverse in form, but they also have something in common: all of these judges were communicating with sets of people and trying to influence the perceptions of those audiences. In quite different ways they all sought to present themselves in a favorable light and, in the case of Judge Luttig, to cast an unfavorable light on a colleague (A. Cooper 2000).

The motivations of the judges in the first two episodes are uncertain, but each judge may have perceived a concrete advantage to his actions. Judge Nadel could anticipate that gaining the maximum publicity for his ruling in favor of a popular figure would enhance his prospects for reelection the next year. Judge Luttig could hope that by calling attention to the differences between his legal positions and those of a possible rival for promotion, he was advancing his candidacy.

Indeed, these judges' career goals might have influenced the substance of their decisions. Judge Nadel had good reason to think that his chances for reelection would improve if his ruling was consistent with the strong views of many Cincinnati voters. Judge Luttig probably would have taken the same general positions even if he had no interest in promotion, because those positions were consistent with his well-established conservatism. But the value of distinguishing himself from Judge Wilkinson may have led Luttig to accentuate his conservative stances on free speech and environmental protection in these cases.[1]

---

[1] Four years later, at a time when Chief Justice Rehnquist's health problems led to the expectation of an imminent vacancy on the Supreme Court, Judge Luttig wrote a concurring opinion in a death penalty case to attack Judge Wilkinson's prodefendant dissent in strong terms. *Humphries v. Ozmint* (4th Cir. 2005). Also of interest are the dueling opinions of Wilkinson and Luttig in *Robles v. Prince George's County* (4th Cir. 2002), a case in which Luttig took the more liberal position.

Of the scholars who study judicial behavior, most would see these possibilities as credible. These scholars typically give limited attention to judges' career goals, in part because their field focuses on the Supreme Court. Still, few would reject the proposition that judges with insecure tenure or prospects for promotion sometimes act with those considerations in mind (but see Posner 1995, 111).

The motivations of the Supreme Court justices in the other three episodes do not have as straightforward an explanation. What did these justices expect to gain from their public expressions? With life terms on the highest court, they could not be seeking retention in their positions or promotion to another position—except, perhaps, chief justice.[2] Students of the Supreme Court emphasize the justices' interest in the substance of legal policy, in making good law or good policy, more or less to the exclusion of other goals. Perhaps these three justices thought they were advancing their conceptions of good law or good policy in some fashion. It is difficult, however, to see how Kennedy or Blackmun could do much to achieve those goals through the public expressions I described earlier.

In the case of Justice Scalia, this explanation is more plausible. Scalia may seek to shape attitudes about legal issues within the public and the legal community, ultimately helping to win judicial support for the policies he favors. But this is a strategy with a highly uncertain and distant payoff, and that potential payoff would not seem to merit even the limited efforts required to undertake it. Moreover, as Scalia's recusal illustrates, the effects can be negative as well as positive.

Yet the behavior of these justices does not defy explanation. Presented with descriptions of the three episodes, most people outside the academic world would have a ready explanation: judges, like other people, get satisfaction from perceiving that other people view them positively. If Justice Kennedy wanted to be seen as a serious and thoughtful jurist, if Justice Blackmun liked to hear that some fellow lawyers appreciated his presence on the Court, if Justice Scalia enjoyed presenting his positions to groups that agreed with him, those motivations accord with what we know about human nature. Nor, I suspect, would most students of judicial behavior

[2] Both Justice Kennedy and Justice Scalia were mentioned as potential candidates for that position. Kennedy's creation of a "Dialogue on Freedom" program in which the participants included Laura Bush and Senator Edward Kennedy aroused speculation that he was subtly campaigning for chief justice (Lane 2002). In 2005 some people thought that Scalia was campaigning for the position by demonstrating his personal charm in public appearances (Carney and Cooper 2005). But Scalia's public expressions of his views and Kennedy's interview would seem more likely to reduce their chances for promotion than to enhance them.

dissent from this interpretation. After all, these scholars seek to explain judges' choices in cases, not the choices they make in other settings.[3]

But what if a desire for approval actually affected the positions these justices took in cases? Perhaps Kennedy's unexpected position in *Planned Parenthood v. Casey*, upholding the bulk of what the Court had decided in *Roe v. Wade*, reflected an interest in approval from the lawyers to whom he was talking through a reporter. Perhaps Blackmun was reinforced in his shift toward a more liberal record by the favorable reactions of liberal groups such as the one to which he spoke. Perhaps Scalia takes more extreme positions than he otherwise would in order to win accolades from conservative groups with which he interacts.

Students of judicial behavior might agree that this type of influence exists. But their research hardly ever takes it into account, because it involves a motivation that does not fit in the models that dominate scholarship on judicial behavior in political science. In those models judges are impervious to influence from others, or they are susceptible to this influence only for instrumental reasons—in the case of the Supreme Court, as a means to help them achieve good legal policy.

This book departs from those conceptions of the relationship between judges and their audiences. I argue that judges care about the regard of salient audiences because they like that regard in itself, not just as a means to other ends.[4] Further, I argue, judges' interest in what their audiences think of them has fundamental effects on their behavior as decision makers. Through their choices in cases, judges engage in self-presentation to audiences whose esteem is important to them.

Because this argument does not fit within the dominant models, it offers a different perspective. The central purpose of this book is to show how that perspective can enhance our understanding of judges' choices. This perspective is intended as a means to think in new ways about issues in judicial behavior and, in the process, to strengthen the dominant models.

The book's inquiry is limited to courts in the United States. I give primary attention to higher courts, especially the Supreme Court.[5] That em-

---

[3] One kind of choice that students of judicial behavior usually leave aside is whether or not to become a judge. With a few exceptions, I follow the same practice. Richard Posner (1995, ch. 3) concluded that the motivations to become a judge may be quite different from the motivations for choosing particular positions in cases. However, Payne and Woshinsky (1972) argued that the motives that bring people into politics affect their behavior as officeholders, and Caldeira (1977) and Sarat (1977) applied that perspective to trial judges.

[4] In the book I use the term *regard* in its meaning of a positive view about a person. I use *esteem* and *approval* as synonyms for regard, and I occasionally refer to popularity and respect as more specific elements of regard.

[5] Of course, the line between higher and lower courts is not sharp. As a group, students of judicial behavior do the preponderance of their research on federal courts and state supreme courts, and I focus on those sets of courts.

phasis mirrors the subject matter of scholarship on judicial behavior. Further, it is in higher courts that the perspective of audiences raises the most serious challenges to existing understandings of judicial behavior. However, my interest extends to lower courts. As I discuss in chapter 6, a perspective based on judges' relationships with their audiences is one means to study lower courts in the same terms as higher courts.[6]

The place to begin my inquiry is with the dominant models.[7] The next three sections of the chapter review those models with the aim of identifying their assumptions, examining the implications of those assumptions, and considering their limitations. The final section sketches out an audience-based perspective as a means to expand our understanding of judicial behavior.

At the outset, I should underline a distinction between the views of scholars and the scope of the models they employ. I emphasize the restrictive assumptions of the dominant models concerning judges' motivations. Models are intended to simplify reality for analytic purposes, and many scholars who adopt those models would accept broader conceptions of judicial motives. Some explicitly caution that their models do not fully encompass the forces that shape judicial behavior (e.g., Maltzman, Spriggs, and Wahlbeck 2000, 27–28; see Epstein and Knight 1998, 49). Thus I characterize not the views of scholars in the field but the models that dominate research in the field.

MODELS OF JUDICIAL BEHAVIOR

The scholarship on higher courts has depicted three ideal types of judicial behavior, typically labeled legal, attitudinal, and strategic. In a pure legal model, judges want only to interpret the law as well as possible. For this reason they choose between alternative case outcomes and doctrinal positions on the basis of their legal merits. In a pure attitudinal model judges want only to make good public policy, so they choose between alternatives on the basis of their merits as policy. In most pure strategic models judges seek to make good policy, but they define good policy in terms of

---

[6] Like judges, other participants in the legal process are influenced by their own audiences. Mather and Yngvesson (1980–81; see Yngvesson and Mather 1983) delineate how audiences shape the development and outcomes of legal disputes. That impact is especially evident in lower courts, though it extends to higher courts as well. Because my subject is judges, the book will not consider this broader impact of audiences.

[7] In this chapter I focus on models and research in political science. To a considerable but lesser degree, students of judicial behavior in other disciplines adopt similar models explicitly or implicitly. As I note later, however, a number of economists and legal scholars have pointed to a wider range of judicial motivations than political scientists typically consider.

outcomes in their court and in government as a whole. Thus they may deviate from their most preferred policy position in a case as a way of helping to secure the best outcome.

In practice, the picture is more complicated. Scholars have developed variants of the three ideal types, and only one of those types—the strategic type—currently has many adherents in its pure form. I begin by considering models based on the strategic type and then turn to the mixed models that developed from the other types.[8]

Strategic Models

Like related terms, *strategic* is used in various ways (see Baum 1997, 90 n. 2; Caminker 1999). My summary of strategic models indicates my own usage of the term. Strategic judges consider the effects of their choices on collective outcomes, both in their own court and in the broader judicial and policy arenas. In other words, they do not simply do the right thing as they see it, such as voting for the most desirable policy on freedom of speech. Rather, they seek to have the right thing triumph in their court's decision and, more important, in public policy as a whole. For this reason, whenever strategic judges choose among alternative courses of action, they think ahead to the prospective consequences and choose the course that does most to advance their goals in the long term.[9]

To achieve this result, judges might vote and write opinions that differ from their own conceptions of the right thing. Thus we cannot assume that a judge's vote in a freedom of speech case fully reflects the judge's conception of good policy. If the goal of an appellate judge is to advance freedom of speech as much as possible, she might take a more moderate position in a particular case in order to win majority support for a pro–free speech ruling by her court. The judge might also try to avoid a decision that provokes Congress to enact legislation limiting free speech.

Judges could act strategically to advance a variety of goals, not just good policy. State judges who lack life terms might balance policy goals against their interest in remaining judges (e.g., M. Hall 1992; Langer 2002). Judges might seek to advance their conceptions of good law (Ferejohn and Weingast 1992) or strive to achieve both good law and good policy (Spiller and Tiller 1996). But in most strategic models that are applied to federal courts, judges act solely on the goal of achieving good policy.

[8] The various positions that students of judicial behavior espouse are examined in Maveety 2003.

[9] I will refer frequently to goals and motives or motivations. Goals can be thought of as ends that people try to achieve, and motives as reasons to pursue those ends, but the two concepts are intertwined.

As suggested already, strategic policy-oriented judges direct their efforts at multiple objects. They consider colleagues on their own court (Maltzman, Spriggs, and Wahlbeck 2000; Hammond, Bonneau, and Sheehan 2005) and judges on other courts (Songer, Segal, and Cameron 1994; Cameron, Segal, and Songer 2000). They also concern themselves with the other branches of government (Spiller and Gely 1992; Schwartz, Spiller, and Urbiztondo 1994; Epstein, Knight, and Martin 2001) and the general public (Epstein and Knight 1998, 157–77). As a result, the strategic judge is subject to influence from a variety of sources. One possible result underlines the impact of strategy: judges who do not care about making good law nonetheless might base their decisions on legal considerations, because they think the public expects them to act on a legal basis. They do so in the belief that if they act in accord with public expectations, the public will be more willing to accept and comply with their decisions (Epstein and Knight 1998, 163–77; see Easterbrook 1992, 287).

Models of strategic judges who are devoted to achieving good policy have some very attractive features. They provide a comprehensive and coherent framework for the analysis of judicial behavior. They also promote rigor in the analysis of that behavior. Primarily because of these virtues, strategic models have become highly influential, and a strategic conception of judicial behavior is now the closest thing to a conventional wisdom about judicial behavior (see Epstein and Knight 2000).

Attitudinal and Quasi-Attitudinal Models

In the terms used in rational choice analysis, judges of pure attitudinal models act sincerely (or naively) rather than strategically. Devoted to good policy as a goal, attitudinal judges act directly on their policy preferences without calculating the consequences of their choices. They cast votes and write opinions that perfectly reflect their own views, regardless of what their court colleagues and other policymakers might do in response. In this model a judge's vote on an issue involving freedom of speech reflects solely what the judge thinks is good policy on the issue in question.

In the judicial behavior scholarship of the 1960s and 1970s, something like a pure attitudinal model was the leading approach to the study of the Supreme Court (e.g., Schubert 1965; Spaeth 1979). Scholars frequently applied attitudinal models to other courts as well, though often implicitly. At the same time, students of judicial behavior—including adherents to attitudinal models—were analyzing strategy in decision making (Schubert 1963; W. Murphy 1964; Rohde and Spaeth 1976, chs. 8–9). For this reason some accounts of judicial behavior appeared to lack theoretical coherence.

Since the 1990s some scholars have overcome this problem by adopting fully strategic models of judicial behavior. Meanwhile, the leading proponents of the attitudinal approach have made more explicit how they integrate strategy into their approach (Segal and Spaeth 2002). They have set aside the original premise of the attitudinal model that judges act sincerely on their policy preferences: as they now see it, judges think strategically. But they argue that in two respects, strategic considerations have only limited impact on the positions of Supreme Court justices. First, justices seldom have to modify their positions to accommodate the preferences of those outside the Court, such as Congress and the general public (Segal and Spaeth 2002, 326–49, 424–48; Segal 1997). Second, while justices act strategically in regard to their colleagues at preliminary stages of decision (such as case selection), they need not do so when they vote on case outcomes, since final votes on outcomes are the last stage in the decision process (Segal and Spaeth 2002, 96–97).

Segal and Spaeth's depiction of the Supreme Court, then, is a hybrid of ideal types. Justices think strategically, but for the most part they act attitudinally. While other scholars have not explicitly adopted this formulation, it is implicit in much of the research on judicial behavior.

Models with a Legal Component

The judge who conforms to the legal ideal type seeks only to make good law. In other words, this judge aims to interpret the law accurately, without concern for the desirability of the policies that result. Faced with a free speech case, the law-minded judge simply seeks the best interpretation of the First Amendment.

This explanation of judicial behavior maintains a foothold in law school teaching and exerts some influence on legal scholarship (Cross and Nelson 2001, 1439–43). But at least since the legal realist movement, few scholars have fully accepted this explanation (W. Fisher, Horwitz, and Reed 1993; R. Smith 1994). However, legal realists differed in the role they ascribed to the law. Those who could be called radical legal realists largely rejected the law as a basis for judicial choice (e.g., J. Frank 1930), a position taken more recently by critical legal theorists (Dalton 1985; D'Amato 1989). In contrast, moderate legal realists left room for the law in judges' decision calculus (e.g., Cardozo 1921). In their conception, judges who decide an issue involving freedom of speech make their choices on the basis of both what they deem to be good policy and how they think the First Amendment is best interpreted.

This moderate version of legal realism is implicit in much of the research by legal scholars. It has also been accepted by some political scientists such as C. Herman Pritchett, a key figure in the movement to analyze judicial behavior systematically (see, e.g., Pritchett 1954). These scholars agree that judges' policy preferences play a substantial part and perhaps the largest part in judicial decisions. But they argue that legal considerations also play a part, chiefly because judges reach decisions within a legal framework.

To a degree, advocates of the other models have kept adherents to moderate realism on the defensive (Gillman 2001b, 466). But their position has achieved something of a revival in a school that is usually labeled historical institutionalism (R. Smith 1988; Clayton 1999; Gillman 1999; "Courts" 1999; Whittington 2000). Moreover, some scholars from outside this school incorporate legal considerations into their analyses of judicial behavior (H. Perry 1991; Songer and Lindquist 1996; D. Klein 2002; Richards and Kritzer 2002; Kritzer and Richards 2003).

Moderate legal realists who focus on the interplay between legal and policy considerations give limited attention to strategy. However, historical institutionalism emphasizes the links between courts and the broader political regime (Gillman 2004). Gillman (1997) and Graber (2004) made explicit what is implicit in some writings by moderate realists: judges act strategically, but their strategic behavior is in the service of both legal and policy goals. Indeed, it has been suggested, much of the strategic interaction that occurs within appellate courts should be understood as an effort to enhance coherence in the law by achieving an opinion that a majority of judges can support (Kornhauser and Sager 1993, 52–53; Edwards 2003).

SHARED ASSUMPTIONS: THE JUDGE AS MR. SPOCK

The competing models of judicial behavior differ on a number of issues, ranging from the place of law in judging to the public's influence on the Supreme Court. Much of the scholarship in the field focuses on these differences, as scholars advocate particular positions and conduct research on points of disagreement among models.

Significant as these differences are, the issues on which these models agree are even more fundamental. All the major models share the premise that policy considerations powerfully influence the choices of higher-court judges. Further, each model allows for judicial strategy.

At a deeper level, these models share a basic premise—so basic that it is hardly ever noticed (but see Baum 1997, 27–28; Schauer 2000, 615–17). Each model incorporates the assumption that Supreme Court justices act solely on their interest in the substance of legal policy, whether that interest is centered on policy or on a combination of law and policy. No other goal has any impact on the justices' behavior. The same assumption is often applied to judges on other federal courts, though not always explicitly.

This is a striking assumption, because it treats judges as people whose choices are based on a very narrow set of goals. If this assumption is accurate, judges' interest in shaping legal policy must be far stronger than other goals that might affect their decisions. To assess this assumption, then, it is necessary to consider both the strength of good legal policy as a type of goal and the potential impact of alternative goals. I will give primary attention to the Supreme Court, because the argument that judges act only on their interest in legal policy is most widely and most fully accepted for the Court.

The Strength of Legal Policy as a Goal

Central to the dominant models of judicial behavior is the premise that judges on higher courts care a great deal about the content of legal policy. The reasons why judges might care so much are hardly ever spelled out. Rather, having observed patterns of judicial behavior that seem consistent with a strong judicial interest in legal policy, scholars see no need to inquire into the bases for this interest.

This does not mean that such bases cannot be identified. Consider first of all the judge who is devoted to making good policy through decisions. Undoubtedly most lawyers who become judges, like other people in law and politics, have strong preferences about a range of policy issues. As a result, they gain satisfaction from the feeling that they are making or contributing to good policy (W. Landes and Posner 1975, 887; Higgins and Rubin 1980, 130; Posner 1995, 131). If commitment to a vision of desirable public policy can motivate political action in other arenas, such as interest group activity (Moe 1980; Verba, Schlozman, and Brady 1995, ch. 4), surely a similar commitment can influence judges' choices. Further, judges who act strategically on their policy goals may enjoy the feeling that they are winning victories and exerting influence.

Similar motivations can spur judges' efforts to make good law as distinct from good policy. Socialized through their legal training and practice, judges gain satisfaction by interpreting the law as well as they can (Stinchcombe 1990; D. Klein 2002, 11–12; Cross 2003, 1473–76). Judge Richard Posner (1995, 131, 133) has suggested that judges enjoy following the rules of the "game" of judging, such as compliance with the strictures of law.

It is very difficult to assess the general strength of these motivations, but it is far from obvious that they are strong enough to dominate judicial decision making. For one thing, a judge does not benefit directly by making good law or good policy. The state of government policy on issues in labor relations or freedom of religion is unlikely to have much effect on a judge's life. Few judges who vote to limit the use of capital punishment expect to become defendants in murder cases.

Thus, working to achieve legal and policy goals does not serve judges' self-interest as conventionally defined. "If one looks only at financial incentives," one legal scholar argues, "it is difficult to explain why most federal judges do not simply decide their cases by flipping a coin, and then take the rest of the day off and go fishing" (Stout 2002, 1606). The same is true of other aspects of self-interest.[10]

The Impact of Other Goals

It might be, however, that the goal of making good legal policy dominates judicial decision making by default. If other goals are pretty much irrelevant to the task of judging, then judges devote themselves to achieving good law or good policy because they have nothing else to do with their power. This is essentially the position of some of the most influential analyses of Supreme Court decision making (Rohde and Spaeth 1976, 72–74; Epstein and Knight 1998, 36–49; Segal and Spaeth 2002, 92–96).

In considering alternative goals, these analyses give nearly exclusive attention to career maintenance and advancement, an obvious possibility for public officials. Students of judicial behavior accept the relevance of this goal to lower-court judges, especially elected state judges (e.g., M. Hall 1992, 1995). In contrast, Supreme Court scholars argue that it has little relevance to the justices (Rohde and Spaeth 1976, 72–74; Epstein and Knight 1998, 36–39; Segal and Spaeth 2002, 93–96). In their view, justices' life terms and the attractiveness of their positions rule out self-interest in the form of career considerations. This answer is a bit too sweeping, in that some justices have been interested in nonjudicial positions or—as noted earlier—elevation to chief justice.[11] Further, it is possible that this interest affects the positions that ambitious justices take in certain cases. Still, for most justices career goals are indeed irrelevant.

---

[10] Self-interest is an elusive concept, and some commentators have defined it so broadly that it encompasses virtually all motivations (see Adam Smith 1759/2000, 449–60). With this usage, judges' satisfaction from taking positions that accord with their conception of good legal policy or from helping to achieve good policy could be considered a form of self-interest. A few scholars label judges' policy goals as self-interested (Spiller and Gely 1992, 464; Schwartz, Spiller, and Urbiztondo 1994, 57), and it might be that they are thinking about this kind of satisfaction. Still, there is a fundamental distinction between concrete or tangible benefits and symbolic or psychic benefits that people obtain from their actions, and that distinction can be maintained by labeling only the pursuit of tangible benefits as self-interested.

[11] Justice William O. Douglas's interest in the presidency and the ambitions of some of his colleagues are discussed in B. Murphy 2003. On Justice Byron White's possible interest in other positions, see Klain 2002.

While political scientists say little about other alternatives to the goal of achieving good legal policy, career goals do not exhaust the possibilities. "Indeed, once salary and tenure are guaranteed, ironically the door is open for many other factors to influence judicial behavior" (Burbank and Friedman 2002, 27). Scholars with an economic orientation have posited a multiplicity of goals for judges on various courts (e.g., Anderson, Shughart, and Tollison 1989; Miceli and Cosgel 1994; Cass 1995; Posner 1995, ch. 3; Toma 1996; Drahozal 1998; Gulati and McCauliff 1998; Georgakopoulos 2000; Bainbridge and Gulati 2002). For the Supreme Court some of these goals, like career goals, can be set aside as very weak at best. The same is true of goals whose impact is idiosyncratic. To take an extreme example, one could imagine a situation in which a Supreme Court justice has an incentive to decide a dispute over a presidential election in a way that makes the justice more comfortable about retiring.[12] But that incentive, decisive though it might be in a major decision, could not be an important component of any theory of judicial behavior.

In contrast, some other goals might have a more regular impact. One candidate is pleasant working relations with colleagues. On appellate courts, judges must work together. Even in an era with limited face-to-face contact among Supreme Court justices, decision making requires considerable interaction among the justices. Frictions are inevitable. The potential for more serious hostility always exists and sometimes comes to fruition (P. Cooper 1995). The justices would be an unusual group indeed if most of them did not prefer to minimize conflict (see Edwards 2003).

In turn, that goal may affect the justices' behavior. This impact should not be exaggerated: occasional reading of dissenting opinions makes it clear that justices sometimes take actions that could foster conflict. Moreover, it can be very difficult to identify the motivations that underlie efforts to minimize conflict: justices who seek to maintain a pleasant environment and justices who seek to win colleagues' support for their legal and policy positions might behave in quite similar ways (see W. Murphy 1964, ch. 3). Yet it is quite plausible that concern for interpersonal relations affects behavior such as opinion writing and joining.

Another possibility is usually called leisure (Posner 1995, 124–25), though perhaps a better label is limiting workload. Judges on any court might seek to maximize leisure time or time for other pursuits by working less rather than more at judging. It is noteworthy that a federal court of

---

[12] Readers may recall the report that Justice Sandra Day O'Connor expressed great dismay on election night in 2000 when she thought that Al Gore had won the election, because she would have to delay her retirement from the Court (E. Thomas and Isikoff 2000–2001, 46). Whether or not this report was accurate, Justice O'Connor's continued tenure on the Court until 2006 suggests that an interest in retirement did not have a strong impact on her position in *Bush v. Gore.*

appeals judge (Posner 1995, ch. 3) has emphasized workload as a goal that can affect judges' choices (see also Macey 1994; Drahozal 1998, 475–76; Gulati and McCauliff 1998, 172; Bainbridge and Gulati 2002). Occasionally, a judge is open about holding this goal. "I didn't get elected to work hard. I worked hard as a trial lawyer" (Flemming, Nardulli, and Eisenstein, 1992, 98). The possibility that Supreme Court justices care about limiting their workloads is supported by the anecdotal evidence that some work less than full days (e.g., Woodward and Armstrong 1979, 270) and by the array of extracurricular activities in which they engage during Court terms, activities that range from law school speeches to duck-hunting expeditions.

Workload considerations affect agenda setting. In courts with discretionary jurisdiction and large numbers of petitions for hearing, there is an unavoidable maximum to the number of cases that judges can accept and handle adequately. The most obvious sign that judges seek to limit their workloads is that they accept substantially fewer cases than that maximum.

This has been the Supreme Court's practice in the last two decades. There was a precipitous decline in the number of certiorari grants per term during the early years of the Rehnquist Court, and the new lower level has been maintained since that time. Commentators have offered various explanations for this decline (Hellman 1996; O'Brien 1997). Some have suggested (though gently, at least in print) that the Rehnquist Court justices preferred doing less work to more (Lacovara 2003). Evidently aware of this interpretation, Justice Ginsburg protested that "the cutback in opinions doesn't mean that the court is becoming a lazy lot" (Biskupic 1994c).

In decisions on the merits, judges' goal of limited workload may result in deference to other people. Judges in some appellate courts strongly defer to the members of central staffs who prepare proposed decisions and opinions (Davies 1981; Stow and Spaeth 1992). Judges may also defer to the colleague who is initially assigned a case, suppressing disagreement in order to avoid writing separate opinions (Wold 1978, 64; Linder 1985, 486; Maltzman, Spriggs, and Wahlbeck 2000, 24). At the extreme, this deference is so great that the outcome of cases largely depends on the identity of the assigned judge (Sickels 1965).

More broadly, workload considerations limit judges' efforts to get decisions "right" as law or policy. This effect is especially important. The distance between a decision and a judge's ideal will tend to decline as the judge devotes more time and effort to the decision. Like people in other positions, judges must determine where to draw the line, at what point to stop working on a case because the likely benefits of additional work are outweighed by the value of spending time on other pursuits. If judges give some priority to their workloads, as they surely do, they stop short of achieving what would be the best possible result as they would define it.[13]

As suggested earlier, still another possible goal for judges is the approval of individuals and groups that are important to them. Under some conditions this goal reinforces judges' interest in good legal policy. Under others it constitutes an alternative basis for judicial choices. The impact of judges' interest in the esteem of others will be considered in the last section of this chapter and in the chapters that follow.

The Realism of the Dominant Models

From this vantage point, all the leading models of judicial behavior share a limitation. Each model portrays Supreme Court justices (and, in some formulations, judges on other courts) as single-minded seekers of good legal policy, whether that means good policy or some combination of good law and good policy. If judges' incentives to pursue this goal are less than overwhelming, and if other motivations are relevant to their work, then the accuracy of this portrayal is questionable.

This limitation is especially relevant to strategic action by judges. As discussed earlier, most students of judicial behavior now believe that judges engage in a good deal of strategic action. Indeed, scholars increasingly accept a model in which judges are fully strategic in acting on their policy goals. For those reasons it is useful to consider the motivational bases for this model in some detail.

One source of the appeal of strategic models is their apparent realism. If judges care about the content of legal policy, then it seems short-sighted or naive for them simply to vote for the alternative that they most prefer in itself. Rather, they should focus on the ultimate consequences of their choices and act to make those consequences as consistent with their preferences as possible. Thus it seems self-evident that judges act strategically to advance their policy goals.

This perception of realism is not necessarily justified. Several scholars have offered formulations of the conditions under which people will adopt the strategies that maximize achievement of their goals (Kreps 1990, 140–45; Kelley 1995, 101; M. Taylor 1995, 225–28; Green and

---

[13] On the great majority of courts, in contrast with the Supreme Court, heavy caseloads limit the time that judges can devote to getting decisions right even if they give a low priority to limiting their workloads. Federal court of appeals judge and legal scholar Frank Easterbrook (1990, 778) offered this judgment: "Much of the judge-centered scholarship in contemporary law schools assumes that judges have the leisure to examine subjects deeply and resolve debates wisely. Professors believe they have this capacity and attribute it to judges. Pfah!"

Shapiro 1995, 267; Cameron 2000, 75–78). Most of these conditions fall into two categories, each more or less obvious. The first is the strength of people's *incentives* to behave strategically. The second is the extent of their *capabilities* to identify and follow the best strategy in any situation. Capabilities might seem relevant only to the effectiveness of strategies, not the choice to behave strategically. But capabilities influence incentives: the more difficult it is to play a strategic game well, the less reason people have to play it at all.

Because incentives are so important, we would expect people to be highly strategic in making economic decisions. Entrepreneurs, employees, and consumers all have a strong self-interest spurring their efforts to maximize their benefits and minimize their costs. Because of their limited capabilities, people frequently deviate from the course that would best serve their economic self-interest (Thaler 1991, 1992; Conlisk 1996; Kahneman and Tversky 2000; Barberis and Thaler 2003). Still, their incentives to behave strategically are strong.

In the political arena, some goals are sufficiently important that people have strong incentives to act strategically on their behalf. Perhaps the most obvious example is reelection, which has received considerable emphasis in studies of Congress (Mayhew 1974; Arnold 1990). Retaining office can serve a variety of important purposes. For that reason most members of Congress have good reason to make the considerable efforts that are required to maximize their chances for reelection. Continued tenure in office is not as fundamental as the basic goals of economic actors; among other things, not all members of Congress want to stay there. Even so, a model of concerted strategic action to secure reelection fits the reality fairly well.

As noted earlier, judges and policy goals are different. Ordinarily, judges gain only intangible benefits from advancing their favored policies. These benefits are meaningful, but they do not seem nearly as substantial as those that accrue to economic actors or even to elected officials who want to retain their positions.

There is also a collective action problem. Whatever benefit judges derive from the state of public policy in a particular field, the choices of a single judge ordinarily have only a marginal impact on the totality of policy. Most directly, multiple judges participate in formulating judicial policy on an issue. An appellate judge faces limits imposed by the actions of colleagues and other courts. Justice William Brennan was widely regarded as someone who could exert significant influence over his fellow justices (Eisler 1993), but in the increasingly conservative Court of the 1970s and 1980s he won fewer and fewer victories.

Further, research on the implementation of judicial decisions has underlined the central role of nonjudicial actors in shaping the ultimate impact of decisions (Rosenberg 1991; Canon and Johnson 1999). To take the classic example, the pace of school desegregation in the South after *Brown v. Board of Education* was determined chiefly by state and local officials and by the other branches of the federal government, not by the Supreme Court. Even with their best efforts, judges can exert only limited influence over the choices of other government officials. In light of this reality, the effort required to act strategically might not be justified by the likely gain for the judge's policy goals.

In this respect, then, strategic models do not seem uniquely realistic. Judges who act strategically do not secure any tangible benefits that are denied to judges who act sincerely. While they may gain intangible benefits when their favored legal policies come closer to attainment, their limited capacity to affect outcomes reduces the quantity of these benefits. Moreover, judges may gain as much or more satisfaction by simply taking what they identify as the right position, regardless of the ultimate outcome. When there is relatively little to be achieved by acting strategically, judges cannot be assumed to engage in fully strategic behavior.

Indeed, if we take judges' interest in their workloads into account, strategic models appear *less* realistic than their competitors. Judges who try to interpret the law as well as possible or to identify the positions that are most consistent with their policy preferences have to work hard, but at least the work of the legal or attitudinal judge ends there. The task of the strategic judge continues, and that judge may need to engage in intensive labor in order to choose something approaching the optimal strategy (see Merrill 2003, 620–21).[14]

Consider, for instance, the job of Supreme Court justices who try to determine whether they should adjust their interpretations of a statute in order to avoid a congressional override of the Court's decision. To estimate whether the current Congress would override a prospective decision is an intricate task, and some of the intricacy is reflected in the complex ideological models that scholars have used to make their own estimates (Segal 1997; Bergara, Richman, and Spiller 2003; Sala and Spriggs 2004).

Other complications arise. For example, Congress can reverse a court decision at any time. So the justice who is committed to avoiding overrides must estimate the ideological composition and political environment of future Congresses. That task requires, among other things, a capacity to predict election results that thus far has eluded skilled political scientists. Another complication is obvious but sufficiently daunting that students of judicial behavior generally ignore it (but see Spiller and Spitzer 1995):

---

[14] Of course, judges have the assistance of law clerks, and like-minded judges on a court can work together. But the labor required to make optimal strategic choices of the sorts described below would still be quite onerous for a judge.

since individual justices differ in their policy preferences, they need to consider each other in developing strategies aimed at Congress. In practice, Court action to avoid an override may produce a policy no closer to the justices' preferences than the policy that would result from an override, without the benefit of delay in its adoption (Cross and Nelson 2001, 1454). Finally, because the Court can respond to congressional overrides and shape their effects (Segal 1997, 32), the conscientious justice needs to calculate outcomes in a multistage game.

Of course, Congress is not the only target for strategic behavior. The strategic justice must face the task of predicting public reactions to the Court's decisions, a task that has its own complexities. One example is the justice who believes that the Court jeopardizes public support for the Court and ultimately its ability to win acceptance for its policies by making decisions that conflict with majority views in the public. If this justice contemplates voting for an outcome that is likely to be unpopular, the justice must estimate how much public support would be lost as a result of that decision and, in turn, how much this loss of support would affect the Court's effectiveness as a policymaker. That estimated effect would then have to be compared with the estimated benefit to the justice's policy goals from the decision in question.

The judgments needed to choose effective intra-Court strategies are a good deal easier to make. This is one reason that justices can be expected to behave more strategically toward colleagues than toward targets outside the Court. But even within the Court, the task of predicting the long-term consequences of different actions may be difficult. Would Justice Scalia ultimately win more support for his policy positions if he traded his hard-line advocacy of those positions for William Brennan's gentler approach? Some very complicated calculations would be required to answer that question with any confidence.[15]

Most research that employs strategic models assumes that justices are willing to take on the burdens of acting strategically. Justices amass all the relevant information and make the calculations needed to determine whether, and how much, they must modify their preferred positions in light of other participants in the policy process. Justices act in this way, sacrificing a large share of the time they might spend in other pursuits, even though there is a good chance that their predictions will be inaccurate. If they do manage to achieve a high level of predictive accuracy, the gains for their preferred policies are likely to be limited. In any event, they derive no concrete benefits from their success.

[15] Whether such a shift in tactics would be possible for Justice Scalia, who once explained that it would be "beyond human nature" to eschew an attack on the arguments in another opinion (*Planned Parenthood v. Casey*, 1992, 981), is a different issue.

In contrast, consider justices who take a different approach. These justices engage in a certain amount of strategic behavior within the Court, aimed at securing majorities for the positions they favor. But for the most part they simply take the positions that accord with their policy preferences. If their positions initially put them on the Court's minority side, they usually accept their minority status and write or join dissenting opinions to disagree with the majority opinion. Nor do they worry much about responses to the Court's decisions by the other branches or the public. While these justices are happy when their colleagues and other policymakers agree with them, they derive satisfaction primarily from casting votes and writing opinions that accord with their sense of what is right.

Because of the approach they take, the job of these justices consumes much less time and effort than the job of the fully strategic justice. It also involves much less frustration. As a result, they can work on cases at a deliberate pace and enjoy a reasonably relaxed life. Advocates of strategic models might label these justices as naive, because they largely eschew strategy. But that label does not seem quite right: these justices know what they are doing, and they are happy with the results.

Even these justices or counterparts who care about law rather than policy might be considered idealistic. Such judges make their choices with the goal of adopting good legal policy, a goal whose achievement brings them no tangible benefits. They need to labor to identify the best choices while recognizing that they may fail to do so. Thus there is an element of Mr. Spock[16] in the judges of the pure legal and attitudinal models, judges who act without emotion or self-interest in order to advance the general good. As the leading expert on Mr. Spock explained, "In the Vulcan culture, one simply does what is right" (Nimoy 1977, 104).

But it is the judges of strategic models who most resemble Mr. Spock. These judges court exhaustion with their arduous and often futile efforts to advance their conceptions of good policy, efforts they expend only for the personal satisfaction of trying to improve public policy. This is a lot to expect of them. People often behave in ways that are not strictly self-interested (Mansbridge 1990; Monroe 1996). Even so, by standards of ordinary behavior the fully strategic judge seems enormously altruistic.

---

[16] It may be that some readers are unfamiliar with Mr. Spock. Played by Leonard Nimoy, he was one of the leading characters in the *Star Trek* television show and movies. Spock was half-Vulcan, and Vulcans were characterized by both their altruism and their devotion to reason.

For those readers who prefer classical allusions, the efforts of the fully strategic judge might be considered Herculean (see Dworkin 1977, 105; 1986, 239; Bainbridge and Gulati 2002, 91–98).

Attractive as Mr. Spock's behavior may be, most human beings—including most judges—do not act like him.[17]

LIMITATIONS OF THE DOMINANT MODELS

The most influential models of judicial behavior share not only a basic assumption but also a limitation, the lack of a persuasive theory of judges' motivations. Each model assumes that judges seek only to achieve good legal policy. Some scholars outside political science have identified motives for pursuing that goal, but these motives seem only moderately strong. Nor does this goal have monopoly status by default; there are other goals that could shape judges' choices. As a result, the dominant models in their current forms are not entirely realistic. That is especially true of strategic models, which have become the leading models in the field.

For many students of judicial behavior, this critique will seem misguided on either (or both) of two grounds. First, as they see it, empirical evidence demonstrates the dominance of good legal policy as a goal and strategy as a means to that goal for judges on higher courts, especially the Supreme Court. Political scientists have amassed a large body of evidence indicating that Supreme Court justices seek to make good policy (see Segal and Spaeth 2002). Increasingly they are amassing evidence of strategic action by the justices to secure good policy, especially in their interactions with other justices (see Maltzman, Spriggs, and Wahlbeck 2000). Given the volume of this evidence, it could be argued that any concerns about motivation are of no particular importance.

Second, models do not need to accord fully with reality in order to advance our understanding. Indeed, their simplification of reality can be a virtue, because it makes analytic problems more tractable. Even if judges are not fully strategic, for instance, that conception of their behavior produces insights and structures empirical analysis in useful ways.

Both points have considerable validity, and the value of the dominant models for an understanding of judicial behavior is quite clear. Models based on the attitudinal ideal type have told us much about the structure of behavior on appellate courts, and they have established fundamental realities about judicial decision making. Models that posit a mix of legal

---

[17] It is true that Supreme Court justice Stephen Breyer refused to disclose the response he gave to a tabloid newspaper reporter who asked Breyer whether he was a space alien (Mauro 1995). It is also true that he later teased an audience about the question of whether judges are human beings (*AU News* 2005). But not all space aliens show the devotion to the common good that characterized Mr. Spock, and some act in truly deplorable ways.

and policy considerations in decisions illuminate the complexities of judges' decision processes and integrate competing conceptions of those processes. Strategic models have encouraged scholars to probe judges' choices in new ways, and they have also brought greater theoretical rigor to the study of judicial behavior. These are hardly trivial contributions, and they continue today with a wave of research that is expanding our understanding of judicial behavior.

Yet these achievements do not dispose of the problem, and both grounds for challenging my critique can be contested. First, the empirical evidence that scholars have amassed proves less than is often thought. This evidence does provide considerable evidence of the kinds of behavior posited by the dominant models. In light of this evidence, to take the Supreme Court as an example, it would be foolish to deny that the justices' policy preferences have strong effects on their choices or that the justices engage in a good deal of strategic behavior.

But the existing evidence does not establish that justices are motivated solely (or even overwhelmingly) by policy goals. What it shows most clearly is quite important but considerably more limited: differences in the positions that the nine justices take in the same cases are best understood as a product of differences in their policy preferences. The evidence on strategic behavior is even less conclusive. It shows that a good deal of what the justices do is consistent with a strategic interpretation, but it falls well short of demonstrating that all judicial behavior takes the forms we would expect if justices are fully strategic. Moreover, much of the evidence of strategic behavior that scholars have found is consistent with non-strategic (or partly strategic) interpretations as well.[18]

Second, the significant benefits of simplifying assumptions in models are accompanied by significant costs. A model of strategic policy-oriented Supreme Court justices can encompass any actions that justices take. There is a beauty to simple, comprehensive models of behavior (see Lave and March 1975, 61–64). But by setting complexities aside these models can limit our comprehension of behavior.

Moreover, there is a cost to employing models whose depiction of motivations is more Vulcan than human. As economist Richard Thaler (1996,

---

[18] Considerable space would be required to make a proper case for these readings of the empirical evidence. I sought to make that case in Baum 1997. See also the assessments of the evidence on judicial behavior in Cross 1997, 1998. In the decade since then the body of empirical evidence on judicial behavior and especially on strategic behavior has grown a good deal, but I think that what this evidence does and does not establish has not changed fundamentally. The primary reason is the difficulty of fully testing the attitudinal or strategic models and especially of testing them against alternative explanations of judicial behavior. A secondary reason is that—to borrow terms from Thomas Mayer (1996, 194)—the dominant models are often tested "compassionately" rather than "mercilessly."

227) describes it, individuals in orthodox economic theory are characterized by "rationality, self-interest, and self-control" in that they "can solve
problems like an economist, care only about themselves, and never suffer
from weakness of will." As Thaler and others have shown, the departure
of this characterization from reality creates difficulties for analysis (Camerer 1997; Thaler 2000; Rabin 2002). Judges in the dominant models of
judicial behavior depart further from reality: they share rationality and
self-control with orthodox economic actors but act on the basis of complete altruism rather than complete self-interest.

Further, the incorporation of certain judicial goals into the dominant
models as basic assumptions limits inquiry into the bases for those goals.
This has been a deliberate choice, based in part on scholars' primary interest in prediction rather than deep explanation (Schubert 1963; Spaeth
1979, 140). This approach is fundamental to most economic analysis
(M. Friedman 1953), and it is quite defensible. But it circumscribes explanations of judicial behavior.

Thus the leading models of judicial behavior teach us a great deal
about why judges do what they do, but their perspective is narrow. That
narrowness limits what these models in their current form can tell us.
By expanding the scope of those models, we can gain a fuller comprehension of the bases for judges' choices. One means to this end is viewing
judicial behavior from other perspectives, and that is the approach I take
in this book.

AUDIENCE AS A PERSPECTIVE

The perspective that I offer is one based on judges' relationships with
their audiences, people whose esteem they care about. Judges' audiences
usually include colleagues on their own courts, but for the most part these
audiences are outside their courts. The impact of external audiences is a
point of disagreement among scholars who work within the dominant
models. For the leading proponents of a quasi-attitudinal model, at least
Supreme Court justices are largely impervious to external influence (Segal
and Spaeth 2002). In contrast, some scholars argue that justices are subject to significant influence from the general public (e.g., Mishler and Sheehan 1996; Flemming and Wood 1997) or Congress (e.g., Epstein, Knight,
and Martin 2001; Bergara, Richman, and Spiller 2003). Studies of lower
appellate courts consider elections as a vehicle of influence for the public
(M. Hall 1987, 1992, 1995; M. Hall and Brace 1992; Brace and Hall
1997; Langer 2002) as well as the impact of Supreme Court review on
the choices of lower-court judges (Songer, Segal, and Cameron 1994;
Cameron, Segal, and Songer 2000).

What scholars who work within the dominant models have in common is the unstated assumption that judges do not care about the regard of their audiences for its own sake. According to this view, judges do not get satisfaction simply from being liked and respected. Rather, judges give attention to audiences as a means to advance their goal of achieving good legal policy. The general public, for instance, functions as a constraint. Judges cannot continue to make policy if they lose elections, and they cannot secure compliance with judicial decisions if they lose legitimacy with the public. But the Spock-like judges of the dominant models have no interest in public approval as an end in itself. If they could best advance what they see as good legal policy by making themselves objects of hatred or contempt, presumably they would do so.

This view of the relationship between judges and their audiences is not universal. One feature of the economic scholarship on judges' goals is its recurring references to judges' interest in securing favorable reactions to their work from other people. In part, this interest is described as a means to other ends, advancement of career goals and effectiveness in policymaking. However, several scholars cite an interest in esteem as a goal in itself (e.g., Cass 1995, 971–74; Posner 1995, 119; Drahozal 1998, 475; see Posner 1990). Some treat concern with reputation as a powerful explanation of judicial behavior (Miceli and Cosgel 1994; see Schauer 2000).

The idea that judges care a great deal about what people think of them is not very radical, and it comports with a commonsense notion of human nature (Harsanyi 1969). As I will discuss in chapter 2, it also comports with a large body of relevant research by psychologists. However, this does not establish that judges' interest in the regard of other people influences their choices on the bench in significant ways. Indeed, because the dominant models of judicial behavior exclude this motivation, arguably the burden of proof lies with anyone who argues for its inclusion.

But perhaps the burden should lie with adherents to these models. After all, the dominant models implicitly treat one of the most fundamental human qualities as irrelevant to judges' choices. Why would judges' interest in approval not affect their choices?

Wherever the burden ought to lie, the case needs to be made. In this book I seek to demonstrate the value of taking into account judges' interest in the esteem of audiences that are important to them. More specifically, I try to show that a perspective based on judges' interest in the approval of their audiences can enhance our understanding of judicial behavior in several related respects.

First, it supplies some of the motivational basis for patterns of judicial behavior that are incorporated into the dominant models. Most important, concern with audiences helps to explain why judges may commit themselves to making what they see as good law or good policy. In the process, familiar patterns of judicial behavior can be understood in a different way.

Second, this perspective provides ways of thinking about debates between competing models. Students of judicial behavior disagree about the relative weights of legal and policy considerations in judges' decisions and about the extent to which judges behave strategically. Relationships between judges and their audiences offer a vantage point on those issues.

Third, an audience-based perspective helps to explain patterns of judicial behavior that diverge from all the leading models. The explanations of decision making that flow from those models are incomplete in some respects and simply wrong in others. The relationships between judges and their audiences fill in some of the gaps and correct some inaccuracies.

Fourth, this perspective points to some new lines of inquiry into judicial behavior. These lines of inquiry relate not just to the impact of judges' audiences but to other issues as well. In this way the scope of empirical research on the bases for judges' choices can be expanded.

As a consequence of these functions, an audience-based perspective suggests ways to modify and expand the dominant models. The value of these models as bases for inquiry has been amply demonstrated. Moreover, they provide a structure for the accumulation of knowledge about judicial behavior. With adaptations, their contributions can be even greater.[19]

I should make explicit what is implicit in that list of functions. I believe that judges' motivation to win the approval of their audiences can explain a good deal about their choices as decision makers, and I seek to demonstrate that explanatory value. But even more important is the value of thinking about judges and their audiences as a means to develop new understandings of judicial behavior.

The book's exploration of relationships between judges and their audiences begins in chapter 2, which considers audiences in broad terms. The chapter examines and draws from the relevant scholarship in social psychology. The concept of self-presentation is used as a link between people's interest in approval and their behavior. The chapter then applies the lessons of that scholarship to judges, discussing judicial self-presentation and its part in judicial behavior.

Chapters 3 through 5 probe the relationships between judges and several audiences that might be relevant to them. Chapter 3 examines the audiences that scholars give substantial attention: court colleagues, the general public, and the other branches of government. In the standard

---

[19] A perspective based on judges' relationships with their audiences might be employed as an alternative model of judicial behavior. But an effort to use audiences as a comprehensive framework would stretch the concept of audience so far that it loses much of its meaning. It is preferable to use this perspective as a way to inform and expand other models.

images of these audiences, judges respond to them for instrumental reasons, as a means to other ends. I raise questions about the strength of
instrumental motives for responding to these audiences. Drawing from
the perspective developed in chapter 2, I also consider personal motives
for responding to these audiences, motives based on an interest in their
esteem for its own sake.

Chapters 4 and 5 discuss other audiences that have received limited
attention from scholars but that may exert influence because of judges'
personal motives for seeking their approval. Chapter 4 considers judges'
social groups and the legal community, including judges on other courts.
Chapter 5 deals with "policy groups," people who share views about legal
policy, and the news media. The chapter also considers the hypothesis of
political conservatives that a "Greenhouse effect" has moved some Supreme Court justices to the left, a hypothesis that pulls together some
themes concerning judges' self-presentation to their audiences.

Chapter 6 examines the ways that an audience-based perspective can
inform our understanding of judges' choices. Drawing on the discussions
in earlier chapters, it suggests how to incorporate the book's inquiries
into the study of judicial behavior. As in the book as a whole, I argue that
drawing out the implications of relationships between judges and their
audiences will lead to richer explanations of that behavior.

Chapter 2

JUDGING AS SELF-PRESENTATION

IN THEIR ESSENCE, the premises of my inquiry into judges and their audiences are simple:

1. People want to be liked and respected by others who are important to them.
2. The desire to be liked and respected affects people's behavior.
3. In these respects, judges are people.

This chapter elaborates on those premises and offers support for them. The first section examines human behavior in general, focusing on the first two premises. I draw from what the scholarship in social psychology has taught us about individuals in a social context, with an emphasis on self-presentation as a link between the social context and individual behavior. In the last part of the section, I apply these lessons to public officials.

The second section discusses judges. The section surveys judicial self-presentation in its various forms. It then examines how judges' interest in the esteem of other people and their self-presentation relate to their choices as decision makers.

People and Their Audiences

The work of social psychologists provides a number of ways to think about the impact of audiences on human behavior. The most useful for my purposes centers on the concept of the self.

The Self and Others

The terms *self* and *selfhood* are at the heart of a substantial body of scholarship in social psychology (Baumeister 1998). The meanings of these terms are complex and at least a little slippery. According to one definition, selfhood means "the thoughts, feelings, and behaviors that arise from the awareness of self as object and agent" (Hoyle et al. 1999, 2).

One key element of people's self-concepts—how they think about themselves—is self-esteem, the "positivity of the person's evaluation of self" (Baumeister 1998, 694; see Owens, Stryker, and Goodman 2001). There is something of a paradox about self-esteem. Contrary to a widespread belief among people in and out of academia, it is not at all certain that high self-esteem brings with it a range of desirable consequences (see Dawes 1994, 9–10, 246–48; Hewitt 1998). Nonetheless, "it is clear that self-esteem is quite important to people" (Baumeister 1998, 695). There is "a basic human need to feel good about ourselves" (Brown 1998, 193), a need that may be the most fundamental (Becker 1968, 328). As two psychologists put it, "in a discipline with few universally accepted principles, the proposition that people are motivated to maintain and enhance their self-esteem has achieved the rare status of an axiom" (Leary and Downs 1995; see Crocker and Park 2003). In a sense, of course, all the research that has made this an axiom simply affirms what observation of human behavior makes obvious.[1]

Research has verified a second obvious truth: an individual's self-concept does not develop in isolation from other people. Rather, self-concepts are based heavily on social relations. "Even a person's most basic sense of his or her own existence seems to depend on interactions with others" (Hoyle et al. 1999, 31). More succinctly, "the self is an interpersonal being" (Baumeister 1998, 682). In her effort to develop a paradigm for the study of political psychology, Kristen Monroe begins with the premise that "it is the actor's perceptions of self *in relation to others*" that are central to an understanding of human behavior (2002a, 400; emphasis in original). Indeed, Monroe argues that building a science of politics requires an understanding of those perceptions (2002a, 414).

There is disagreement about the extent to which self-esteem is socially determined (see Brown 1998, 196–209). However, most scholars conclude that self-esteem, like people's sense of themselves as a whole, is defined largely or primarily in social terms. Indeed, scholars have argued that people act to maintain their self-esteem as a means "to avoid social exclusion" (Leary and Downs 1995, 129; see K. Williams 2001; Leary 2001).

Individuals, then, are not isolated from each other. Nor are they interdependent solely because they want to get concrete things from each other. Rather, people's identities, their conceptions of themselves, rest fundamentally on their relations with each other. And the need for others to validate people's self-conceptions does not end at some point. Rather, it continues throughout life (Fels 2004, 77–78).

---

[1] Arguably, the importance of self-esteem is not universal but a product of culture. Americans may be more concerned with themselves and with self-esteem than people in some other cultures (Hewitt 1998, ch. 2). Because this book is specifically about judges in the United States, that issue need not be addressed here.

Much of the research in social psychology implicitly treats the impact of social relations as a constant across individuals. In contrast, some scholars suggest that people differ in the balance between autonomy and interdependence (Triandis 1989; Markus and Oyserman 1989). The best-known formulation of such differences is David Riesman's (1950, ch. 1) distinction between "inner-directed" and "other-directed" people. But this variation is a matter of degree; the self-concepts of all people depend in part on the people around them (see Riesman 1950, 25).

Models of human behavior can have explanatory value even if they do not take this reality into account. The value of such models has been amply demonstrated by scholarship with a rational choice perspective, which typically does not incorporate emotional ties between people. However, such models are necessarily incomplete. The connections between individual selves and other people provide a basis for more comprehensive explanations of behavior, including political behavior (Schuessler 2000).

Groups and Social Identities

The people in an individual's environment are not of equal importance, and their relative salience stems largely from the individual's group identifications. The part that such identifications play in individual behavior is a long-standing interest in sociology and social psychology. For example, the concept of reference groups has received wide application (Singer 1981; R. Hall, Varca, and Fisher 1986; Lau 1989; see Stets and Burke 2003).

Many social psychologists analyze the impact of group identifications on individuals in terms of social identity theory (Tajfel 1978; Deaux 1993; Abrams and Hogg 1999; Brewer 2001; see Akerlof and Kranton 2000). This body of theory emphasizes the role of group identifications in shaping people's sense of themselves. As defined by the scholar who first conceptualized social identity, it is "that *part* of an individual's self-concept which derives from his knowledge of his membership of a social group (or groups) together with the value and emotional significance attached to that membership" (Tajfel 1978, 63; emphasis in original). Group memberships need not be formal, nor do they necessarily involve direct contact with other group members. People usually identify with multiple groups, a condition that can result in complex social identities (Roccas and Brewer 2002).

An important element of social identity is the distinction between "us" and "them," "between the individual's own group and the outgroups which are compared or contrasted with it" (Tajfel 1978, 62). People need to belong to some groups and to feel distinctive from other groups

(Brewer 1991, 2003). One result of this need can be to strengthen a sense of intergroup competition.

Social psychologists who have developed and used identity theory differ in their views about the bases for social identification, the relationship between personal and social identity, and other issues. But they agree that people's identifications with groups are important to their self-concepts (Turner 1982, 18–19). For this reason, people's sense of social identity affects their self-esteem.

Thus social identity theory underlines the extent to which people's perceptions of themselves are group-oriented. It is less certain to what extent, and in what ways, other attitudes and behavior are functions of group identifications. But to take one example, it is clear that these identifications shape people's political thinking (Conover 1984, 1988; Dawson 1994; Koch 1994; R. A. Jackson and Carsey 2002; K. Walsh 2004; see Symposium 2001).

Self-Presentation

People want to be liked and respected by others, especially those who are most important to their social identities. What they do to win popularity and respect can be understood as efforts to make favorable impressions. These efforts have been conceptualized as self-presentation or, alternatively, impression management (Goffman 1959; Schlenker and Weigold 1992; Leary 1996; Schlenker and Pontari 2000). The concept of self-presentation might be limited to intentional actions (Weary and Arkin 1981, 225), but the concept usefully can be broadened to include people's less conscious efforts to present themselves in a positive light (Tetlock and Manstead 1985, 61–62). Indeed, much of people's self-presentation may be semiconscious and habitual (Schlenker 1980, 41; see Chartrand and Bargh 2002).

The goals that underlie self-presentation have been conceptualized in different ways (Baumeister 1982, 3–4; Tetlock and Manstead 1985, 61; Leary 1996, 40–44). In broad terms, these goals may be put into two categories, instrumental and personal.[2] I will refer to audiences whose relevance is based primarily on one category of goals or the other as instrumental and personal.

Instrumental self-presentation is easy to describe: people present themselves in certain ways in order to gain something concrete from an audience. To put it another way, they seek to ingratiate themselves with others as a means to secure a gain (E. Jones 1964). This kind of behavior has

---

[2] This is a modified version of Baumeister's (1998, 704–5) instrumental and expressive categories of motives for self-presentation.

been called "strategic self-presentation" (E. Jones and Pittman 1982; E. Jones 1990, ch. 7).

Personal self-presentation is more difficult to describe because its aims are more diffuse. Most directly, people engage in self-presentation because they seek popularity and respect as ends in themselves, not as means to other ends. At a deeper level, personal self-presentation is aimed at building a desirable self-concept. When people perceive they have achieved a favorable image with others, that perception tends to boost their self-esteem.

But the link between self-presentation and self-concepts runs even deeper than that. To a degree, people internalize the images of themselves that they present to others (Schlenker 1980, 194–96; Tice and Wallace 2003). In effect, then, presentation to others is also presentation to one-self, a way to help develop a desired self-image (Arkin 1980, 179–81; Greenwald and Breckler 1985; Leary 1996, 167–68). In other words, self-presentation helps people to create their identities.

Instrumental and personal motives for self-presentation often are inter-twined, so that they reinforce each other.[3] As a result, it can be difficult to determine their relative weights or to differentiate their impact. But there is a clear conceptual difference between the two motives, and that difference is central to the argument of this book. Accounts of judicial behavior that rule out personal goals for self-presentation miss much of the motivation that underlies judges' choices.

Just as individuals vary in their dependence on others for their self-images, they differ, Mark Snyder (1987) argues, in the level of effort they give to impression management. Snyder makes a distinction that is paral-lel to Riesman's distinction between other-directed and inner-directed people. What Snyder calls "high self-monitors" oversee the ways they present themselves more or less constantly, and they adjust the images they present as appropriate. "Low self-monitors" give less attention to the impressions they make; as a result, they are more consistent in the images they present.

Yet this consistency can be understood as a form of self-presentation—presentation of a desired image to oneself. High self-monitors may be more concerned with how others view them, low self-monitors with how they view themselves (M. Snyder 1987, 57; Greenwald and Breckler 1985). Moreover, even low self-monitors seek to create a self-image that

[3] One way in which they are intertwined is obvious: the esteem of other people often leads to concrete benefits. People who are well-liked or highly respected may receive all sorts of benefits as a result, from attractive job offers to good tables in trendy restaurants. Still, if the primary motives for seeking esteem are personal, these kinds of concrete benefits are ancillary.

ultimately will impress other people (Schlenker and Pontari 2000, 214–18). The fiercely independent person—Justice William O. Douglas comes to mind—may be very concerned with presenting an image of fierce independence (see Simon 1980; B. Murphy 2003).

In the scholarship on self-presentation, theatrical metaphors arise with some frequency (e.g., Schlenker 1980, ch. 2; M. Snyder 1987, 5–6, 185–86; E. Jones 1990, 172). These metaphors were integral to the classic work on self-presentation, Erving Goffman's *The Presentation of Self in Everyday Life* (1959). Goffman wrote that "the perspective employed in this report is that of the theatrical performance; the principles derived are dramaturgical ones" (1959, xi). One theatrical metaphor is reflected in the title of this book. Metaphors can easily obscure reality rather than illuminate it, but I think this one helps in understanding the process of self-presentation. With varying degrees of self-consciousness, people perform in ways intended to give other people the impressions they seek.

Self-Presentation by Public Officials

Goffman's reference to "everyday life" in the title of his book is a reminder that the preponderance of psychological research deals with ordinary people in ordinary situations. People in high public positions operate in extraordinary situations. Thus the choices of public officials in their work might have bases that differ from those of most other people.

Yet there are good reasons to conclude that the lessons of social psychology apply to public officials. Although political psychologists give primary attention to mass behavior, there is a substantial body of work dealing with officials and politicians (e.g., Barber 1965; Hermann 1986; D. Winter 1987; Renshon 1995; Sylvan and Voss 1998; see Monroe 2002b; Kuklinski 2002; Sears, Huddy, and Jervis 2003). This work establishes that concepts and theories in social psychology are relevant to the behavior of political leaders.

The concept of self-presentation applies especially well to public officials. To achieve their positions, most officials had to work hard to appeal to some combination of higher officials, politicians, and voters. Once in office, they continue to engage in impression management. That is especially true of elected officials. Scholars have documented the high priority that presidents (Miroff 1995; Kernell 1997) and members of Congress (Mayhew 1974; Fenno 1996; see Jewell 1982) give to maintaining and enhancing their public support.

The connection between these efforts and the concept of self-presentation has been made explicit in some of the scholarship on public officials and their audiences. Several students of presidential image-making have referred to self-presentation (Nakamura 1977–78, 647; Citrin and Green 1986, 450; Guttieri, Wallace, and Suedfeld 1995, 607, 616). In describing House members' visits to their districts in his classic *Home Style*, Richard Fenno said that "much of what they do is captured by Erving Goffman's idea of *the presentation of self*" (1978, 54; emphasis in original). Charles Goodsell (1977) argued that administrative agencies use physical objects in their public offices as a form of collective self-presentation.

Goffman's theatrical metaphor has also worked its way into depictions of self-presentation by political leaders. Goodsell found it applicable to bureaucracy, and one scholar applied it more broadly to political elites (Combs 1980, esp. ch. 4). One book of essays on Congress applied the metaphor to the functioning of Congress (Weisberg and Patterson 1998).

For public officials, the most proximate goals underlying self-presentation are instrumental. This is especially true of those who must win elections to maintain their positions. That goal gives elected officials strong incentives to engage in strategic self-presentation, and personal motives sometimes have little relevance. It is doubtful that members of Congress feel a personal attachment to most of the interest groups from which they solicit campaign contributions. For some officials, such as the reluctant campaigners described in some of Fenno's vignettes, reelection may be the only motive for efforts to win the approval of constituents.

But for most political leaders, the quest for public support undoubtedly serves personal goals as well. In a world in which success is measured largely by electoral margins and public approval ratings, it is natural for evidence about public approval to affect self-esteem. This effect is enhanced by direct contact between officeholders and members of the public. For these reasons, even self-presentation that is undertaken chiefly for electoral purposes seems almost certain to affect leaders' self-concepts.

It is not just constituents and other elements of their electoral coalitions to whom public officials present themselves. They seek to win the regard of other political leaders, occupational colleagues, and longtime associates. These efforts may be primarily strategic, intended to advance goals such as political success. But here too, personal motives come into play as well. Naturally, people want to be liked and respected by those with whom they work.

All this would be true even if public officials were a random sample of the population. But on the whole, those who seek and accept public positions are especially interested in the esteem that winning and holding prestigious positions provides. Indeed, some political leaders may look to the mass public for a personal validation that other sources have not provided (see Goodwin 1991). In any event, it would be a reasonable guess that

most people who hold significant public positions are among Snyder's
high self-monitors.[4]

Judicial Self-Presentation: A First Look

The picture of human perceptions and behavior that emerges from the
scholarship in social psychology is not very surprising, and it is easy to
see how that picture applies to public officials. But this picture differs
from the images that are implicit in the dominant models of judicial behavior. For that reason, what social psychologists tell us about people and
their audiences provides a different perspective on judges and judging.[5]

General Implications of an Audience-Based Perspective

In each of the dominant models of judicial behavior, judges are social
isolates. The world around them influences their choices on the bench,
but only because they have strategic reasons to take that world into account. Strategic considerations aside, judges do not care what people
think of them.

This depiction of judges is unrealistic, in that few people are so removed
from their social environment. If judges are like other people, they care
about the regard in which they are held for its own sake. In turn, their
interest in the esteem of others can be expected to influence their work
as judges.

As with other public officials, the selection processes that determine
which people become judges tend to favor those with an especially strong
interest in the esteem of other people. Lawyers who become judges often
give up substantial income to do so (see M. Frank 2003). To varying
degrees they accept constraints on their activities as well. The prestige of

---

[4] Occasionally an individual achieves high political office despite a dearth of skills in
dealing with other people; Richard Nixon was such a person (Reeves 2001). But those individuals still may be very concerned with how other people regard them. Indeed, Nixon was
a classic example of a high self-monitor.

[5] Just as the lessons of social psychology apply to other public officials, their application
to judges has been amply demonstrated. Although students of judicial behavior have made
only limited use of psychological theory, the research that does employ it demonstrates its
utility for understanding judges' choices (Wrightsman 1999, chs. 1–5; Baum 1997, 136–
41). Examples include work that draws from psychoanalytic perspectives on personality
(Lasswell 1948; Hirsch 1981), self-esteem (Atkins, Alpert, and Ziller 1980; Gibson 1981),
small-group behavior (Walker and Main 1973; Walker 1976), and cognition (Segal 1986;
Rowland and Carp 1996). Attitude theory was central to development of the attitudinal
model of decision making (Schubert 1965; Spaeth and Parker 1969; Rohde and Spaeth
1976).

being a judge is one of the benefits that outweigh these costs for those who pursue or accept judicial positions. Further, gregarious people who are effective in social settings have an advantage in securing judgeships.

This recruitment pattern should be especially pronounced at higher levels of the judiciary. On average, the sacrifice of income for enhanced prestige is greatest for federal appellate judges. Undoubtedly, the power to shape legal policy is an important attraction for many judges on higher courts. But the opportunity to win deference and admiration may be even more important.

If the people who become judges care more about the esteem of others than do most other people, that difference will affect their behavior on the bench. The same traits that make judgeships especially attractive to certain people give them a strong interest in how their actions as judges are evaluated. If those evaluations are positive, they provide an individualized recognition that goes beyond the diffuse prestige attached to judgeships (see Fels 2004, 9–10).

The psychological scholarship has a second implication that diverges sharply from the dominant models of judicial behavior. These models typically allow for variation among judges in the bases for their choices, but that variation exists only because courts vary in institutional characteristics that affect judges' instrumental motives. For instance, judges who hold life terms and those who regularly face the electorate are expected to give different weights to public opinion in reaching decisions. In these models, however, it is assumed that judges in the same institutional situations—judges on a particular court or at the same court level—respond to the same mixes of influences.

This assumption is questionable if judges have personal motives to seek approval from people outside their courts.[6] The audiences that judges care most about depend on their social identities, identities that inevitably differ from judge to judge. Thus two judges whose objective situations are identical may have different sets of personal audiences, so that they act on different mixes of influences.

The potential for interpersonal differences in the bases for judges' choices is central to the inquiry in this book. The discussions of various types of audiences in the chapters that follow emphasize differences among judges. In chapter 6, I consider the implications of these differences for the study of judicial behavior.

---

[6] This is not the only ground on which that assumption can be questioned. So long as judges differ in their goals or the ways they seek to achieve those goals, no matter what form these differences take, the mix of considerations that shape their decisions can be expected to differ as well.

Modes of Self-Presentation

The various forms of judicial self-presentations are familiar to scholars and other observers of the courts, even if they do not use that label. Still, it is useful to survey activities of judges that can be understood as self-presentation. That survey provides a starting point for consideration of the motives that underlie judicial self-presentation as well as the impact of audiences on judicial behavior.

For judges on the job, opportunities for self-presentation arise during court proceedings and in the announcement of decisions. Because they preside alone, trial judges have especially broad freedom to conduct proceedings as they wish. The classic studies by Harold Lasswell (1948, ch. 4) and by Alexander Smith and Abraham Blumberg (1967; Blumberg 1967, ch. 6) give a sense of the differing ways that judges express themselves before their more or less captive courtroom audiences (see Conley and O'Barr 1987–88).

To a degree, oral argument provides similar opportunities to appellate judges. Accounts of the Supreme Court regularly describe the ways that justices express their individual styles through their questions and comments in argument sessions (e.g., Biskupic 1998a; Lithwick 2002). Even Clarence Thomas's usual silence during oral argument is a form of self-presentation.

Announcements of decisions also allow judges to express themselves. Judges often use sentencing decisions to indicate outrage about criminal behavior and to portray themselves as strong enforcers of the criminal law. In one of the incidents described at the beginning of chapter 1, a Cincinnati judge employed his announcement in the Pete Rose case to call attention to a decision that he expected to be popular.

Announcements of decisions in written opinions are an attractive way for judges to present themselves, because their written form widens their circulation and increases their longevity. Scholars and judges have said a good deal about the functions of opinions as a communication form (Bosmajian 1992; Tushnet 1994; Schauer 1995; Wald 1995). A reading of opinions themselves makes it clear that one function is as a vehicle for self-presentation, especially evident when judges go beyond the standard forms of expression in judicial opinions.[7] To take two examples, judges sometimes engage in humor (Jordan 1987; Rudolph 1989) or creativity in writing.

---

[7] In assessing self-expression in judicial opinions, it is important to keep in mind that law clerks do much of the drafting of opinions. As a result, opinions reflect the writing styles of both clerks and judges (Wahlbeck, Spriggs, and Sigelman 2002). However, some judges (including several discussed in this section) have distinctive styles that clearly reflect their own interest in self-expression.

Both of these attributes were reflected in some recent allusions to music in opinions. A federal judge likened a criminal defendant's dilemma to that of the protagonist in a song by The Clash (*United States v. Jackson* 2004, 396 n. 3). In a dispute between two Yellow Cab companies, another federal judge cited lyrics by Joni Mitchell and Chuck Berry (*Yellow Cab Company of Sacramento v. Yellow Cab of Elk Grove* 2005, 926–27). A Michigan judge included a rap verse in an opinion dismissing a lawsuit against Eminem (Halcom 2003). In a case involving a doctor who was connected with George Harrison, a New York judge granted a change of venue in an opinion that parodied one of Harrison's songs for the Beatles (Goldiner 2004). In each instance the judge went beyond what was necessary to decide the case in order to engage in a bit of self-expression that perhaps was aimed at impressing readers of the opinion.

Some judges regularly use opinions as vehicles for their distinctive forms of self-expression. Michael Musmanno of the Pennsylvania Supreme Court expressed his views in elaborate language, often with elements of humor (Musmanno and Brown 1966). Bruce Selya of the federal court of appeals for the First Circuit inserts puns and obscure words into his opinions (e.g., *United States v. Hussein* 2003; see Margolick 1992). Federal district judge Samuel Kent of Galveston portrays himself in some opinions as a long-suffering trial judge who can find humor in the difficulties he faces.[8] Among these difficulties are the foibles and shortcomings of the lawyers in his court:

> Before proceeding further, the Court notes that this case involves two extremely likable lawyers, who have together delivered some of the most amateurish pleadings ever to cross the hallowed causeway into Galveston, an effort which leads the Court to surmise but one plausible explanation. Both attorneys have obviously entered into a secret pact—complete with hats, handshakes and cryptic words—to draft their pleadings entirely in crayon on the back sides of gravy-stained paper place mats, in the hope that the Court would be so charmed by their child-like efforts that the utter dearth of legal authorities in their briefing would go unnoticed. Whatever actually occurred, the Court is now faced with the daunting task of deciphering their submissions. *Bradshaw v. Unity Marine Corporation, Inc.* (2001, 670)

Among Supreme Court justices, perhaps the classic example of self-presentation came in opinions by Felix Frankfurter. Justice Frankfurter depicted himself as a jurist devoted to the law, regardless of his own preferences and in contrast with less high-minded colleagues:

[8] See, for instance, *Smith v. Colonial Penn Insurance Company* (S.D. Texas 1996) and *Republic of Bolivia v. Philip Morris Companies, Inc.* (S.D. Texas 1999).

Were my purely personal attitude relevant I should wholeheartedly associate myself with the general libertarian views in the Court's opinion, representing as they do the thought and action of a lifetime. . . . As a member of this Court I am not justified in writing my private notions of policy into the Constitution, no matter how deeply I may cherish them or how mischievous I may deem their disregard. *West Virginia Board of Education v. Barnette* (1943, 646–47)

Outside of court, judges have ample opportunities to present themselves to audiences in forums such as speeches, articles, and interviews. Most judges make some use of these forums, and some use them actively. In a 1977 survey of judges on state trial courts of general jurisdiction, 14 percent reported that they spent more than eight hours a month on community relations (Ryan et al. 1980, 42). The proportion is probably higher today.

Judges on higher courts collectively engage in a large volume of academic writing (Abrahamson, Fieber, and Lessard 1993; O'Brien 2003). Federal court of appeals judge John Noonan (2000, 8) has estimated "that at least 25 percent of active and senior appellate judges and 10 percent of active and senior district judges are among the scholarly writers." Noonan himself is a good example. A legal scholar before his judicial appointment, he has continued academic writing that includes a book expressing his disagreement with the Supreme Court on issues of constitutional federalism (Noonan 2002). Some federal judges produce a sufficient volume of writing, or speeches turned into writing, to be compiled in books (e.g., Medina 1954, 1959; Friendly 1967; Miller 1984). State judges are less prolific, but many write books or articles (e.g., Linde 1980; Kaye 1986; Satter 1990; Moyer 2003).

Supreme Court justices are in sufficient demand that they have a wide choice of public appearances outside the Court. Most make a good many appearances. Sandra Day O'Connor reported that she had spoken in every state (O'Connor 2003, xvi). Justice Frankfurter wrote a good many articles for law reviews and other publications (see Frankfurter 1956). Justice O'Connor (2003; O'Connor and Day 2002) and William Rehnquist (1992, 1998, 2001, 2004) published multiple books,[9] and William O. Douglas was a very prolific book author (see Wasby 1990, 315–16).

---

[9] Chief Justice Rehnquist's 2004 book about the aftermath of the 1876 presidential election is especially interesting. When Rehnquist wrote about the parallels between the roles of Supreme Court justices in the elections of 1876 and 2000, some readers surmised that he was seeking to dampen criticism of the Court's decision in *Bush v. Gore* (Donald 2004; Wittes 2004; see G. White 2004). By the time Rehnquist wrote his book, it was clear that the Court's legitimacy did not need to be rescued. However, a persuasive (if indirect) defense of the decision might improve the images of the justices who supported it.

Occasionally a justice talks with a reporter on the record, as Anthony Kennedy did in the 1992 interview that was quoted at the beginning of chapter 1. Federal district judge Thomas Penfield Jackson gave a series of interviews while he was presiding over the federal government's antitrust case against Microsoft in 1999 and 2000 (Auletta 2001b; see *United States v. Microsoft Corp.* 2001, 197–209). Judges sometimes offer direct defenses of their decisions in public forums (e.g., Shatzkin 1997), and in a law school talk Judge Jackson once criticized four of the jurors in a completed criminal case (Gellman 1990).

Most of what judges say in their extracurricular speaking and writing reveals little about them personally. Even so, they communicate something about themselves—that they are friendly or thoughtful or think in certain ways about public issues. The willingness of many judges to devote significant time to self-expression off the bench indicates that it has considerable value to them.

Some judges stand out for the volume and content of their self-expression both on and off the job. Justice Antonin Scalia's off-the-bench comments on legal issues were discussed at the beginning of chapter 1. One journalist noted that "circumspection is not a word in the otherwise limitless Scalia vocabulary" (Lithwick 2003b). Another, describing the justices' public appearances, said that "Scalia is the most likely to offer the jurisprudential equivalent of smashing a guitar onstage" (Talbot 2005, 41).

On the bench, Justice Scalia is more than content to stand in the minority. "I find myself in a large majority and I feel uncomfortable. It questions the premises I'm operating on" (Foskett 2004, 266). That point of view is reflected in his opinions, which often emphasize his differences with other justices. The image that emerges from some of his opinions is of a judge who understands the best course for the Court but who must suffer the pain of watching other justices err because of their lesser skills or questionable motives:

> Beyond that brief summary of the essence of my position, I will not swell the United States Reports with repetition of what I have said before. . . . I must, however, respond to a few of the more outrageous arguments in today's opinion, which it is beyond human nature to leave unanswered. *Planned Parenthood v. Casey* (1992, 981)

Justice Scalia frequently uses strong language to attack opinions by erring colleagues, even in multiples: "A few words are appropriate in response to the concurrence, which finds VMI unconstitutional on a basis that is more moderate than the Court's but only at the expense of being even more implausible" (*United States v. Virginia* 1996, 592).

Less prominent than Scalia but even more active in self-expression— and more self-revealing (Kozinski 1997b)—is Judge Alex Kozinski, who has served on the federal court of appeals for the Ninth Circuit since 1985 (Bazelon 2004). Kozinski has written more than two dozen law review articles, many based on speeches and talks, as well as articles for nonacademic magazines that include the *New Yorker* (1997c), *New Republic* (1993a), and *National Review* (1995). With his Ninth Circuit colleague Stephen Reinhardt, Kozinski toured law schools and other forums for a series of debates about legal issues (Albert 1992). In his articles Kozinski presents an image of himself as someone who speaks plainly, who thinks creatively about issues, who sees the humor in himself and his work, and whose interests go well beyond the law—in sum, a judge who departs from the conventional image of judges (see Kozinski 1991, 1994, 1997a, 2001; Kozinski and Gallagher 1995).[10]

Kozinski uses opinions in the same way, writing in a lively style that attracts attention:

> Long after the public spotlight has moved on in search of fresh intrigue, the lawyers remain. And so we find ourselves adjudicating a decade-old dispute between Gennifer Flowers and what she affectionately refers to as the "Clinton smear machine." *Flowers v. Carville* (2002, 1122)

> MCA filed a counterclaim for defamation based on the Mattel representative's use of the words "bank robber," "heist," "crime" and "theft." But all of these are variants of the invective most often hurled at accused infringers, namely "piracy." No one hearing this accusation understands intellectual property owners to be saying that infringers are nautical cutthroats with eyepatches and peg legs who board galleons to plunder cargo. In context, all these terms are nonactionable "rhetorical hyperbole." The parties are advised to chill. *Mattel, Inc. v. MCA Records, Inc.* (2002, 908) (citation omitted)

> That a company called "Online Classifieds" would have no Internet connection is beyond implausible. Yet NSI made no effort to contact Kremen before giving away the domain name. It's a bit as if Judge Reinhardt sent a letter to the DMV saying, "Judge Kozinski wants you to transfer title to his Lamborghini to me—he'd write to you himself, but he's out of stamps." *Kremen v. Cohen* (2003, 1044 n. 2)

Judge Richard Posner was a leading legal scholar before his 1981 appointment to the federal court of appeals for the Seventh Circuit. He is well known and widely admired for his work as a judge, work that in-

---

[10] Judge Kozinski's interest in his reputation is further demonstrated by his eloquent letter of self-nomination as a candidate in "Superhotties of the Federal Judiciary," a contest conducted by a weblog (underneaththeirrobes.blogs.com/main/2004/06/courthouse_forum.html accessed July 19, 2004). Perhaps because of his eloquence, Kozinski finished first in the male division by a large margin.

cludes considerable creativity in opinion writing. Studies have found him to be the most cited court of appeals judge (e.g., Gulati and Sanchez 2002, 1157–61; Choi and Gulati 2004, 50–51, 60). Posner also stands out for his extracurricular writing; he has maintained a pace of writing for both academic and popular outlets that is best described as staggering. Exaggerating somewhat, one writer reported that Posner "publishes a book every half hour" (MacFarquhar 2001, 78). He also shares a weblog with economist Gary Becker.[11]

The array of topics on which Posner writes is as striking as his volume of publication. While much of his writing is on issues of interest chiefly to scholars, he has published books on the impeachment of President Clinton (1999), the role of the courts in the 2000 presidential election (2001), and policies to deal with risks of catastrophe (2004). Some of Posner's scholarly writing takes controversial positions on issues of social and public policy. In 1987, for instance, he revisited the question of appropriate policy for adoptions of children, a question on which his earlier article with another scholar had been caricatured as advocacy of "baby selling" (Posner 1987, 59–60; see E. Landes and Posner 1978).

The judges whom I have highlighted are hardly typical. The judges of some courts, such as intermediate state courts, work in an obscurity that would be difficult for them to transcend.[12] Some judges who could be prominent prefer to remain relatively obscure.

Yet all judges engage in self-presentation. Presiding over court, participating in oral argument, announcing rules, and writing opinions, they put forward images of themselves. Whether the audiences that pay attention to a judge are large or small, they are still audiences, and judges choose how to present themselves to their audiences.

Motives for Judicial Self-Presentation

The ways that judges choose to present themselves could reflect a wide array of motives. Of the possible instrumental motives, the most powerful is probably judges' interest in advancing their career goals. When elected judges publicize popular decisions or seek to justify unpopular rulings, they usually have their eye on the electorate. In one of the episodes described at the beginning of chapter 1, a federal judge may have used his opinions to enhance his prospects for promotion to the Supreme

---

[11] The blog, "The Becker-Posner Blog," is at http://becker-posner-blog.com.

[12] But not impossible. Judge William Bedsworth of the California Court of Appeal has gained considerable notice from his articles and other extracurricular activities (Judicial Council of California 2005).

Court. Some appearances in public forums are intended to serve the same purposes.

A second instrumental motive that can underlie self-presentation is an effort to advance a judge's legal or policy goals, an effort that fits into strategic models of judicial behavior. Inherent in the writing of opinions for a court is an effort to win support for a decision. Effective opinions might enhance the prospects for compliance with a decision or reduce the chances of reversal by a higher court. Opinion writers may have the additional aim of underlining a court's adherence to legal norms in order to maintain support for the court as an institution (Epstein and Knight 1998, 157–77). Writers of minority opinions may seek to garner support for their positions outside of their court and, in the long run, within it.

Expressions outside court can also be used to win support for judges' conceptions of good judicial policy. That is one purpose of extracurricular expressions by Supreme Court justices. One noteworthy example is the law review article in which Justice William Brennan (1977) advocated that state supreme courts use their own constitutions to broaden legal support for civil liberties.

These instrumental motives undoubtedly account for much of what judges do in presenting themselves to their audiences. This is especially true of elected judges who have a strong stake in keeping their offices. But an explanation of judicial self-presentation based on these motives would be highly incomplete. The limits of an instrumental explanation can be identified by thinking about judges as opinion writers.

Consider, for example, the career goals of Samuel Kent and Alex Kozinski. Almost certainly, each would welcome promotion to a higher federal court. "Kozinski used to joke about being a member of OOPPSSCA, the Organization of People Patiently Seeking Supreme Court Appointments" (Bazelon 2004, 32). Their flamboyant expressions in opinions enhance their visibility, and visibility can help in winning promotion. Even so, their opinions probably work against their promotion. Like other judges who employ humor at the expense of litigants or lawyers, Judge Kent risks annoying both the targets of his words and others who disapprove of their tone. Judge Kozinski's free expression of his views in opinions and out of court makes him controversial and probably rules him out as a candidate for the Supreme Court. He is aware of that effect, explaining,

> I decided a long time ago that it ain't worth it. If I don't live the job for all it's worth, I cheat myself and the public. So I write my opinions and I try to say something. (Bazelon 2004, 32)

Justice Scalia's opinions illustrate the limits of a policy-based explanation of self-presentation. Scalia's strongly worded dissents might advance his conception of good legal policy by winning over his colleagues and legal audiences outside the Court. In this way his opinions could be part of a strategy for shaping the law. Judge Kozinski, who knows Scalia personally, argued early in Scalia's Supreme Court tenure that he was creating the conditions for long-term influence over legal doctrine (Kozinski 1991, 1586–91).

Yet Scalia could write forceful opinions without the vitriolic language that he frequently includes in them. It is difficult to see how that language enhances his influence. Indeed, it carries the risk of alienating the colleagues at whom it is directed as well as other judges who find it unseemly. Scalia himself surely recognizes that reality. A justice who was concerned solely with advancing policy goals would write opinions in ways that minimized this risk.

If these judges do not advance their instrumental goals through the ways they present themselves in opinions, what do they gain? Several Supreme Court justices have provided a sense of the benefits when they discuss dissenting opinions. Oliver Wendell Holmes wrote that "one of the advantages of a dissent is that one can say what one thinks without having to blunt the edges and cut off the corners to suit someone else" (Howe 1953, 646–67). Similarly, Justice Blackmun said that it was "fun to dissent. . . . You have all the enjoyment without the responsibility" (Barbash and Kamen 1984, A42; see also B. Murphy 2003, 402). Justice Scalia (1994, 42; emphasis in original) was especially eloquent on this point:

> To be able to write an opinion solely for oneself, without the need to accommodate, to any degree whatever, the more-or-less differing views of one's colleagues; to address precisely the points of law that one considers important and *no others*; to express precisely the degree of quibble, or foreboding, or disbelief, or indignation that one believes the majority's disposition should engender—that is indeed an unparalleled pleasure.[13]

If he chose, Scalia could write such opinions and then file them for his own future reference rather than disseminating them through the *United States Reports*. Clearly, part of his pleasure derives from the knowledge that other people will read what he writes. Indeed, Scalia's style of opinion writing has won him an admiring audience,[14] an audience that he clearly enjoys (see Tushnet 2005, 147).

---

[13] The same may be true of Scalia's oral announcements of his dissents. William Suter, the head of the Court clerk's office, disputed press reports that Scalia read his "angry dissent" in one case. "'He didn't look angry,' said Suter. . . . 'He looked happy'" (Ringel 2003).

[14] One example is the "Cult of Scalia" website, now out of date, whose text begins: "Overcome by unadulterated awe . . . " (members.aol.com/schwenkler/scalia/, accessed July 20, 2004). A wide-ranging blog by a law school professor at Regent University is entitled

The same can be said of the other judges whose opinions I excerpted. Judge Kent undoubtedly enjoys injecting humor into his opinions, regardless of any audience, but his writing style has also attracted attention in the legal community—attention that, undoubtedly, he also enjoys (e.g., Cox 2001). In combination with his off-the-court expressions, Judge Kozinski's opinions have given him an unusual degree of celebrity for a lower-court judge and the kind of reputation that he seeks.[15]

Justice Frankfurter used opinions as a means to reinforce the image of a self-denying judge devoted to principle over personal preferences (Hirsch 1981). This self-concept was linked with his social identity, in that Frankfurter expected it to win approval from those whose approval he most valued. That self-concept also strengthened his identification with the judges, living and dead, whom he admired and treated as his peer group: Learned Hand, Louis Brandeis, and Oliver Wendell Holmes (Hirsch 1981, 129, 181–82).

Nor can instrumental motives fully explain judges' self-presentation off the bench. This is especially true of judges whose positions are secure, so that they need not campaign to maintain those positions. It is true that judges sometimes can advance their policy goals through their off-the-court speaking or writing. Justice Brennan's advocacy of action by state courts to expand civil liberties probably helped to stimulate that action. But on the whole, judges' off-the-court expressions do not have much impact on public policy. Occasionally they even work against judges' chances to achieve their policy goals. Justice Scalia had to recuse himself from *Elk Grove v. Newdow*, the pledge of allegiance case. Judge Jackson's interviews during the Microsoft case resulted in his removal from the case by the court of appeals (*United States v. Microsoft Corporation*, 2001). Commitments to off-the-bench activities have another cost that is more prosaic but more pervasive: judges who spend substantial time on nonjudicial pursuits have less time to advance their policy positions through their court work.

On the whole, then, judges' willingness to expend this time is better understood in personal rather than instrumental terms. Judges seek approval, and at a deeper level they seek to establish self-concepts that they find pleasing. In their activities off the bench, as in their judicial work, they present themselves to audiences they care about in an effort to achieve those fundamental ends.

"Ninomania" in honor of Justice Scalia, using his nickname (ninomania.blogspot.com/, accessed February 22, 2005). See also Ring 2004.

[15] Judge Kozinski is also the subject of a website, "The Unofficial Judge Alex Kozinski Site," albeit one that is not as effusive in its praise as the one honoring Justice Scalia (see note 14). (notabug.com/kozinski, accessed July 30, 2004).

Audiences and Judicial Behavior

If judges seek the regard of their personal audiences, it is certainly plausible that this goal influences their behavior as decision makers. Indeed, as noted in chapter 1, this is the view of some scholars and observers of the courts. Sheldon Goldman and Austin Sarat (1978, 336) argued that judges are moved by their sense of "what will be acceptable to . . . those people whom the judge respects and looks to for approval." Frank Askin, a litigating attorney, made the same point in stronger form:

> Even lifetime-appointed Supreme Court justices have a constituency to answer to: the bar from which they come, the social and cultural elite with whom they mix; and the general public, whose acclaim they desire. Nobody likes to be a pariah. Faced with disapproval from close associates and disdain from others, only the hardiest ideologue remains true to the faith. (1997, 202)

The dominant models of judicial behavior implicitly disagree with this view, in that they give no consideration to judges' interest in esteem for its own sake. In research based on these models, the existence of this influence on judges' choices is not refuted; it simply is not considered. Thus it is necessary to anticipate possible arguments against a linkage between an interest in approval and judicial behavior.

Two arguments stand out. The first rests on a distinction between judges' self-presentation and the positions they take in decisions. The second rests on the premise that judges can choose the audiences they seek to impress, so that their audiences are endogenous to their preferences. Addressing these arguments provides a way to probe the links between personal audiences and judicial behavior.

Self-Presentation and Decision Making

Even those who agree that judges seek the approval of their personal audiences could argue that this interest in approval has no impact on their choices as decision makers. According to this argument, judges act on the basis of other goals when they adopt their positions in cases. In the dominant models of judicial behavior, the primary (or only) goal is to make good policy or some combination of good law and good policy. Only after judges have chosen their positions do they present those positions and themselves in ways intended to appeal to their personal audiences.

Thus the judge who reaches a decision that will disappoint important audiences could use an opinion to reduce that disappointment. Anthony Kennedy joined in the Supreme Court's decision to strike down the Texas statute prohibiting flag burning in *Texas v. Johnson* (1989). He then wrote a short concurring opinion that declared his unhappiness about helping to let Gregory Johnson go free: "The hard fact is that sometimes we must make decisions we do not like" (420). Presumably, Kennedy's vote reflected his conception of good legal policy in this case. His opinion can be interpreted as an effort to limit the negative reactions to his vote among audiences that he cared about, ranging from personal friends to the segment of the public that became aware of his position.

From the same perspective, Felix Frankfurter might be considered someone who used opinions and other forms of communication to shore up his image among his old associates in the legal and political communities. Perhaps Frankfurter became a conservative on judicial protection of civil liberties early in his Supreme Court tenure, a stance reflected in his votes on case outcomes. Yet he wanted to be perceived as someone who held his liberal beliefs in check because of his commitment to judicial restraint. Thus he explained his votes in that way in his opinions and other communications. Among students of judicial behavior, this is a widely accepted interpretation of Frankfurter's behavior (e.g., Spaeth 1964).

These interpretations of the two justices' behavior may well be accurate. Undoubtedly, some judges in some situations take personal audiences into account only after they reach decisions based on other motives. But this does not mean that there is usually such a clear separation between decision making and self-presentation. To the contrary, there are reasons to doubt that such a clear separation exists.

One reason is the limited strength of good legal policy as a goal. It should be kept in mind that judges seldom gain anything concrete by trying to achieve good legal policy. For this reason it seems doubtful that their concern with the content of legal policy is sufficiently powerful to exclude other considerations from the decision-making process.

Like good legal policy, the esteem of personal audiences in itself is not a source of concrete benefits. But to be liked and respected is of fundamental importance to people. In light of this reality, there is no reason to think that judges invariably give precedence to legal policy over the approval of others. When there is a direct trade-off between the two kinds of goals, judges could be expected to depart from their most preferred policies on some occasions in order to appeal to audiences they care about.[16]

For students of judicial behavior, this should not be all that strange an idea. Within the framework of strategic models it seems natural—even inevitable—that judges depart from their most preferred policy positions

---

[16] In Timur Kuran's terms (1995, 30–31), judges are willing to sacrifice some "expressive utility" that they gain from expressing their own views to gain "reputational utility" from expressing views that important audiences approve. Kuran uses the term "expressive" differently from Alexander Schuessler (2000), whose perspective is discussed shortly.

when doing so would advance their careers or their policy goals. It is at least equally natural for judges to modify their positions when their motives are personal rather than instrumental.

Alexander Schuessler (2000) provides a way to understand such behavior with his concept of expressive choice. Schuessler analyzed mass behavior in arenas such as elections as a form of choice by which people express their identities and attach themselves to others who make the same choices. Judges' choices occur in a context very different from that of voting: their participation in decisions is not optional but required, they act publicly rather than privately, and their individual votes in cases affect outcomes far more than individual votes in elections. For these reasons, Schuessler's analysis may not seem relevant to judicial behavior.

But judges' choices are expressive in their own way, because votes and opinions link judges to particular values and to other people who hold those values. The ultimate impact of a decision is uncertain and contingent; in contrast, a judge's choice between alternative positions is direct. Moreover, by taking positions, judges align themselves implicitly with groups whose positions are consistent with theirs. Kuran's (1995, 30–31) concept of reputational utility is a reminder that the very publicness of judges' choices enhances this function: unlike citizens' votes in mass elections, judges' votes and opinions in cases are known to their audiences.

In the discussion thus far, I have depicted judges who make deliberate trade-offs between the approval of personal audiences and other considerations. The reality is more complicated than that image in at least two ways. First, the desire for esteem is not fully parallel with judges' legal and policy goals or entirely separate from those goals. For instance, judges' social identities may underlie their interest in making good legal policy or condition the impact of that interest on their choices. Of course, judges' preferences themselves are shaped by their reference groups; attitudes develop within a social context (Eagly and Chaiken 1993, ch. 13).

Second, the impact of judges' social identities on their choices generally does not result from a fully conscious process. When judges try to appeal to audiences for instrumental reasons, that response is usually deliberate: they decide to take a particular position in a case in order to avoid retaliation from Congress or the disapproval of voters. But personal motives for responses to audiences typically operate more subtly and at deeper levels. In general, judges who take certain positions to solidify their ties with a social group are not fully aware of that motive and its effects on their behavior.

These complications suggest why there could not be a sharp line between judges' self-presentation to their personal audiences and their choices in cases. If judges' interest in approval is intertwined with other motives, and if it is not fully conscious, this interest inevitably affects what judges decide and not just how they depict what they decide.

Choosing Audiences

Even if it is clear that judges' interest in esteem affects their choices, the strength of this effect can be debated. A second possible argument against a linkage between personal audiences and judicial behavior is that these audiences typically want the same things that judges themselves want. According to this argument, judges choose to link their social identities with individuals and groups whose preferences are similar to their own. As a result, judicial behavior that is consistent with judges' own preferences also enhances regard for them among their most important audiences, so judges' social identities exert little independent impact on their choices (see Rosenberg 2000, 647).

This line of analysis clearly has some validity (see Finifter 1974, 608). People with strong views about policy, especially people who are politically active, tend to gravitate toward reference groups whose members have similar views. During their tenure on the bench judges can continue to form ties with like-minded audiences. And no matter what positions a judge takes, the judge will find people and groups who applaud those positions. If Clarence Thomas is unlikely to win accolades from the American Civil Liberties Union, he can expect an enthusiastic welcome from the Federalist Society.

But the validity of this argument is limited by two realities. First, people do not have complete freedom to choose the audiences that are important to them, to select a particular social identity. People who become judges may be strongly oriented toward a local community or a segment of the legal profession for reasons that have little to do with their self-interest or their policy preferences. Those kinds of identifications can be difficult to shed, even when they create cross-pressures that complicate decision making.

Further, judges sometimes have limited choices among audiences when they seek a particular kind of approval. The federal judge who wants to be well regarded by legal scholars must take legal academia as it is. The same is true of the Supreme Court justice who seeks favorable coverage from the reporters who cover the Court. If legal scholars or Supreme Court reporters lean toward certain positions on the issues the Court addresses, that leaning does not necessarily coincide with a justices' own preferences.

The second reality is that reference groups can influence a judge even when their preferences are similar. A judge and a legal audience may share an inclination toward decisions that adhere to certain standards of legal interpretation. Similarly, a judge and a policy-oriented audience may share a commitment to conservative legal policies. On the surface, audiences of this type would seem to have no independent impact on a judge's choices; judges who seek to please them need do only what they wanted to do anyway.

But such audiences still exert influence by reinforcing tendencies in judges' behavior. Awareness of a legal audience can strengthen a judge's commitment to good legal interpretation as a goal and thereby reduce the weight of policy considerations that might compete with this goal. Judges who identify with a politically liberal audience may feel subtle pressures from that audience against deviation from liberal positions in particular cases. Not surprisingly, consistency between an individual's attitudes and behavior is enhanced by support for those attitudes from important reference groups (Terry, Hogg, and Duck 1999). For this reason even a judge whose audiences perfectly mirror the judge's preferences could be influenced by an interest in maintaining the approval of those audiences.

An audience that accords with a judge's preferences can have more fundamental effects on that judge's behavior. Most important, judges' interest in the approval of their personal audiences helps to solve the motivational problem described in chapter 1: judges gain nothing concrete by trying to achieve good legal policy, so why should they devote themselves to this goal? At least part of the answer is that such devotion can serve judges' interest in establishing a desired image with their audiences and ultimately with themselves. Achieving a desired self-image is not a tangible self-interest, but few things are so important to people. It follows that judges may be willing to work to achieve what they see as good law or good policy, even to undertake some of the difficult labor required by strategic models, if they think those efforts foster the image they want.

Further, judges' links with their audiences help to determine their choices between good law and good policy and between sincere and strategic behavior in the pursuit of those goals. For that matter, personal audiences may encourage judges to pursue goals other than advancing good legal policy. And all these effects can occur even if judges and their reference groups agree fully about what constitutes good law or good policy.

Taking an Audience-Based Perspective

If judges' interest in the esteem of their audiences affects their choices as decision makers, then much can be gained from thinking about judicial behavior from the perspective of judges' audiences. One way to frame that inquiry is in terms of two questions.

First, for a single judge or a set of judges in a particular situation, what audiences are likely to be salient? The answer to this question depends on the attributes of both judges and the situations in which they make decisions. Inferences about the answer can be made on the basis of what we know about human motivation in general, about the experiences and expressions of individual judges and broader groups of judges, and about the opportunities and constraints created by the contexts in which they work. For example, a judge whose career has been entirely within the legal community is likely to identify with that community. On a different level, the requirement that most judges win elections to retain their positions orients judges toward the voting public.

Second, how is a judge's concern with approval from those audiences likely to affect the judge's behavior? The answer rests in part on what is valued by the people who constitute an audience and thus what kinds of behavior would win their approval. It also depends on the salience of a particular audience, both in absolute terms and relative to other audiences. Winning the esteem of audiences is a matter of fundamental importance to human beings; even so, it is not the only thing people want. Further, audiences are not equal in importance. I have emphasized the distinction between instrumental and personal audiences. Those audiences whose esteem is important to judges chiefly for personal reasons are typically more salient and thus have greater potential impact on judicial behavior.

Simply describing these questions makes clear the difficulties involved in ascertaining the influence of judges' audiences—and especially personal audiences—on their behavior. A judge's salient audiences can be difficult to identify, and their boundaries may be amorphous. The influence of these audiences is likely to be subtle and connected with other influences on judicial behavior. Variation in the salience of audiences across judges complicates any effort to analyze their impact.

Because of these difficulties, even those who agree that judges' personal audiences influence their choices might object that there is no point in trying to identify their impact. Scholars have found it challenging to analyze issues that seem considerably more tractable, such as the relationship between judges' policy preferences and their votes on case outcomes; how could they possibly analyze the impact of personal audiences?

For the most part, I will leave this question aside for the moment. Some pieces of an answer emerge in the chapters that follow, and chapter 6 addresses the question directly. At this point, however, three things can be said. First, the difficulties of ascertaining the impact of judges' personal audiences do not rule out meaningful analysis of that impact. There are ways to test for the effects that would be expected if judges act to win the esteem of those who are important to them. Indeed, this task may not be substantially more difficult than the analytic tasks that already occupy students of judicial behavior.

Second, the importance of the task makes it worthwhile to confront its difficulty. I argue that personal audiences have a substantial impact on judges' choices. Indeed, their impact may be more fundamental than the impact of some forces on which scholars currently focus. If that argument is credible, eschewing the study of personal audiences for more tractable issues would be something like the choice of the man in the old joke who searches for his car keys not where he lost them but where the light is better (Chun 2002, 16).

The final and most fundamental point is on a different level. Whether or not it is possible to ascertain the impact of judges' personal audiences on their choices, it is useful to consider judicial behavior from the perspective of the relationships between judges and their audiences. That perspective offers new ways to think about the forces that shape judges' choices and about what we have learned from scholarship on judicial behavior. Indeed, that is the most important benefit of taking this perspective.

The approach taken in the next three chapters is exploratory. Those chapters consider the potential and actual impact of several judicial audiences, employing the theoretical perspectives developed in the first two chapters. Empirical evidence relating to the salience and influence of these audiences is drawn from a range of primary and secondary sources. Among the types of evidence used are judges' opinions and votes on case outcomes, reports of their off-the-bench expressions and activities in the legal and mass media, information on their perspectives and behavior in biographies, and the findings of scholarly analyses of patterns in judicial behavior. The explorations of various audiences provide a basis for tentative judgments about their impact and identify implications of that impact for our understanding of judicial behavior.

These explorations begin in chapter 3 with the audiences that are most familiar to students of judicial behavior. Chapters 4 and 5 examine audiences that receive less attention, in large part because their connections to judicial behavior rest chiefly on personal rather than instrumental goals. In those chapters the effects of taking an audience-based perspective will become especially clear.

COURT COLLEAGUES, THE PUBLIC,

AND THE OTHER BRANCHES OF GOVERNMENT

WHEN JUDGES ENGAGE in self-presentation, they have a wide array of potential audiences. Students of judicial behavior concentrate their attention on three of those audiences. Two are elements of a court's environment, the mass public and the other branches of government.[1] Interest in those two audiences, already substantial, has grown with the popularity of strategic models. The third, judges' colleagues on their own court, is not conceptualized as an audience. But most scholars think of court colleagues as a powerful influence on judges' choices.

Different as these three audiences are, their influence over judges' choices is usually seen as resting on similar bases. Scholars interpret their influence as a product of judges' instrumental motives, primarily their interest in achieving good legal policy. As suggested in chapter 1, there are reasons to be skeptical about the strength of that interest as a motive. Because judges gain nothing for themselves by advancing good policy as they perceive it, their incentives to pursue this goal are not overwhelming.

This does not mean that these audiences do not influence judicial behavior. They do derive some influence from judges' interest in legal policy, and some audiences can be important to judges' achievement of their career goals. Judges' personal motives provide another source of influence that has not been fully recognized, though one whose relevance varies among these audiences. In this chapter, I examine each audience in turn, gauging and interpreting its influence on judges in relation to the full range of judicial motives.

COURT COLLEAGUES

Some trial judges sit alone on a court, but most trial judges and all appellate judges work alongside other judges. Colleagues[2] can influence both

---

[1] Scholars also give considerable attention to a third element of the courts' environments, interest groups. The impact of interest groups is thought to derive chiefly from their part in setting judicial agendas and their provision of information about cases rather than from their serving as audiences for judges (Caldeira and Wright 1988; Spriggs and Wahlbeck 1997; Epstein and Knight 1999). For that reason I do not consider interest groups as a general category, though the section on political groups in chapter 5 discusses interest groups that can serve as judicial audiences.

[2] When I use the term *colleagues* in this section, it refers solely to judges on the same court.

the ways that judges do their jobs and the substance of their decisions. While influence among judges is hardly absent from trial courts (see Flemming, Nardulli, and Eisenstein 1992, ch. 3), I will focus on the appellate level, where there is greater room for such influence.

Because the scholarship on appellate courts as groups is so extensive, we have learned a good deal about the impact of colleagues on judges' choices. Even so, scholars disagree about the extent of that impact and the conditions under which it operates. They also differ on the motives that underlie interpersonal influence, though typically agreeing on the primacy of judges' legal or policy goals. I argue, in contrast, that the impact of court colleagues on each other's behavior rests heavily on their interest in the esteem of other people.

Conceptions of Influence within Courts

Appellate court decisions are inherently collective products. The outcome for the litigants and the legal doctrine that a court promulgates are determined by where a majority of judges stand. Even so, a court might be atomistic in the sense that each judge adopts a position in each case without taking colleagues into account. Under this condition, outcomes and doctrines would simply be the additive result of votes and opinions that individuals choose by themselves. Courts in which every judge writes an opinion in each case, such as the early Supreme Court (Casto 1995, 110–11), may approximate this model.

On the whole, appellate courts in the United States depart substantially from this pattern, in that judges regularly take each other into account during the decision process. The greatest opportunities for influence among colleagues arise during the stages of decision that begin with writing of the court's tentative opinion and end with the final positions of each judge. The opinion writer may incorporate colleagues' views into the first opinion draft. That draft may persuade other judges to change their positions. And give-and-take can occur as opinions are redrafted to win the support of colleagues.

The existence of interpersonal influence in these stages has been well documented for the Supreme Court. Drawing from the justices' papers and other sources, histories of the Court and biographies of justices depict shifts in votes and doctrinal positions that resulted from anticipated and

---

Judges interact with court personnel other than colleagues. Probably most important are law clerks, with whom judges work closely. Law clerks might constitute an important audience for a judge, primarily because judges want to be viewed positively by the people they work with (see Kozinski 1993b, 994). Further, former law clerks help to influence judges' reputations within the legal community. However, law clerks will not be discussed as a discrete audience.

actual actions by colleagues (e.g., J. Howard 1968a; B. Schwartz 1983; Jeffries 1994). Walter Murphy's *Elements of Judicial Strategy* (1964, ch. 3) pulled together evidence on persuasion within the Court from historical and biographical sources. Using similar evidence, J. Woodford Howard (1968b) portrayed what he called fluidity in justices' positions during the decision process, fluidity that derived in part from interactions within the Court.

More recent work provides systematic evidence on behavior related to influence among the justices: shifts of votes (Brenner 1980, 1982), efforts by justices to secure changes in draft opinions (Maltzman, Spriggs, and Wahlbeck 2000, ch. 3; Epstein and Knight 1998, 70–76), and changes in opinions that respond to actual or anticipated objections (Maltzman, Spriggs, and Wahlbeck 2000, ch. 4). This evidence is open to multiple interpretations. One example is the finding that 7.5 percent of the justices' votes on case outcomes during the Burger Court shifted during the decision process (Maltzman and Wahlbeck 1996, 587). That finding can be read to support a conception of the justices as mostly independent or one in which they are highly interdependent.

It does seem clear that the justices exert significant influence on each other. Perhaps the most striking evidence of this influence is movement toward consensus, as justices abandon dissenting votes or sign on to majority opinions they did not originally accept (Dorff and Brenner 1992). Although the evidence on other courts is more limited, the Supreme Court clearly is not the only one in which judges respond to their colleagues' positions. In some courts group decision making takes a form similar to that in the Court (Schick 1970). In others, its primary form is strong deference to the assigned opinion writer (Sickels 1965; Wold 1978).

Scholars who work within the dominant models of judicial behavior interpret the influence of judges on their colleagues in terms of two categories of motives. The first might be labeled *competitive*. Each judge has preferences about court outputs, most often depicted as policy preferences. Judges compete to bring outputs as close as possible to their own preferences. In other words, they behave strategically on behalf of their policy goals (W. Murphy 1964).

Of course, intracourt strategy is an integral part of strategic models of judicial behavior (Epstein and Knight 1998; Maltzman, Spriggs, and Wahlbeck 2000; Hammond, Bonneau, and Sheehan 2005). But models that grow out of the legal and attitudinal ideal types also contain elements of strategy. To varying degrees, adherents to each model view judges as working to achieve what they regard as good legal policy in the collective outputs of their court.

The second category of motives can be labeled *cooperative*.[3] In this conception a court's judges work together to achieve the best feasible decision. "Best" could mean at least two things. One is clarity and coherence in the law, advanced through consensual support for the court's opinions. This goal is central to traditional conceptions of the judicial role (Kornhauser and Sager 1993, 52–53), so it is most closely identified with legal models.

The second meaning is desirable public policy in the judiciary or government as a whole. A court's judges may collaborate to advance their shared conceptions of good policy. If unanimity gives a Supreme Court decision greater strength in other forums, as some justices believe, then one good collective strategy is to pursue unanimity when justices anticipate negative reactions to a decision (Rohde 1972). Like unanimity, other strategies to secure desired responses from the legislature or general public are likely to require cooperation among judges.

The competitive and cooperative interpretations of intracourt influence both involve judges who act instrumentally to achieve good legal policy. Absent from these interpretations is the human element in courts as work groups (see J. Levine and Moreland 1991). It is not that students of the courts ignore this element altogether. There is considerable interest in the inner life of courts, and biographical research often documents the emotions that shape interactions among judges (e.g., Schick 1970; Hirsch 1981; see P. Cooper 1995). But there is little of this human element in efforts to describe and explain intracourt influence.

Colleagues as a Personal Audience

One important human element in the interactions between judicial colleagues is the function of colleagues as a personal audience, one whose relevance does not depend on instrumental motives. Colleagues are likely to be an important personal audience for at least the great majority of judges.

For one thing, judges interact directly with each other. In appellate courts a certain minimum of interaction is required simply to reach collective decisions. For some judges the interaction extends well beyond that minimum, both in decision making and beyond it. The diary of Elizabeth Black, Hugo Black's wife, provides a good picture of life on the Supreme Court in the late 1960s and early 1970s (Black and Black 1986). One

---

[3] An alternative label, derived from scholarship in economics, is *team behavior* (Marschak and Radner 1972; see Kornhauser 1995; Cameron 1997). Kornhauser and Sager (1993, 3–7) offer a somewhat different conception.

striking theme of her account is the frequency with which the justices and their spouses saw each other in formal and informal social settings.

The judges on a trial court could function quite separately from each other most of the time, but even they may interact regularly. Robert Satter, a Connecticut trial judge, has written of "the loneliness of being a judge" that he felt after his appointment to the bench. Ultimately "I hunkered down with my fellow judges, realizing that, after all, we had only each other" (Satter 1990, 35, 37). In part, the isolation of which Judge Satter spoke reflects the constraints on judges' interactions with practicing lawyers and other people outside their courts (Carp and Wheeler 1972, 372–73). The freedom of contact and conversation between court colleagues undoubtedly strengthens the bonds between them. Further, the difficulties of learning and adjusting to the job of judging—difficulties that are greatest at the trial level—lead to bonds between new judges and experienced colleagues who assist in their socialization (Carp and Wheeler 1972).

Colleagues would be an important audience even in the absence of frequent interaction. They function as a true peer group, people who share the same position and work in the same situation. In appellate courts, they are especially well situated to assess each other's work. Not surprisingly, one member of a federal court of appeals cited "the respect of our fellow judges" as one limit on judges' choices (Wald 1984, 10). Two legal scholars argued that, at least below the Supreme Court, judges' "primary audience" is the judges on their own court (Bainbridge and Gulati 2002, 108). If so, court colleagues must constitute a major object of judges' self-presentation.

Presumably, the qualities that most judges want their colleagues to perceive in them are of two types. First, they want to be liked as individuals, pleasant to interact with and easy to work with. Second, they want to be respected as professionals who are capable of doing their work well and who adhere to the norms of their job. That formulation is far more obvious than profound, but it provides a vantage point on some issues in collective decision making.

One of these issues is the balance between legal and policy considerations. On many courts judges differ considerably in their policy preferences. But they have undergone training and socialization that creates a shared belief in the value of interpreting the law well. This shared belief gives judges an incentive to demonstrate to their colleagues that they are skilled interpreters of the law and thus worthy of respect (Kozinski 1993b, 994–95; see J. Cohen 2002, 178–80). In conjunction with judges' interest in the regard of the broader legal community, this incentive adds to the weight of legal considerations in decision making.

One effect is on the content of internal deliberations within the Supreme Court. Scholars who have studied these deliberations note that justices regularly cite legal factors such as precedent. One reason may be that the justices want to fashion decisions that are persuasive to groups outside the Court (Epstein and Knight 1998, 165–71). A more basic reason is that the justices themselves think largely in legal terms (W. Murphy 1964, 44 n. *). But for any individual justice, that legal orientation is strengthened by recognition of how other justices think. An argument will be more persuasive to court colleagues if it is legally strong. And justices will best gain the respect of their colleagues if they make effective legal arguments within the Court. In this way the justices reinforce each other in thinking about cases largely in legal terms.

A second set of issues concerns intracourt strategy. In chapter 1, I questioned the strength of judges' motivations to act strategically. Judges can gain satisfaction from advancing their conceptions of good legal policy in their court or in government as a whole, but they also can gain satisfaction from taking the positions they most prefer. Why take the first path rather than the second, when strategic action requires greater effort and success is hardly guaranteed?

Yet judges do a good deal to win support for their positions in cases from colleagues, and their doing so requires explanation. Much of the explanation lies in judges' concern with the esteem of those colleagues, which provides a noninstrumental basis for competition over the content of decisions.[4] In the interplay that produces a court's decision and opinion, some judges get more of what they want than others. Put differently, judges win and lose to varying degrees. Most judges can be expected to get caught up in that competition, seeking to gain the satisfactions of winning and avoid the frustrations of losing.

These satisfactions and frustrations would exist even if judges did not care what their fellow judges thought of them. But concern for the regard of colleagues strengthens these reactions, and this concern may even be their primary source. Colleagues are well aware of a judge's degree of success in shaping court outputs, and people want to be perceived as skillful and effective by those with whom they work. As a result, it can be difficult for judges to avoid competing with their colleagues to gain support for their positions.

The difference between this conception of strategic behavior and the standard conception in strategic models should be underlined. In the standard conception, judges act strategically within their courts only because they care about the content of court decisions. In this alternative concep-

---

[4] Another part of the explanation relates to the relative ease of engaging in intracourt strategy. Through their regular interactions, judges learn a lot about their colleagues and about how to deal with them, greatly easing the task of devising effective strategies (W. Murphy 1964, 67).

tion, judges care not only about the content of decisions but about winning and losing, because wins and losses affect their standing with colleagues and thus their own self-images.

This is not a very remarkable idea, because it accords with what we know about human behavior. For instance, economists have shown that people will act directly contrary to their concrete self-interest in order to avoid accepting a result that marks them as the loser in a game (Thaler 1988; Camerer and Thaler 1995).[5] Judges would be unusual people if the desire to gain wins and avoid losses did not affect their behavior.

In this way judges' interest in the esteem of their colleagues fills some of the motivational gap in strategic accounts of decision making in appellate courts. Yet that interest also raises questions about some strategic interpretations of intracourt interactions. One example is Walter Murphy's (1964, 49–54) suggestion that Supreme Court justices could try to increase their colleagues' "personal regard" for them as a tactic to win support for their policy positions.

Without question, judges sometimes engage in that tactic. But it is difficult to imagine that strategic motives outweigh personal motives in judges' efforts to appeal to each other. For one thing, most judges are sufficiently perceptive to see through colleagues who behave in an exclusively instrumental fashion toward them. Justice Potter Stewart reported that Felix Frankfurter "courted" him when Stewart joined the Supreme Court, but "Felix was so unsubtle and obvious that it was counterproductive" (Simon 1989, 249). William Brennan has been cited as someone who was considerably more effective in courting his colleagues (Eisler 1993; Clark 1995), but he was effective in part because he enjoyed interactions with colleagues aside from their effects on the Court's decisions.

Brennan aside, most judges undoubtedly care about the esteem of their colleagues as a good in itself. Judges who deal regularly with their co-workers and professional colleagues are unlikely to treat those people solely as votes to be won. Such behavior requires an ability to set aside ordinary emotions that is not very common among human beings.

Another form of intracourt behavior that merits reconsideration is the movement toward consensus that frequently occurs in courts such as the Supreme Court. This movement is usually interpreted in strategic terms, as the result of bargaining over the content of opinions among policy-oriented judges. Certainly that interpretation has some validity, but it cannot fully account for some aspects of the movement toward consensus. One aspect is the building of large majorities. Not surprisingly, the Court's assigned opinion writer is much less likely to accommodate col-

---

[5] The authors of these studies explained the behavior in question in terms that are somewhat different from mine, but I think the explanations are compatible.

leagues with changes in the opinion once majority support is achieved (Maltzman, Spriggs, and Wahlbeck 2000, 121). But such accommodation still occurs with considerable frequency, and it is puzzling: why compromise with someone whose assent is not needed for a majority?

A second aspect of the movement toward consensus concerns pivotal judges. The judge who stands in the pivotal position in a case often joins an opinion to create a majority in exchange for some accommodation on doctrine. In strategic terms, that behavior seems counterproductive. If a judge is pivotal, the judge could simply write a concurring opinion whose position would be decisive (see *Marks v. United States* 1977, 193–94). Justice Lewis Powell wrote only for himself in *Regents v. Bakke* (1978), but his opinion established the legal rules on affirmative education in college admissions for the next quarter century.

Thus movement toward consensus does not fully fit within standard views of intracourt strategy. One alternative explanation is judges' role conceptions, which usually encompass the value of consensus and coherence in decisions. Another is a different kind of strategic consideration, an interest in presenting a united front to other institutions. For that matter, judges' interest in limiting their workloads contributes to consensus.

One important explanation may be personal: judges want colleagues to perceive them as cooperative, as good team players. Because judges gain nothing tangible from the content of their court's decisions as legal policy, they may find it easy to yield some of the benefit of getting the decisions they most prefer for enhanced esteem from their colleagues. Even if there were no other reasons to seek consensus, this motive would lead courts toward agreement.

Variation in Influence among Colleagues

Patterns of influence within courts can vary along several lines. The most obvious of these, the level of influence that different judges wield, has been the subject of some inquiries (Spaeth and Altfeld 1985). Consideration of court colleagues as an audience points to other forms of variation.

One form is the susceptibility of individual judges to the influence of colleagues. Undoubtedly, judges differ in the salience of colleagues as an audience. We can get hints about that salience from judges' choices about their interactions. The haste with which Justice William O. Douglas departed from Washington at (or before) the end of the Supreme Court's term was one visible indicator that he was not as strongly oriented toward his colleagues as, say, Hugo Black (Simon 1980; B. Murphy 2003; see Black and Black 1986). The greater a judge's integration into a court, the more open the judge is to colleagues' influence.

Further, a judge may care far more about the esteem of some colleagues than of others. Judge Jerome Frank of the federal court of appeals for the Second Circuit was a leading legal realist who was often critical of judges and others. He engaged in a fairly bitter rivalry with one judge on his court. Yet toward his colleague Learned Hand he was a "hero-worshiper" (Schick 1970, 244).

Of course, Frank's personal conflict with a colleague was not unusual. Frictions within the Supreme Court over its history are well documented (P. Cooper 1995). In other appellate courts, and even in trial courts, judges sometimes get enmeshed in serious conflicts with each other (e.g., Magagnini 1996; Slind-Flor 1998; Fuetsch 1999; Mitchell 2003; Liptak 2003). Conflict within a court gives special weight to the esteem of allies in that conflict.

Especially when conflict exists in a court, influence may operate primarily within subgroups of judges rather than in the court as a whole. Further, judges' identifications with subgroups enhance perceptions of competition within their court. The result can be to elevate the importance of policy goals as a basis for choices, because judges become more committed to the shared values that link them with some judges and distinguish them from others. The higher stakes in competition over outcomes also foster forms of strategic behavior such as preconference caucuses within factions (W. Murphy 1964, 79).

Courts vary in the overall level of interpersonal influence. Research has shown that institutional rules on matters such as voting and selection of chief judges can affect collective decision making on appellate courts (Brace and Hall 1990). By the same token, court characteristics that help to determine the salience of judges to each other affect the level of influence among them.

One of these characteristics is spatial proximity. The operation of some courts puts judges in frequent direct contact with each other, while arrangements on other courts put distance between them. It is true that today, with easy electronic communication and larger staffs of law clerks, geography has less impact on the work of an appellate court than might be expected (J. Cohen 2002, 153–60). For one thing, even judges who live and work in the same place may interact relatively little with each other. But proximity tends to enhance the personal salience of judges to each other. "Thus, it appears that the correlation between physical distance and social distance is large and positive" (J. Cohen 2002, 167).

At one extreme is the federal court of appeals for the Ninth Circuit as of 2005 (see Hellman 1990). (Congress might divide the Ninth Circuit in the near future.) The court had twenty-eight authorized judgeships, twenty-four of which were filled at the beginning of 2005, and almost that many senior judges. The judges were widely scattered across the vast territory of the circuit, from Arizona to Alaska and Montana to Hawaii; in 2005 the active judges were in fourteen different cities. Groups of three judges met in one of the circuit's courthouses to hear arguments in a set of cases and then separated for the remainder of the decision process. The number of judges on the court made it unlikely that the same three judges would join again in the near future. The court's full complement of active judges never got together to hear cases, because en banc decisions were made by a subgroup of eleven judges.

In contrast, in most state supreme courts and some other courts, a single set of judges sits in one place to hear and decide cases. The judges in some courts reside in the same city. In others, judges converge on the state capital or the home city of a federal circuit to hear and decide cases. As a member of the New York Court of Appeals noted (Kaye 1986, 166), that arrangement enhances the salience of colleagues.

> The fact that we are a nonresident, plenary bench promotes quick bonding. In Albany, we are all away from hearth and home, with a huge caseload and the same seven of us to work our way through it.

This is even more true when judges "work, eat and sleep in the same building, a situation that keeps them in almost constant contact" (Egler 1984). That situation existed in the early Supreme Court under Chief Justice John Marshall, when the justices shared the same boardinghouse (Beveridge 1919, vol. 4, 86–87; Young 1966, 76–77). The justices' continuous interactions and their isolation from others in Washington promoted consensus in their decisions and enhanced Marshall's influence over his colleagues.

It can be posited that the importance of fellow Supreme Court justices as a reference group changed over time with the justices' working arrangements—from the boardinghouse to separate residences and workplaces to offices in proximity with each other at the Supreme Court building. More recently, the development of a practice in which justices work within what Justice Powell called "nine small, independent law firms" (*American Bar Association Journal* 1976, 1454) likely reduced the salience of the justices to each other. If working arrangements have had this impact, they have also shaped the potential for intracourt influence in decision making.

Assessing Court Colleagues as an Audience

With the partial exception of adherents to quasi-attitudinal models, scholars agree that interactions among judges shape the decisions of appellate courts. They disagree about the motives that underlie this influence, but there is a broad consensus that those motives are primarily instrumental: influence operates through judges' interest in the content of legal policy.

This consensual view leaves out judges' interest in the esteem of colleagues. That interest provides a motivational basis for strategic behavior within courts, behavior that would otherwise be difficult to explain fully. It also provides an alternative explanation for some forms of behavior that have been interpreted in strategic terms, such as the citation of legal materials in court deliberations.

Perhaps more important, a perspective that incorporates judges' interest in what their colleagues think of them leads to expectations that differ from those of strategic models. First, judges can be expected to cooperate with their colleagues more than strategic considerations alone would dictate. Because judges value the regard of their colleagues for its own sake, they take opportunities to demonstrate friendliness and good will.

Second, influence within courts can be posited to vary along lines that are unrelated to strategic considerations. A judge will be more open to influence from colleagues who are more relevant at a personal level. Geographic and structural conditions that strengthen personal ties among judges also enhance their impact on each other's choices.

Interest in the regard of colleagues is only one of the human elements that exist in work groups such as courts. Research on courts as small groups, once fairly abundant (see Ulmer 1971), has become rare. Understanding of competition and cooperation in collective decision making would be enhanced by new analyses that depart from the image of Spock-like emotionless judges.

The General Public

The heavy emphasis on the Supreme Court in political science scholarship has produced a curious result: the largest body of research on relationships between judges and the public concerns a court whose members were appointed to their positions and who retain those positions for life. Scholars do study the electoral connection for state judges, and attention to elected judges is growing. I consider these two sets of judges.[6]

---

[6] The situation of federal district judges should be noted. District judges are formally independent of the public, but they reside in the areas affected by their decisions and often have close ties with people there. The resulting pressures were most evident for southern judges in the 1950s and 1960s (Peltason 1971). Some aspects of their situation are discussed in chapter 4. District judges occasionally become national figures, and perceptions of public views may affect their choices. This impact is evident in Judge John Sirica's (1979) account of his involvement in the Watergate cases. Judge Harold Medina of New York, who presided over the major prosecution of Communist Party leaders in 1949, became a visible public

Elected Judges

According to one count (Schotland 1998), 87 percent of all state judges must win voter approval to remain judges when their terms expire. The strongest reason for those judges to take the public into account is the most obvious, their interest in retaining their positions. As with other elected officials, the impact of future elections on judicial behavior depends chiefly on how much judges want to remain judges, how vulnerable to defeat they feel, and their perceptions of linkages between their choices in cases and their electoral fates (see Mayhew 1974, ch. 1).

Most judges want to remain judges when their terms expire (see M. Hall 2001b), and undoubtedly a high proportion have a strong interest in retaining their positions. Their actual vulnerability to defeat varies enormously. Some of the variation is across states, largely due to differences among formal selection systems. Melinda Gann Hall (2001a, 319) found a 19 percent rate of defeat for supreme court justices in partisan elections but only a 2 percent rate in retention elections. There is also variation across court levels, with fragmentary evidence indicating that supreme court justices fare worse than judges on lower courts (Hannah 1978; Baum 1983; Dubois 1984; M. Hall 2001a; see Aspin et al. 2000).

For members of Congress, even a low rate of defeat is sufficient to create a sense of vulnerability, in part because seemingly safe incumbents suffer defeats from time to time (Mann 1978, 3; Parker 1986, 22). Surely the same is true of judges. In light of the one-fifth rate of defeat that Hall found in partisan elections, supreme court justices who serve in states with that system have very good reason to feel vulnerable. Across all courts, judges who face retention elections lose only 1 percent of the time (Aspin 1999, 79). Yet in a survey of those judges, a substantial proportion acknowledged that the existence of retention elections affected judges' choices (Aspin and Hall 1994, 312–13).

Many judges perceive that their chances of defeat depend in part on their decisions. This perception is symbolized by the oft-quoted statement of Otto Kaus, a former California Supreme Court justice, that "there's no way a judge is going to be able to ignore the political consequences of certain decisions, especially if he or she has to make them near election time. That would be like ignoring a crocodile in your bathtub" (Reidinger 1987, 58). Judges' perception of a link between their decisions and their electoral prospects undoubtedly has strengthened with the frequency of campaigns that attack incumbents' decisions (Glaberson 2000; D. Goldberg, Holman, and Sanchez 2002).

---

figure as a result. Medina's speeches after the trial make it clear that even nonelected judges may derive enormous satisfaction from public adulation (Medina 1954, 1959).

Cases vary in their electoral sensitivity. Judges are most vulnerable to attack for perceived leniency in criminal justice, so they have the strongest incentives to take the public into account when they decide criminal cases. Thus it is not surprising that Pennsylvania trial judges become increasingly severe in their sentencing as they get closer to the next election (Huber and Gordon 2004; see Gordon and Huber 2005) or that the prospect of elections affects state supreme court decisions on death sentences (M. Hall 1987, 1992).

The impact of the public stops there for many elected judges. They came to the bench without much interest in what the mass public thinks, and they resent having to take the public into account when they reach decisions. As a result, they respond to the public only to the extent they think necessary to keep their jobs. Judges who express resentment about the need to consider public views in their decisions or to campaign for reelection fall into this category.

For some elected judges, however, the general public is not just an instrumental audience but also serves as an important reference group. Elections can create what Luttbeg (1981, 6–10) called "noncoercive" linkages between officials and the public, linkages that enhance interest in popularity as an end in itself. These linkages were noted in the preceding chapter, and their sources can be considered more fully here.

First, formal and informal campaigning increases contact between judges and the electorate. In turn, that contact can strengthen judges' sense of links with the public. This is especially true of trial judges who serve small constituencies, whose contacts with the people in their jurisdiction are typically more intense than those of their big-city counterparts.

Second, election returns are one of the few concrete indicators of judges' success, and they are by far the most visible. Surely most judges believe that the public is uninformed about the quality of their work and that votes in judicial elections are based chiefly on other considerations. But the public vote still exists as a well-publicized evaluation, and it can be important to judges' self-esteem that they secure as positive an evaluation as possible even if they do not fear defeat. As with legislators, this consideration helps to account for seeming overreaction to the prospect of facing the voters.

Finally, in the states that elect judges, selection effects in judicial recruitment favor lawyers who feel some affinity with the public. On average, lawyers who are willing to face the electorate as judicial candidates have a relatively strong interest in the esteem of the mass public. A task that requires winning votes will be more attractive to lawyers who care what the public thinks of them than it is to lawyers with no interest in public approval. Moreover, in many places active participation in electoral politics enhances the chances of achieving a judgeship.

The strength of these selection effects varies from place to place. Martin Levin (1972; 1977, ch. 8) found that Pittsburgh judges were more strongly oriented toward the public than those in Minneapolis, because they had much greater pre-judicial political involvement. In some states initial accession to the bench comes primarily through interim appointments; in others, most judges have to win elections to take office. The judges in the second group may have stronger ties to the public than those in the first group, because lawyers who care little about public approval are more likely to be deterred by the need to run for office as nonincumbents.

Thus the impact of elective systems on judicial behavior goes beyond creating concerns about tenure on the bench. Rather, the institution of judicial elections serves as a catalyst for several processes that strengthen the link between judges and the public (see Kuklinski and Stanga 1979; Gibson 1980). Judges who identify with the public feel drawn to take public opinion into account. Identification with the public also makes it easier for judges to reconcile their interest in reelection with their own conceptions of good decisions. For these reasons, differences between the behavior of elected and appointed judges do not result solely from fear of electoral defeat.[7]

The importance of the public as a reference group for elected judges should not be overstated. Whether or not they face elections, surely most judges identify more closely with narrower groups than they do with the general public. Still, judges' interest in public approval for its own sake strengthens the impact of the public on the decisions of elected judges.

Supreme Court Justices

The individual self-interest that helps connect elected judges to the general public is essentially irrelevant to Supreme Court justices. Few justices have career ambitions that would be furthered by public support. Yet many students of the Court believe that the justices pay considerable attention to public opinion.

As these scholars see it, the primary reason for concern with the public is instrumental but not narrowly self-interested: the justices seek to maximize the Court's effectiveness as a policymaker. Approval of the Court within the mass public leads to better implementation of its decisions, reduces the chances that the other branches will limit or reverse those decisions, and deters action by the legislature and executive against the Court itself. Thus, it is thought, the justices have strong incentives to se-

---

[7] The behavior of elected and appointed judges is compared in Atkins and Glick 1974; Pinello 1995; Blume and Eisenberg 1999; Hanssen 1999; Tabarrok and Helland 1999; and Helland and Tabarrok 2002.

cure public support (Mishler and Sheehan 1993, 89; Stimson, MacKuen, and Erikson 1995, 555; Flemming and Wood 1997, 494; Mondak and Smithey 1997, 1114; see B. Friedman 2003).

Despite its widespread acceptance, this conception is questionable. It is not clear that the Court as a body benefits much from responding to public opinion. Moreover, the justices' incentives as individuals incline them toward giving little weight to the Court's public standing when they make choices as decision makers.

The difficulties with this conception begin with the collective benefits that might accrue to the Court from trying to maximize favorable attitudes toward the Court. The public support that arguably strengthens the Court is usually characterized as diffuse support or legitimacy, generalized "favorable attitudes" or "good will" toward an institution (Easton 1965, 273; Gibson, Caldeira, and Spence 2003a, 356). Aside from what they do outside the Court, justices could try to foster diffuse support through their decisions in any of several ways.

First, they might avoid specific decisions that adopt highly unpopular policies. Such decisions run counter to a consensus in public opinion on an issue that arouses strong public feelings. The Court's rulings on school prayer and flag burning are well-known examples of decisions that meet those criteria.

Second, they might refrain from decisions that are perceived as inappropriate on procedural rather than substantive grounds. Epstein and Knight (1998, 159–77; see Epstein, Segal, and Johnson 1996) argued that justices avoid overturning precedents and introducing new issues into cases because the public sees such actions as inappropriate.

Finally, justices might try to keep the Court's general pattern of decisions in agreement with the ideological tenor of public opinion, what Stimson (1992) labeled the public mood. These efforts could be reflected in congruence between the Court's decisions as a whole and the public mood. Alternatively, the result might be that the Court shifts ideologically in tandem with the public and in response to the public's shifts (see Songer, Segal, and Cameron 1994, 674–75).

It could make sense for the justices to act in these ways if two conditions are met: the level of diffuse support for the Court affects its institutional strength and effectiveness, and the Court's decisions affect that level of support. On the first condition, the main issue is the extent to which policymakers consider public attitudes toward the Court when they decide on their responses to the Court's decisions and their treatment of the Court as an institution. A perception of diffuse public support for the Court probably deters Congress from making very strong attacks on the Court, such as the one embodied in Franklin Roosevelt's Court-packing plan (see Caldeira 1987). Similarly, that perception may deter policymakers from engaging in highly visible noncompliance with the Court's decisions. One example is the noncompliance that President Nixon considered after *United States v. Nixon* (1974) required that he turn over audiotapes of his conversations. In contrast, it is doubtful that assessments of public support for the Court have much impact on more mundane responses to decisions, such as overrides of statutory decisions.[8]

Despite extensive research,[9] we do not have a clear picture of the second condition, the impact of the Court's decisions on diffuse support for the Court. On the whole, however, the evidence suggests that this impact is limited. Diffuse support tends to remain high, higher than that enjoyed by the other branches (see Gibson, Caldeira, and Spence 2003a), and it recovers from the short-term effects of disagreement with specific rulings (Mondak and Smithey 1997). Even a decision as visible, consequential, and controversial as *Bush v. Gore* seemed to have minimal impact on public attitudes toward the Court (Gibson, Caldeira, and Spence 2003b; Nicholson and Howard 2003).[10] The justices probably have little reason to fear that unpopular decisions or lines of policy will weaken their institutional shield.

Moreover, as suggested earlier, the justices probably give little weight to any potential impact of prospective decisions on the Court's legitimacy. This conclusion follows from three related characteristics of legitimacy. First, it is a collective benefit rather than one that accrues to individual justices. Second, any loss of legitimacy due to the Court's decisions and any consequences of that loss are uncertain. Finally, if those effects do occur, they will come in the future, perhaps at a time when the justice is no longer serving. Thus, justices who depart from their preferred positions to protect the Court's legitimacy are giving up something in the present for a speculative benefit in the future, a future that people tend to discount heavily (Loewenstein and Thaler 1989; Loewenstein and Elster 1992).

Consider a justice who believes that the Court's legitimacy suffers if its policies are too distant ideologically from the views of the public. The justice might respond by spending a career casting votes and writing opinions aimed at bringing the Court closer to the public's position. In doing

---

[8] Two studies of school prayer (R. Johnson 1967; Muir 1967) suggest that policymakers' own diffuse support for the Court affects their responses to decisions, but this is different from their perceptions of public support.

[9] This research includes W. Murphy and Tanenhaus 1968; Casey 1976; Caldeira 1986; Caldeira and Gibson 1992; Gibson and Caldeira 1992; Mondak and Smithey 1997; Grosskopf and Mondak 1998; Hoekstra 2000, 2003; and Durr, Martin, and Wolbrecht 2000.

[10] Price and Romantan (2004) did find some ideological and partisan polarization of attitudes toward the Court shortly after *Bush v. Gore*, but aggregate confidence in the Court changed little.

so, the justice regularly deviates from personal preferences for a possible increase in public support that accrues to the Court as a collectivity. This seems like a quite poor strategy, and in any event it could not be very appealing to most justices.

Under unusual circumstances, a potential threat to legitimacy appears to be substantial and immediate. Perhaps this was the perception of some of the justices who ultimately formed the majority in *Bush v. Gore*. Before the decision was issued, they may have concluded that a ruling in favor of Governor Bush would damage the Court's legitimacy. But if those justices had strong rooting interests in the outcome of the election, those interests could be expected to outweigh their concern with legitimacy. Which was worse, to tarnish the Court's standing or to leave open the possibility that a liberal president would come into office and—among other things—appoint liberal justices to the Court? As it turned out, the majority reached the decision it wanted without measurable damage to the Court's legitimacy.

All this being true, it is likely that some justices exaggerate the impact of the Court's decisions on its public support or the impact of the Court's support on its efficacy as a policymaker. Perhaps some justices are highly risk-averse. In either case, they might actually give more weight than necessary to public opinion. But the justices' incentives, reinforced by the Court's record of maintaining public support, do not seem to run in that direction.

Justices might respond to public opinion for another reason altogether, their interest in personal approval from the mass public. Scholars have essentially ignored this possibility. They set it aside because justices who have no interest in elective office lack both instrumental motives for courting the public and the links with the public that flow from elections. Yet it is possible that the public functions as an important reference group for some justices.

It is difficult to assess this possibility. On the one hand, the individual benefit of popularity provides a stronger incentive than the collective benefit of effectiveness in policymaking. Thus, if justices use their votes and opinions to win public support, an interest in popularity is the more likely motive for these efforts. On the other hand, it is not clear that most justices care very much about the public's view of them. Because of their pre-Court experiences, Supreme Court justices are likely to orient themselves toward elite groups rather than the general public.

However, the justices are not homogeneous in their experiences. Some were immersed in electoral politics before reaching the Court, while others had little contact with the general public. Justices who were active in politics are more likely to identify with the public than those who spent their careers in elite law practice and the judiciary.

TABLE 3.1

Background Characteristics of Supreme Court Justices,
by Year of Appointment

Years	Lifetime Experience			Position at Appointment	
	N	Electoral Candidacy	Judgeship	Political Position	Judgeship
1861–1895	22	86.4%	68.2%	13.6%	45.5%
1896–1932	19	57.9	57.9	26.3	42.1
1933–1968	21	38.1	47.6	61.9	28.6
1969–2005	13	7.7	84.6	7.7	84.6

Sources: Biskupic and Witt 1997; Epstein et al. 2003; biographies of justices.

Table reprinted, with modification and updating, from Lawrence Baum, "Recruitment and the Motivations of Supreme Court Justices," in *Supreme Court Decision-Making: New Institutionalist Approaches*, ed. Cornell W. Clayton and Howard Gillman (Chicago: University of Chicago Press, 1999), 210. © 1999 by the University of Chicago.

Note: For justices with multiple appointments to the Court, only the first is counted. "Electoral Candidacy" refers to candidacy for any nonjudicial office in government that was, or appears to have been, elective. Seats in the U.S. Senate are counted as elective in all periods. The proportions in this column may be slightly inaccurate because of incomplete information. "Political Position" refers to any official, full-time position in the executive or legislative branches. "Judgeship" refers to any judgeship, including part-time positions.

In this respect the backgrounds of justices in the current era are distinctive. Beginning with Richard Nixon, presidents have given Court appointments chiefly to people whose involvement in political activity was relatively limited. This development is the culmination of a longer-term change in recruitment paths to the Court (Schmidhauser 1959, 1979; Baum 1999; Epstein, Knight, and Martin 2003; see Silverstein 2003).

The pattern of change is shown in table 3.1. Increasingly, justices come to the Court from careers in the legal system as practicing lawyers and judges rather than from careers in politics. In the successive periods since the 1860s, the proportion of justices who ran for elective office at some point has declined precipitously. The proportion who held some kind of political position (as defined in the table) when they were appointed to the Court was at its highest in the 1933–68 period, but that proportion reached its lowest point in the most recent period. Of the justices appointed from 1969 to 2005, only Sandra Day O'Connor had run for office, and only William Rehnquist held a political position at the time of appointment. Justices who reach the Court after careers in elective office have become rare, while those who spent their pre-Court careers in some combination of legal practice, law teaching, and judgeships predominate.

This trend has contributed to a decline in the number of justices with an interest in moving to an elective office. William O. Douglas may have been the last justice with that ambition (Simon 1980, 261–62; Eisler 1993, 123). But more important is the likely decline in justices' identifications with the mass public.

The possible impact of this change is suggested by the example of Hugo Black. Some commentators have speculated that an interest in public approval shaped Black's behavior as a justice: he embraced civil liberties in part to dispel the image of him as a former Ku Klux Klan member, and he became more conservative late in his tenure with an eye to his reputation among white southerners (Davis 1994, 43; Domnarski 1996, 67; Hutchinson 1999, 167). These speculations may simply be wrong. But Black had been a very active politician and officeholder until his Court appointment (Newman 1997), experience that undoubtedly oriented him toward the public. And as a justice Black paid attention to the public, even answering hostile mail about one of the Court's school prayer decisions (Black and Black 1986, 95–96). Although his political ambitions probably ended when he reached the Court, his public career reflected and reinforced an interest in approval from the general public. Thus the speculations about his motives are more credible than they would be for a justice without much political experience.

For most of the Court's history, a career politician such as Black would not have stood out. Today he would. It remains true that appointment to the Court is unlikely without some participation in politics. But among today's justices, the level of participation is typically far below the central part that politics played in Black's life. As a consequence, the public is now less likely to serve as an important reference group for members of the Court.

Even if the justices of the current era sought public approval, its pursuit could be viewed as futile. After all, individual justices are not very visible to the public. For instance, only small proportions of survey respondents can recall the names of most justices (Biskupic 1995a; Madigan 2002).

To a degree, this lack of visibility is a matter of choice: most justices seem wary of exposure to the mass public. This wariness is one reason for the continuing refusal to allow televising of Court sessions and the unwillingness of most justices to give interviews on broadcast television. These practices help maintain a protective anonymity for the justices.

And yet interest in public regard is not entirely absent in the current era. Some justices devote time and energy to activities that put them in contact with the general public. Because these activities are hardly mandatory, the willingness to engage in them is not simply a matter of duty. Indeed, some justices believe they have a public reputation and care about it (Koh 1994, 20; Davis 1994, 106; Domnarski 1996, 67; Rosen 1997,

65; J. Williams 1998, 369–70; A. Thomas 2001, 485). This interest in public reputations is understandable: even justices who recognize and appreciate their limited visibility can enjoy acclaim.

This appears to be the case with Sandra Day O'Connor, who stands out among recent justices for the strength of her relationship with the public. For one thing, she was unusually well known. Surveys indicated that she had greater public visibility than any of her colleagues during her last decade on the Court (Biskupic 1995a; Polling Company 2002). (Clarence Thomas ranked second.) More than any of her colleagues, she was a public figure.

Moreover, O'Connor showed considerable interest in the public, and one commentator referred to her "cultivating her public persona" (Rosen 2001, 35). That interest was reflected in her public appearances, books for a mass audience (O'Connor and Day 2002; O'Connor 2003; see McElroy 1999), and television interviews. At least in her first year on the Court, she tried to answer all the mail she received, more than five hundred letters a week (Rosen 2001, 35).

O'Connor also indicated that she cared what the public thought. In a television interview, she referred to the strong views of people on both sides of the abortion issue. "And I'm very much aware of that when we have a case in that area" (*Dateline NBC* 2002). In all likelihood, most justices would not acknowledge that awareness. It is plausible that on highly visible issues, O'Connor's thinking about prospective public reactions affected her judgments. In particular, a desire to be perceived as moderate may have influenced her positions on issues such as affirmative action (*Grutter v. Bollinger* 2003).

It is relevant that O'Connor was the only justice in the current era to run for public office. She did give up a leadership position in the Arizona legislature to become a judge, a decision that someone with a strong interest in mainstream politics would not have made. Still, her political career linked her to the public in a way that the careers of other recent and current justices did not. This background may be related to the strength of O'Connor's relationship with the general public.

Whatever may be their motives for interest in public approval, to what extent do justices actually take the public into account when they make choices in cases? Earlier I noted three ways that a concern with institutional legitimacy might affect the Court's decisions. Justices who care about their public standing as individuals might respond in the same ways. In the first two, justices avoid taking individual positions or contributing to collective decisions that establish highly unpopular policies or that violate norms such as adherence to precedent. It is very difficult to ascertain whether the justices actually act in these ways.

For instance, justices sometimes mention the Court's legitimacy in their opinions.[11] In *Planned Parenthood v. Casey* (1992), the three justices who wrote the Court's pivotal opinion emphasized their view that overturning *Roe v. Wade* would damage the Court's legitimacy. Dissenters occasionally charge that the Court's decision will damage its standing (e.g., *Payne v. Tennessee* 1991, 856; *Bush v. Gore* 2000, 158). But there is no clear evidence that concerns about legitimacy actually affected the justices' positions in such cases rather than reinforcing positions based on other considerations.

Almost surely, justices sometimes avoid decisions that would be highly unpopular in the country. This was the perception of Justice William O. Douglas (1980, 38, 92–93), for instance. But the Court often does make very unpopular decisions, and it is uncertain how often the justices shrink from putting themselves in direct conflict with public attitudes.

The overall relationship between the public mood and the Court's ideological position is more susceptible to inquiry, and several studies have analyzed this third form of public influence. The largest body of research focuses on covariation between the public's ideological mood (Stimson 1992) and the Court's decisional record in broad fields of policy or across all fields. A series of studies has concluded that to a degree, some individual justices or the Court as a whole respond to changes in the public's ideological position.[12]

The findings of these studies are subject to multiple interpretations. Most important, it is difficult to distinguish between the effect of changes in the public's ideological mood and changes in the justices' own attitudes. The events and trends that produce one kind of change might bring about the other as well. For the reasons discussed earlier, it seems more likely that the justices' own preferences change than that the justices respond systematically to changes in mass public opinion.

One complication in analyzing the impact of public opinion on the Court is that justices might respond to subsets of the public that are especially salient to them rather than the public as a whole. It would be reasonable for them to focus on the segment of the public that is most attentive to the Court's work. Alternatively, justices might try to win the approval of groups that are especially relevant to their personal identities. Justice

---

[11] They sometimes mention legitimacy in other places. The most famous off-the-bench statement of concern about legitimacy is former justice (and future chief justice) Charles Evans Hughes's (1928, 50–54) citing of three "self-inflicted wounds," ill-advised decisions that he thought had weakened the Court's legitimacy.

[12] These studies include Mishler and Sheehan 1993, 1996; Marshall and Ignagni 1994; Link 1995; Stimson, MacKuen, and Erikson 1995; Flemming and Wood 1997; and McGuire and Stimson 2004. Norpoth and Segal (1994) concluded that the public exerts no systematic effect on the justices.

O'Connor's choices of public appearances and her expressions suggest that she had a particular interest in approval from women (O'Connor 2003, part 4; see Lane 2004b). Clarence Thomas's efforts to counter criticism of him in the African-American community make it clear that he cares a great deal about his standing in that community (Biskupic 1994a; A. Williams 1995; N. Lewis 1995; Foskett 2004, 288–93).

Interest in the support of a subset of the public could lead justices in directions that diverge from the views of the public as a whole. For instance, Justice O'Connor had an incentive to avoid taking positions that would jeopardize the adulation she received from well-educated women—women who tend to support feminist goals. As a result her position on abortion might have responded to attitudes in this segment of society, attitudes that do not coincide with mass public opinion (see Blackmun 1994–95, 504–5).

Assessing the General Public as an Audience

It seems safe to conclude that most judges care about how the public views them. It is less certain how much they care and why they care. It is even less certain how much and in what ways judges' interest in the public affects their behavior as decision makers.

Scholars have emphasized instrumental reasons for judges to respond to public opinion. Elected judges want to remain in office. Supreme Court justices want to maintain the Court's legitimacy and thus its efficacy as a policymaker. Certainly the interest of elected judges in maintaining their positions makes the public salient to them. The assumption that an interest in efficacy makes the public salient to Supreme Court justices is more questionable.

Scholars have more or less ignored judges' interest in public approval for its own sake. That omission may do no great harm: the mass public is probably not of great importance to the social identities of most judges. Yet this motivation should not be dismissed out of hand. A personal interest in public regard can reinforce career goals in making public approval relevant to elected judges. For Supreme Court justices, this interest may be the primary basis for any influence the public actually exerts on the justices' choices.

Institutional attributes of courts affect the degree and form of public influence on judges. Elected judges pay more attention to the public than do their appointed counterparts. Because they serve smaller and more homogeneous constituencies, trial judges probably have stronger links to the public than do appellate judges.

Institutional attributes aside, individual judges surely differ in the weight they give to public approval. This variation probably correlates with judges' backgrounds. Some judges reach their positions after immersing themselves in electoral politics as a vocation or avocation. The choice to take that path may reflect interest in public approval, an interest that judges would bring to the bench. Further, political experience in itself enhances the relevance of the public to a judge. Those who achieve judgeships without that experience and those whose pre-judicial careers are in elite settings such as corporate law practice are less likely to think about how they are viewed by the general public. Thus the influence of public opinion on judges can be posited to increase with their prior experience in electoral politics.

For any given judge the impact of the public is likely to vary with case characteristics and other circumstances. Elected judges may respond to electoral considerations primarily in criminal cases. Supreme Court justices are most likely to take the Court's legitimacy into account when the Court is under unusually strong pressure. Judges who court popularity for its own sake may do so through the occasional decisions that are highly visible. Efforts to ascertain the public's importance as a judicial audience should take these complications into account rather than looking only at across-the-board effects.

Another type of complication is potentially quite important. As Fenno (1978, ch. 1) emphasized, some constituents are more important to legislators than others. Undoubtedly that is true of elected judges as well. Judges who do not face the voters are even more likely to seek the approval of segments of the public rather than the public at large. As a result, the overall relationship between mass public opinion and judges' decisional choices may not fully capture the impact of the public on those choices.

THE OTHER BRANCHES

Compared with the mass public, the legislative and executive branches of government are far smaller, more proximate to the courts, and more attentive to judicial decisions. Moreover, the other branches are relevant to judges in multiple ways: they shape the impact of decisions, they hold powers over courts as institutions, they select judges for some courts, their members have personal ties with judges, and the executive branch is the most frequent litigant. Each of these linkages provides a potential source of influence over judges' choices.

I will not discuss the role of government as a litigant, a subject that has been studied extensively. In this role government bodies can have considerable impact on the courts, but at most this impact is strengthened marginally by their serving as an audience for judges.[13] Each of the other linkages will be examined in terms of the bases for influence that it may provide.

The first two linkages are widely thought to provide substantial influence for the legislature and executive. Because the other branches can modify or overturn court decisions, several scholars have posited that judges routinely take these potential responses into account when they make decisions. And because the other branches can attack courts and their judges, most scholars believe that judges act to avoid or ameliorate serious conflicts with the other branches. The first source of influence is thought to derive from judges' interest in the content of legal policy, the second largely but not exclusively from that interest. As I will discuss, there are reasons to be skeptical about influence for the other branches that is based on judges' interest in legal policy.

The power of the other branches to select judges and personal ties between judges and other policymakers have received less attention. The influence over judges that derives from these sources is highly uncertain, and that influence may not be substantial. However, the motivational bases for these sources of influence are relatively strong—in all likelihood, stronger than judges' interest in the content of legal policy.

Routine Adjustment

A number of scholars who use strategic models of judicial behavior have argued that the Supreme Court engages in what can be called routine adjustment of statutory decisions.[14] Although other courts could also engage in routine adjustment, the Court provides a good focus for consideration of it. In this strategy policy-oriented justices determine in each case whether taking their most preferred doctrinal position would result in congressional action to override the Court's decision with a new statute. When they expect an override, they modify their position to prevent it.

---

[13] Scholars who are interested in government as a litigant have focused primarily on the success of the federal government in the Supreme Court and the sources of that success (Scigliano 1971; Caplan 1987; Segal 1990, 1991; Salokar 1992; McGuire 1998; Ditslear 2002; Yates 2002; Pacelle 2003).

Some students of judicial politics in other nations have argued that concern with the power of the other branches leads judges to favor government as a litigant. But even in systems in which the courts are highly vulnerable, their responses may be more complex (Helmke 2005). That certainly is true in the United States, where legislators do not necessarily favor the positions taken by the executive branch in litigation.

[14] Examples include Eskridge 1991b; Spiller and Gely 1992; Eskridge and Frickey 1994; Schwartz, Spiller, and Urbiztondo 1994; Epstein and Knight 1998, 139–45; and Bergara, Richman, and Spiller 2003. This discussion of routine adjustment draws from Baum and Hausegger (2004).

The posited benefit of this strategy is that judges thereby obtain the best possible result, since a Court decision that departs somewhat from their ideal is preferable to the larger departure that would result from a congressional override.

The motivational assumptions that underlie this conception of judicial strategy were discussed in chapter 1. In that discussion I questioned whether the benefit derived from action to avoid congressional overrides could outweigh the costs. By avoiding overrides, justices can gain only the symbolic benefits of advancing the policies they prefer. In the process, they yield the somewhat different symbolic benefits of adhering to their preferred positions. Serious efforts to avoid overrides also increase the time and energy that judges put into decision making.

A closer look at routine adjustment raises additional questions about its attractiveness. For one thing, the symbolic benefits that actually accrue to a justice from routine adjustment are limited. The efforts of a single justice to shape congressional responses to decisions can have only a very limited impact on the totality of government policy on an issue.

The satisfaction that justices derive from this form of strategy might be enhanced by the enjoyment of playing an implicit game with Congress. But this does not seem like a very satisfying game: it puts the justices in a subordinate and dependent position, one that undoubtedly runs contrary to the self-concepts that most justices want. Moreover, in contrast with intracourt strategy, winning and losing are not immediately apparent, and the close interactions that can heighten a sense of competition are absent. This is one reason to posit that strategic behavior is more common within the Court than in relation to other institutions.

Further, the difficulty of predicting overrides goes beyond the ideological calculations described in chapter 1. Like any other kind of congressional action, overrides result from a complex process that greatly complicates efforts at forecasting. One thorny problem for a justice who seeks to predict congressional action is that, more often than not, overrides are provisions of broader bills (Solimine and Walker 1992, 449; Hausegger and Baum 1998, 228–29; but see Barnes 2004). It is difficult even to count overrides because so many are buried in omnibus legislation (Melnick 1994, 331 n. 13), and members of Congress themselves are often unaware of these provisions. This practice increases the element of idiosyncrasy in overrides and aggravates the task of prediction.

The uncertainty of congressional response reduces the strategic value of routine adjustment. A justice who always acts to avoid predicted overrides sometimes will compromise implicitly with Congress when compromise is unnecessary. Similarly, calibration of decisions to minimize the chances of an override is inherently inexact, so justices frequently would give up more than necessary (or not enough to avoid an override) when they modify their positions with Congress in mind.

Meanwhile, the costs of failing to prevent an override are not especially severe. An override often moves policy on an issue away from what a justice would prefer. But the difference between the policy that results from an override and the policy that the Court would have adopted to prevent an override is seldom great, and the Court retains the ability to shape policy by interpreting the new legislation.

For these reasons, even a highly strategic justice probably would not engage in routine adjustment (Segal 1997, 31–33; Cross 1998, 527–29). Taken together, the various pieces of relevant empirical evidence support this judgment. One piece comes from studies of routine adjustment that test for the impact of the ideological makeup of the other branches on the ideological content of Supreme Court votes and decisions where justices might have strategic reasons to adjust their positions (Spiller and Gely 1992; Segal 1997; Martin 1998, ch. 4; Bergara, Richman, and Spiller 2003; see Hansford and Damore 2000).

These tests are meaningful but far from definitive. For one thing, their findings conflict. More fundamentally, they do not fully overcome the difficulties of measuring strategic behavior. For example, they incorporate the assumption that justices who seek to avoid overrides consider only the ideological positions of the other branches. But interest groups play an important part in getting overrides on the congressional agenda and determining their success (Eskridge 1991a; Solimine and Walker 1992; Hausegger and Baum 1998; Barnes 2004; Hettinger and Zorn 2005). A justice who wants to avoid overrides would not ignore the evidence of potential interest group initiatives that amicus briefs make readily available.

Two other pieces of evidence are inconsistent with routine adjustment. The first is the number of congressional overrides of statutory decisions. The most thorough effort to identify overrides (Eskridge 1991a), updated by a half dozen years, found that a minimum of 5.6 percent of the Court's statutory decisions in the 1978–89 terms were overridden substantially or completely (Hausegger and Baum 1998, 228). Because Congress would leave most statutory decisions standing even if the justices simply adopted their most preferred policies, even a 5.6 percent override rate represents a substantial proportion of the cases in which an override could have occurred.

In light of this finding, it may be that justices do their best to avoid overrides but are simply not very successful. It seems more likely that the justices do not work very hard to avoid overrides. These two possibilities are related. If justices learn that overrides are difficult to predict, and if there is not much to be gained from avoiding overrides, the most reasonable response is to stop trying to predict them.

The second piece of evidence that questions routine adjustment is the frequency with which majority opinions invite Congress to consider overriding statutory decisions (Hausegger and Baum 1999). These invitations might be interpreted as the product of a complex policy-oriented strategy (Spiller and Spitzer 1995; Spiller and Tiller 1996). More likely, they reflect multiple considerations (Hausegger and Baum 1999). But whatever their sources, the use of invitations argues against the conception that justices uniformly seek to avoid overrides.

For the most part, attention has focused on routine adjustment in statutory decisions. This strategy might also be used in constitutional decisions, since Congress could enact new statutes to limit or nullify the impact of some of these decisions as well (Dahl 1957; Meernik and Ignagni 1997; Pickerill 2004, ch. 2). Scholars have begun to investigate this possibility (Martin 1998, ch. 4; Martin 2001; Epstein, Knight, and Martin 2001; Sala and Spriggs 2004). Yet the reasons to doubt that routine adjustment occurs in statutory law apply to the constitutional arena as well.

Arguably, justices have a stronger incentive to avoid overrides of constitutional decisions because such overrides are more likely to involve serious institutional conflict (Epstein, Knight, and Martin 2001). In practice, however, most constitutional overrides are similar to statutory overrides in the lack of serious conflict. Even in the rare instances when Congress proposes a constitutional amendment to overturn a decision, the justices do not necessarily feel great heat. This was true, for instance, when Congress and the states enacted the Twenty-sixth Amendment on the eighteen-year-old vote after *Oregon v. Mitchell* (1970). Thus justices who care about the Court's standing and powers may perceive little threat from the possibility that the other branches will overturn constitutional decisions or limit their impact.

All this does not mean that the justices never seek to influence legislation. Invitations to Congress are one form of such action. Justices can act in other ways to achieve good policy by taking Congress into account. Walter Murphy (1964, 125–32) discussed various tactics that might be aimed at "securing positive action" from Congress, and these tactics receive some use. For example, the justices reportedly avoided a constitutional issue in a 1964 case stemming from a racial demonstration so they would not interfere with the debate over the Civil Rights Act of 1964 (Hutchinson 1998, 350). In 1965 the Court decided a conscientious objector case in a way that avoided striking down a federal statute, apparently because some justices feared that Congress would not adopt a new statute and thereby would eliminate conscientious objector status (Cray 1997, 482).

Occasional use of such tactics seems more consistent with justices' desired self-concepts than does routine adjustment. It does not require regular subordination to Congress. Indeed, such occasional action may allow the justices to feel a degree of control over their political environment. In motivational terms, selective efforts to influence congressional action are more reasonable than constant efforts to avoid overrides.

Avoiding and Defusing Conflict

One form of selective response to the power of the other branches is action to avoid serious conflicts or to defuse conflict when it does occur. Indeed, a standard image of the Supreme Court is that the Court collectively engages in strategic retreats under pressure from the other branches. This image is widely accepted; even the strongest supporters of a quasi-attitudinal model agree that on a few occasions, "the Court arguably has backed down in the face of real danger from Congress" (Segal and Spaeth 2002, 350 n. 102).

It is certainly plausible that judges back down, because they have two kinds of motives to limit conflict with the other branches. The first derives from the powers that the legislature and executive branch hold over courts as policymakers, powers exemplified by congressional control over federal court jurisdiction. To the extent that judges care about their capacity to make policy, they would prefer to avoid limits on that capacity.

The second kind of motive concerns the impact of the other branches on judges as individuals. Control over court budgets affects their work lives, and control over salary increases affects their incomes. Personal attacks by people in the other branches can make life less pleasant, and at the extreme a legislature could remove a judge through impeachment (see Kalman 1990, 359–76). Weakening of a court could reduce the prestige attached to its members, prestige that surely is important to the self-esteem of most judges.

Because these motives can be powerful, scholars have argued that fear of sanctions from the other branches has substantial impact on Supreme Court justices (Rosenberg 1992; Peretti 1999, ch. 5; Cross and Nelson 2001, 1459–73). Yet the extent of this impact is quite uncertain. The primary source of this uncertainty is the difficulty of isolating concern with Congress and the president from other considerations in the justices' choices. This difficulty is analogous to the problems in determining whether concern about public support deters the justices from making unpopular decisions.

Several historical episodes are regularly cited as examples of Supreme Court retreats under pressure. John Marshall carefully limited his confrontations with the hostile Jeffersonians in the presidency and Congress

(M. Graber 1998; McCloskey and Levinson 2000). The Court accepted
the withdrawal of its jurisdiction over a challenge to the post–Civil War
Reconstruction policies (*Ex parte McCardle* 1869; see Epstein and Walker
1995). When conflict with President Roosevelt over his New Deal policies
reached a height, one or perhaps two pivotal justices engaged in the
"switch in time" to ease the conflict. The Warren Court of the 1950s
undertook a "tactical withdrawal" (W. Murphy 1962, 246; see Pritchett
1961) under the threat of adverse congressional action.

These episodes are subject to differing interpretations. For instance, not
all commentators accept the standard account of the New Deal episode,
and there are reasons to question that account (B. Cushman 1998). But
in all probability some justices in some of the episodes acted on their
concern about the other branches.

In less dramatic circumstances there is sometimes evidence that justices
worried about congressional hostility or concrete action against the Court
when they considered cases (e.g., Cray 1997, 486; B. Schwartz 1998, 43).
In some of these instances concern with Congress may have been decisive
in determining the positions that justices took. There are other cases in
which it is a reasonable guess that some justices tried to avoid negative
action by the other branches. In *Elk Grove v. Newdow* (2004), for instance, some of the Court's more liberal justices might have voted to
obliquely reverse the Ninth Circuit's ruling against inclusion of the words
"under God" in the Pledge of Allegiance in order to avoid the congressional pique that would have resulted from voting to affirm that ruling.[15]

On the other hand, the Court often reaches decisions that seem likely
to arouse conflict with the other branches. For example, the justices who
struck down a flag-burning law in *Texas v. Johnson* (1989) surely could
predict that they would stir up opposition in the other branches. The
Court's decisions on policies concerning suspected terrorists in *Hamdi v.
Rumsfeld* (2004) and *Rasul v. Bush* (2004) were guaranteed to displease
the executive branch. The same is true of broader lines of policy. The
justices who voted to invalidate a series of New Deal laws prior to 1937
understood quite well that they were creating a confrontation with Congress and the president. The range of Warren Court decisions that ran
counter to strong sentiment in the legislative branch is striking.[16] For their

[15] Action to avoid negative responses from the other branches may be easiest when it
involves avoiding the controversial issue in a case, as in *Newdow*, or simply not hearing a
case. In these situations justices are not required to support policies with which they disagree
in order to minimize interbranch conflict.

[16] It has been argued that the Warren Court was really affirming national values when it
struck down policies of the states, especially those of southern states (Shapiro 1978, 182–
84; Powe 2000). This argument has some validity, but it should not be overstated. The
Court's decisions on issues such as criminal procedure and school religious practices invali-
dated state rather than national policies, but they were still unpopular in Congress.

part, state supreme courts frequently reach decisions that are likely to produce conflict with the other branches, most notably the series of decisions that struck down state systems for the funding of public schools (Reed 2001).

Further, judges often adhere to policies that have angered legislators and chief executives. Such adherence is exemplified by the Supreme Court's striking down the new federal law against flag burning in *United States v. Eichman* (1990) even after the furor aroused by *Texas v. Johnson*. This behavior suggests a degree of resistance to pressures from the other branches.

If judges are sometimes willing to accept conflict with the other branches rather than avoiding it, how can this behavior be explained? Part of the answer is that the other branches seldom follow through on serious threats against courts and judges. For instance, in the current era proposals to withdraw the Supreme Court's jurisdiction over areas in which it has made controversial decisions are routinely introduced in Congress, sometimes considered seriously, but (thus far) never enacted (see Curry 2005, chs. 6–7). If the justices are even moderately risk-acceptant, they can endure criticism and even confrontation as the price of following their preferred course.[17]

Another part of the answer is that the threat from the other branches often is to the Court as a policymaker, so that the threat has only symbolic consequences for the justices. But the importance of this attribute should not be overstated. Narrowing the Court's jurisdiction surely has a greater sting than overriding a statutory decision, and justices who face such a threat may fear that the prestige attached to their positions will decline.

In any event, conflicts with the other branches have not been without costs for Supreme Court justices. They pay at least a small monetary cost in limited salary increases for displeasing Congress too often over the past half century, a cost that was made explicit in the early 1960s (Schmidhauser and Berg 1972, 8–12). The complaints by some justices about the salaries of federal judges indicate that this matter concerns them.

But this cost illustrates the limits on judges' incentives to retreat from conflict with the other branches. Suppose that justices on the Warren

---

[17] The dearth of strong congressional attacks on the Court and its justices could be interpreted to mean that the justices anticipate and thus avoid lines of policy that would actually precipitate those attacks. This interpretation is not inherently unreasonable. But the record indicates that the justices have (and use) very broad freedom to decide cases as they wish without suffering serious sanctions from the other branches. Moreover, on the whole, the kinds of decisions that would actually trigger serious sanctions from the other branches are probably unattractive to the justices on their merits; differences in policy preferences between the justices and other policymakers may be substantial, but they are unlikely to be overwhelming (Dahl 1957; Peretti 1999, ch. 4). For these reasons, justices generally need not depart from their preferred positions in order to avoid sanctions.

Court had the prescience to recognize that civil libertarian policies would have the effect of depressing increases in their salaries. Would some of those justices have forsaken whole lines of policy that they found desirable in order to avoid this cost? To take that course would exchange independence for subordination, and the resulting damage to justices' self-esteem likely would have exceeded the value of the lost salary increases. In reality, the impact of Court policies on congressional salary decisions is uncertain, making judicial retreat even less attractive.

The justices' calculations about actual and potential conflict with the other branches probably would be different if Congress more frequently used its powers against the Court. In that situation, the justices would have greater reason to avoid conflict and to retreat under pressure. This may be the situation at the state level. Anecdotal evidence suggests that in at least some states, legislators and governors are more inclined to take adverse action against judges and courts than are their federal counterparts. One example was the 2000 impeachment (but not conviction) of the New Hampshire chief justice, largely a result of his court's unpopular decisions on school funding (see Toobin 2000). However, state governments may appear to be more aggressive in using their powers against the courts simply because there are fifty of them, automatically producing more examples of aggressive action. In any event, we have only a limited understanding of how state supreme court justices respond to the powers of the other branches (see Langer 2002).

The outcome of the current conflicts between Congress and the federal courts will be instructive. Threats of congressional action against the courts and their judges have grown since 2000. In 2004, for instance, the House responded to the court of appeals decision in *Newdow v. United States Congress* (2002) by approving a bill that prohibited lower federal courts from ruling on issues relating to the Pledge of Allegiance (H.R. 2028), and it passed another bill prohibiting federal courts from ruling on the constitutional validity of the 1996 Defense of Marriage Act (H.R. 3313). Threats against the judiciary became more intense after all three levels of federal courts declined a congressional invitation to intervene in the Florida case involving the medical treatment of Terri Schiavo (*Schiavo ex rel. Schindler v. Schiavo* 2005). Members of Congress suggested a wide range of serious anticourt measures and denounced the courts in strong terms (S. Levine 2005; Marcus 2005).

The ferocity of these attacks might lead federal judges to avoid making decisions that could heighten congressional wrath. But it is noteworthy that several judges risked that wrath with their rulings in the *Schiavo* cases. And the threats to act against the courts aroused considerable criticism in and out of Congress, reducing the chances that they would be carried out and thus limiting pressure on the courts. If Congress does take significant actions against the courts or individual judges, judicial responses to that action will tell us more about the impact of pressures from the other branches.

The absence of clear evidence on that impact rules out firm conclusions about its strength. Undoubtedly some judges at some times act on their fear of negative consequences from displeasing the other branches. Yet their incentives to take this course are limited in important respects, and by no means do judges automatically bend under pressure. Action to avoid or defuse conflict with the other branches is episodic, and it may be exceptional as well.

Career Considerations

The other branches of government have considerable impact on judges' careers. In several states the governor, legislature, or the two together determine whether judges serve additional terms.[18] In most states and the federal system, the other branches have full or partial control over judicial promotions. Thus, like the electorate in most states, the other branches might affect judicial decisions through their impact on judges' achievement of their career goals.

The federal courts provide a good setting in which to consider ambition for judicial promotions (see Klerman 1999). Presumably, the great majority of judges would happily accept a promotion: "Every magistrate judge is a district judge in waiting; every district judge is a circuit judge in waiting; every circuit judge is an associate justice in waiting" (Kozinski 2004, 1104). Promotion enhances judges' prestige and sometimes their power. Promotion to the Supreme Court ensures at least a small place in history.

One difference between a state judge who seeks reelection and a federal judge who hopes for promotion is the attention of the relevant audience. Administration officials are far more cognizant of judges' decisional records than are the voters. This is especially true in the current era. Judges can expect their records to be scrutinized closely by the presidential staff members and Justice Department officials who work on appellate nominations. As one federal judge said about those who want promotions, "they know their votes are being watched, their decisions are being analyzed" (*Judicature* 1996, 81). Thus ambitious judges have reason to think about the relationship between their choices in cases and their prospects for promotion.

---

[18] We know little about denial of new terms by governors and legislatures. It appears that such denials are uncommon, even more so than electoral defeats. However, judges occasionally fail to win new terms as a result of their decisional records, and it may be that such defeats are becoming more common.

However, the impact of judges' decisional behavior on their prospects for promotion is both small and uncertain. As Judge Posner (1995, 111) pointed out, "Some decisions have no impact at all on those prospects, and in the case of almost all the remaining ones the impact is unpredictable—the decision may offend as many influential people as it delights." His point is all the stronger now that senators look more closely at nominees to the courts of appeals; a record that wins a nomination may preclude confirmation. Moreover, the odds against promotion to a court of appeals are fairly long, the odds against promotion to the Supreme Court very long, and the chances of either promotion are nearly zero when the wrong party holds the presidency.

Under these circumstances it might make little sense for judges to modify their policy positions in order to enhance their candidacy for promotion. Judges want to be promoted, just as they want the legislature to leave their decisions standing. Still, the benefits of maximizing the chance of a favorable outcome (promotion), like the benefits of minimizing the chance of an unfavorable outcome (override of a decision), may be insufficient to justify departures from a judge's most preferred positions.

But there is a difference. Judges receive far greater benefits from promotion than they do from advancing their preferred policies or even protecting their court's institutional standing. Judges might be willing to sacrifice some of their preferred policies, which provide no tangible benefits, for even a small improvement in the odds of elevation to a higher court.[19] This possibility is difficult to assess in the abstract. A few studies analyze whether judges with relatively good prospects for promotion are more likely than their peers to reach decisions that might enhance those prospects. Their findings provide some evidence of a link between promotion prospects and decisional behavior, but the evidence is limited and mixed (M. Cohen 1991, 1992; Sisk, Heise, and Morriss 1998; Morriss, Heise, and Sisk 2005). In light of the importance of promotion to some judges, its impact on judicial behavior merits further inquiry.

Personal Ties

One of the strangest episodes in recent Supreme Court history arose from the Louisiana duck-hunting trip that included Vice President Richard Cheney and Justice Antonin Scalia. Cheney and Scalia were friends from their service in the Ford administration, and Cheney was invited on the trip at Scalia's suggestion. At the time, oral argument was pending in

---

[19] When a judge advertises a policy position rather than departing from a preferred position, the costs of doing so are minimal. This may describe Judge Luttig's calculus in the episode discussed in chapter 1.

Cheney v. United States District Court (2004c), which concerned the activities of an energy task force over which the vice president presided in
2001. Two groups went to federal court to seek information about those
activities, a court of appeals reached a decision that was mostly favorable
to the groups, and the Supreme Court granted certiorari in late 2003. The
duck-hunting trip occurred shortly after that grant. After an enterprising
reporter discovered the trip, it became the subject of considerable commentary, including a large number of disapproving editorials and editorial
cartoons. The primary theme of the disapproval was that for Cheney and
Scalia to come together in a situation that involved the vice president's
hospitality (Scalia flew to Louisiana on Cheney's plane) compromised
Scalia's impartiality in Cheney's case.

One of Cheney's opponents in the case, the Sierra Club, filed a motion
asking Justice Scalia to recuse himself from the case in light of the trip.
Scalia responded with a lengthy memorandum explaining why he would
not do so.[20] The memorandum argued against the need for recusal on
several grounds. One ground was that this instance of contact between a
justice and an administration official with interest in a Supreme Court
case was hardly unique. Scalia pointed out that

> many Justices have reached this Court precisely because they were friends of
> the incumbent President or other senior officials—and from the earliest days
> down to modern times Justices have had close personal relationships with
> the President and other officers of the Executive. (*Cheney v. United States
> District Court*, 2004b, 916)

Scalia discussed two instances in which justices socialized with administration officials (an attorney general and a president) while cases in which
those officials were parties or had a political interest were pending before
the Court. In neither case, Scalia noted, was there even a motion for recusal (*Cheney v. United States District Court*, 2004b, 924–26).

Whatever may be the merits of the recusal issue in this case, Justice
Scalia's memorandum is a reminder that judges sometimes have close connections with government officials who have a stake in cases they decide.
Relationships between Supreme Court justices and presidents have been
documented extensively (Scigliano 1971, ch. 3). For instance, Justice Harlan Fiske Stone was close to Herbert Hoover (Mason 1956, 262–74, 287–
89), Felix Frankfurter to Franklin Roosevelt (Silber 2004, 75, 83, 86,
101–2).[21] Justice Abe Fortas was even closer to Lyndon Johnson. For most

---

[20] The Sierra Club's motion and attached materials document the controversy. See
Cheney v. United States District Court (2004a). Other accounts can be found in Savage and
Serrano 2004 and Janofsky 2004.

[21] Frankfurter was only one of several Roosevelt appointees who retained social contact
with President Roosevelt and members of his administration. Ironically, it was Coolidge

of his time on the Court, according to another justice, "Abe was sitting in Lyndon Johnson's lap" (Kalman 1990, 293). This raises the question of whether social ties might influence the responses of judges to cases that presidents care about.[22]

In a nuanced discussion of this question, Scigliano (1971, 135–37) offered a qualified "yes" to that question. His conclusion was well founded. If a Supreme Court justice values social ties with the president, those ties can have a subtle impact on the justice's assessment of cases that the president cares about. Even if a justice gains nothing tangible from a relationship with the president, the intangible benefits of an important relationship could be sufficient to exert a marginal impact on judge's decisional behavior.

With the exception of Harriet Miers's nomination in 2005, presidents since 1969 have refrained from nominating Supreme Court justices who were personal associates. While this change in practice has much to recommend it, it might not constitute good strategy. From the president's perspective, cronyism can be a virtue if the value of the president's friendship is sufficient to influence the crony's thinking. What we know about social identities makes such influence plausible.

There is little information on personal ties between state supreme court justices and officials in the other branches. In all likelihood, cronyism in gubernatorial appointments to judgeships has not declined as it has at the federal level. Moreover, the barriers to continued interaction between justices and other officials may be lower in the states. If so, officials in the other branches may be a more significant audience at the state level than the federal.

---

appointee Stone (later promoted by Roosevelt to chief justice) who supplied the most important extracurricular assistance to the administration, in a conversation with Secretary of Labor Frances Perkins at a social occasion. In response to Perkins's jocular complaint that she was unsure how to design a social security system that the Court would accept, Stone advised her that "the taxing power is sufficient for everything you want and need" (Perkins 1946, 286).

[22] A related question is whether gratitude induces a president's or governor's appointees to judgeships to favor the chief executive's interests (Little 1995). One study found that Supreme Court justices are not substantially more likely to support the government in litigation when their appointing president is still in office (Segal 1990). Anecdotal evidence on Supreme Court cases that affected presidents' interests is mixed, but *United States v. Nixon* (1974) and *Clinton v. Jones* (1997) make it clear that a president's appointees do not automatically line up behind the president even in cases that are quite important to the president. The apostasy of President Nixon's three appointees in *U.S. v. Nixon* elicited a characteristically profane response from the president, who apparently had overestimated the impact of gratitude (Lukas 1976, 569). In contrast, it was widely perceived that judges who were effectively chosen by the first Mayor Daley's political machine in Chicago, even those on the federal bench, had sufficient gratitude to support the machine's interests reliably (Goulden 1974, ch. 3).

Assessing the Other Branches as an Audience

Courts and judges are linked with the other branches of government in several ways. In themselves, these links do not mean that legislators and chief executives influence judges' choices. Rather, any influence for them must have a motivational basis.

The power of the other branches over the fate of judicial decisions and over courts themselves may give judges incentives to take the legislature and executive into account. Students of judicial behavior have emphasized these incentives. They tend to see judges as supplicants who act fearfully or as strategists who act carefully to avoid negative reactions from the other branches.

But these incentives may not be as strong as they appear. The value of adjusting decisions to avoid legislative overrides is limited, in part because the costs of overrides are not great. Judges have greater reason to avoid serious attacks by the other branches on their courts or themselves, but the Supreme Court's record suggests that the justices are usually willing to accept the risk of such attacks.

The power of the other branches over judicial careers can tap into stronger incentives for individual judges. Those who want very much to retain office or win a promotion have reason to please people who help determine whether they achieve these ambitions. But the magnitude of this impact, little studied so far, remains an open question.

For some judges, officials in the other branches constitute personal audiences. Continuing relationships with those officials might affect a judge's choices in certain cases. Across the judiciary as a whole, however, this is probably not an important influence. To the extent that this influence exists, it does not reflect any special position of the other branches so much as the general impact of judges' social groups on their perceptions and choices.

CONCLUSIONS

Of all the groups that might influence judges, court colleagues, the general public, and the other branches of government receive the greatest attention from scholars. Though not thought of as an audience, colleagues are widely viewed as highly influential. This is especially true of strategic models in which appellate judges seek to advance their policy goals through the collective decisions of their courts.

Judges' policy goals do not seem sufficient to fully motivate their efforts to influence their colleagues. When personal motives are added to the equation, strategic behavior is easier to explain. Judges who want their colleagues to perceive them as skillful and effective have strong incentives to seek victories in their courts. An interest in the regard of fellow judges shapes other forms of intracourt behavior and patterns of influence among judges. For this reason, recognition of personal motives for self-presentation leads to a better understanding of courts as small groups.

The general public and the other branches of government are often analyzed as judicial audiences. There are theoretical reasons to give attention to these audiences, but methodological considerations also come into play: both audiences are clearly defined, so their influence is easier to analyze than that of some other audiences.

Yet we still know relatively little about the impact of the public and the other branches on judges' choices. What we can surmise about judges' incentives, however, leads to some tentative judgments. First, this impact is more situational than pervasive. Elected judges have far more reason to take the public into account when they decide criminal cases than when they decide contract cases. Supreme Court justices have greater reason to take Congress into account when the two branches are in serious conflict than they do in ordinary times.

Second, the sources of influence for these audiences may be somewhat different from the ones that are emphasized in research on judicial behavior. This is especially true of federal judges, for whom scholars emphasize the motive of achieving good legal policy. In itself, that motive may not do a great deal to orient judges toward the other branches or the general public. In contrast, the interest of some judges in popularity for its own sake may provide the public with a significant basis for influence. The career goals of some lower-court judges may give meaningful influence to the president and members of Congress.

The research on state judges is closer to the mark, because there is a strong motivational basis for its emphasis on career goals as a source of influence for the electorate. Even so, judges' desire for public approval may be strongly reinforced by their interest in that approval for its own sake. Thus in Luttbeg's terms, the impact of judicial elections may be not just to create coercive linkages between the public and judges but to strengthen noncoercive linkages as well.

The most important tentative judgment about the public and the other branches is that their impact on judicial behavior is more limited than much of the scholarship suggests. This is especially true of judges whose career goals are irrelevant, most notably Supreme Court justices. At first glance, then, the discussions of the public and the other branches in this chapter support the assumption of autonomy in quasi-attitudinal models of the Supreme Court. After all, these two groups are usually thought to have the greatest influence of any audiences outside the Court. If they actually exert only limited influence on the justices, then Supreme Court justices would appear to be quite independent. To a lesser degree, the same is true of other judges who do not worry much about maintaining their judicial tenure or achieving promotion.

But this is not the end of the inquiry, because the public and the other branches are not necessarily the most important audiences for judges. Indeed, one lesson of chapter 2 is that the most consequential audiences are likely to be those with the greatest relevance to judges' social identities, audiences whose bases for influence are chiefly personal rather than instrumental. Court colleagues are one such audience. Chapters 4 and 5 consider the impact of other personal audiences on judges' choices.

Chapter 4

SOCIAL AND PROFESSIONAL GROUPS

CHAPTER 3 EXAMINED COURT COLLEAGUES, the general public, and the other branches of government, the most familiar judicial audiences. This chapter and chapter 5 consider another set of audiences. These audiences are quite diverse, but they have two characteristics in common. First, they receive little attention from students of judicial behavior. Second, their influence stems primarily from their status as personal audiences for judges. Thus these audiences are especially relevant to an inquiry into judges' social identities and their impact on decision making.

The audiences examined in these two chapters fall into several categories. First are social groups: judges' families, friends, and acquaintances. Second are professional groups, the legal profession and its subsets. Those two types of audiences, considered in this chapter, can be expected to have the greatest impact across the judiciary as a whole. Third are policy groups, people who share ideological orientations or policy positions. The last is a different kind of audience, the news media. The media serve as intermediaries between judges and other audiences and as an object of judges' interest in themselves. Policy groups and the media are considered in chapter 5.

These audiences will be examined in somewhat different ways, but the inquiry into each has two broad purposes. First, I seek to establish that judges have a motivational basis for self-presentation to each audience, in turn giving these audiences a basis for influence over judges' choices. The second purpose is to show how taking these audiences into consideration enhances our ability to explain judicial behavior.

SOCIAL GROUPS

In October 1973, Attorney General Elliot Richardson refused to carry out President Nixon's order to fire Special Prosecutor Archibald Cox. Instead, Richardson resigned from his position. One observer offered this explanation: "I think at the bottom of it, if Elliot fired Archie, it meant that he could never walk down Beacon Street or across Harvard Yard again and hold his head high when he met friends" (T. White 1975, 253).

This explanation captures the impact that social groups can exert on the decisions of public officials. People with whom officials have close personal ties are usually quite important to their social identities. Because social groups are so integral to people's sense of themselves, people have strong incentives to please members of these groups and to avoid alienating them.

Social groups are also the best situated to shape people's values and beliefs. Because of intense interaction and high credibility, family, friends, and acquaintances have ample opportunity to influence a person's ways of thinking about the world, including politics and public policy. This influence has been well documented for the mass public,[1] and it undoubtedly operates for people in government as well.

Research on relationships between background characteristics and decisional behavior touches on the influence of social groups on judges' values (Goldman 1975; Tate 1981; Ulmer 1986; Brudney, Schiavoni, and Merritt 1999; George 2001). Some of the variables whose impact has been tested, such as religious affiliation and father's occupation, encompass elements of family socialization. Some studies have found evidence that variables of this type are correlated with judicial votes on a liberal-conservative scale, correlations that are usually interpreted as reflections of group influence on judges' values.

An implicit assumption of scholarship on judicial behavior is that the influence of social groups is complete by the time judges reach the bench. This assumption probably reflects two premises. First, judges' values are well formed by early in their adult lives, so those values are no longer subject to influence. Second, social groups are not a significant audience for judges because they possess no concrete sources of leverage. Legislators can override decisions; judges' friends cannot.

Both these premises can be questioned, and the second is especially dubious if judges are similar to other people. Scholars often argue that judges make choices with the public or the other branches of government in mind. The impact of these audiences can be debated, but it is certainly credible to think that judges try to maintain their support. On the whole, however, judges have much stronger incentives to maintain the esteem of the most important people in their lives.

Of course, judges' social groups are not a random sample of society. Schmidhauser (1959; 1979, ch. 3) showed that historically, most federal appellate judges shared elite social origins. These origins affected judges' own values, but they also ensured that most of the people in judges' social groups had high socioeconomic status. Even today judges (and especially those on higher courts) remain something of an elite group in origins. And whatever their family backgrounds may be, judges on all but the

---

[1] Niemi, Hedges, and Jennings 1977; Jennings and Niemi 1981; Beck and Jennings 1991; Huckfeldt et al. 1995.

lowest courts are highly educated. Because of their schooling and their careers, judges usually have highly educated spouses, friends, and acquaintances. Judges and the people around them are also likely to enjoy high economic status. Of the federal judges appointed by Bill Clinton and by George W. Bush in his first term, nearly half were millionaires (Goldman et al. 2005, 269, 274).

This reality is consequential because the opinions and values of economic and educational elites differ in some respects from those of society as a whole (Erikson and Tedin 2005, 177–86). Justice Antonin Scalia has complained that the Supreme Court's decisions on sexual orientation under the law reflect the values of "the elite class from which the Members of this institution are selected" (*Romer v. Evans* 1996, 636; see *Lawrence v. Texas* 2003, 602). Leaving aside the merits of Justice Scalia's specific complaint, he surely is right in suggesting that the justices tend to share elite values. This tendency results not just from judges' own backgrounds but also from the status of people with whom they associate. However, as Scalia's complaint reminds us, the views of elite groups on social and political issues are not homogeneous.

The composition of a judge's social group can change over time. Selection as a judge or promotion to a higher court sometimes triggers change by bringing a judge to a new location and exposing the judge to a new set of people. One possible effect of the Supreme Court's social environment on new justices will be discussed in the next chapter.

As an audience, social groups can affect judges in multiple ways. To take one example, judges may want their families and friends to perceive them as people who embody virtues such as impartiality that they associate with good judges. This goal could move judges to act in ways that emphasize their fealty to the law as a basis for judgment. Alternatively, judges may want to be seen as acting consistently with the policy views that predominate in their social circles. This second type of impact is not necessarily the more powerful, but its potential effects are easier to trace. Two episodes in the recent past show how the influence of social groups can help to explain patterns of judicial policy.

Racial Equality in the Federal Courts

One familiar episode in legal history is the civil rights era of the 1950s and 1960s. During that era southern federal judges responded to issues of racial discrimination in the context of social and political turmoil. The most prominent of these issues was school segregation, brought to the lower courts chiefly in the aftermath of *Brown v. Board of Education*. The record of the federal courts in that era has been read in different ways (Sanders 1995). However, it is clear that many southern district judges offered no more than grudging compliance with *Brown* (Peltason 1971), and litigants with other civil rights claims also encountered considerable resistance in the district courts.

This resistance reflected both the personal values of many southern district judges and external pressures on all of them. The sources of these pressures included public officials, the white portion of the general public, and interest groups opposed to civil rights. But also influential were the people with whom judges interacted directly in their social lives. For most judges, wholehearted support for school desegregation or other forms of racial equality would jeopardize relationships with people in their social circles. As Peltason (1971, 9) wrote,

> A judge who makes rulings adverse to segregation is not so likely to be honored by testimonial dinners, or to read flattering editorials in the local press, or to partake of the fellowship at the club. He will no longer be invited to certain homes; former friends will avoid him when they meet on the street.

Judge Skelly Wright in New Orleans, who sought to enforce *Brown v. Board of Education*, attested to that kind of ostracism:

> I never have been a gregarious type, and I've become much less so in the past few years. You never know whether people really want to talk with you and I don't see a lot of people any more. (Peltason 1971, 9)

Similarly, a Florida federal judge said that he had "lost more friends in the last four years following the Constitution of the United States than I made in the first forty" (Carp and Wheeler 1972, 373). Even Supreme Court justice Hugo Black suffered a degree of isolation from friends and acquaintances in Alabama after the Court decided *Brown*. One niece did not speak to him for fifteen years (Black and Black 1986, 234; Newman 1997, 440–44).

The prospective loss of such relationships was a high price to pay. Indeed, the likelihood that pro–civil rights decisions would alienate friends and acquaintances was probably a good deal more troubling to many judges than the expected opprobrium from other quarters. In any event, the attitudes of their social groups helped to deter southern judges from ruling in favor of school desegregation and other civil rights.

On the whole, federal district judges in the North responded more positively to lawsuits on behalf of school desegregation in the 1970s. They frequently ordered school busing programs to implement desegregation, sometimes extending remedies further than the Supreme Court thought appropriate (*Milliken v. Bradley* 1974; *Pasadena City Board of Education v. Spangler* 1976). In one respect, this line of policy is surprising. Most orders that required large-scale busing of public school students in northern cities were unpopular, and judges who issued such orders suffered a degree (often a considerable degree) of hostility from the general public. One example was Arthur Garrity, who ordered and supervised desegregation in Boston. Garrity was the target of both death threats and actual murder attempts (C. Goldberg 1999).

But at the same time the people who comprised the social groups of northern judges in the 1970s were unlikely to harbor the strong antipathy toward civil rights that most southern judges encountered in the 1950s and 1960s. In the North, support for racial equality was relatively high among the well-educated people with whom federal judges associated,[2] and desegregation of public schools in central cities had relatively little personal impact on people of high status. This difference between the social groups of southern and northern judges helps to account for the difference in their responses to lawsuits over school segregation.

Of special interest are the southern district judges who took pro–civil rights positions in a hostile environment. The primary attributes that distinguished these judges from more recalcitrant colleagues were courage and personal conviction. But this was not the whole story. On average, these judges were less dependent on the regard of people who disapproved of civil rights than were most of their colleagues. District judges who supported racial equality were not as well integrated into the mainstream of their communities as other southern judges by such measures as party and religious affiliation (Vines 1964). This social distance had some effect on judges' values, and it also reduced the chances that judges' social groups were hostile to racial equality. Social groups can "serve as protective environments for individuals whose attitudes deviate from those of the culture around them" (Finifter 1974, 608), and that was the case for some district judges in the South. It was true as well of court of appeals judge John Minor Wisdom, who had "developed a network of friendships with people who circulated within the 'eastern establishment'" (Bass 1981, 48).

One southern judge provides a good case with which to consider the impact of judges' social groups (Grafton 1950; Yarbrough 1987). J. Waties Waring served as a federal district judge in South Carolina from 1942 to 1952. For most of his life Waring seemed to hold the standard racial views of upper-status southern white men. But after becoming a federal judge he showed signs of racial liberalism, and eventually he became a strong advocate of civil rights. On the bench he ruled that the South Carolina white primary was unconstitutional (*Elmore v. Rice* 1947), and he dissented from the decision of a three-judge court upholding school segre-

---

[2] Greeley and Sheatsley 1974; Sears, Hensler, and Speer 1979; Sears and Allen 1984; Schuman, Steeh, and Bobo 1985. But see Jackman 1978, 1981; and Campbell 1971, 54–67.

gation in a South Carolina district (*Briggs v. Elliott* 1951). He worked actively for racial equality off the bench as well, and some of those activities went so far that they compromised his impartiality as a judge (Yarbrough 1987, 201).

Inevitably, Waring's support for civil rights brought him a good deal of hostility. He was subjected to threats and harassment, and the hostility at least contributed to his decision to retire and depart for New York. His story undoubtedly served as a cautionary tale for other southern judges who faced civil rights issues in the 1950s.

The evolution in Waring's thinking and behavior was complex, but one element was a change in his social environment. In 1945 he divorced his wife and married a woman from the North with liberal racial views. The divorce and remarriage in themselves threatened Waring's ties with his circle of acquaintances. He seemed almost to welcome the breaking of these ties, and he developed a new and racially mixed social circle that supported civil rights. He looked to this set of people for reinforcement, and his decisions favoring civil rights clearly constituted a form of self-presentation aimed at that audience. To a considerable degree, the approval he received from his new set of friends and acquaintances insulated him from the very negative reactions of other South Carolinians to his decisions. The praise that he sought and received from other sources, such as the northern mass media, provided reinforcement as well.

Judge Waring's change in social environment does not fully account for his liberalism in civil rights. For one thing, even before his divorce and remarriage he demonstrated greater liberalism on civil rights than one would expect from a southern judge in that era. Moreover, his racial attitudes largely determined the composition of his new social circle. But the creation of that circle, especially his remarriage, reinforced the changes in his thinking that had already occurred. The fact that his primary audience became one favorable to civil rights facilitated his taking positions that diverged radically from the norm among the white citizens of South Carolina.[3]

District judge Frank Johnson of Alabama provides another, somewhat different example (Kennedy 1978; Yarbrough 1981; Bass 1993). Appointed by Eisenhower in 1955, Johnson was a relatively strong supporter of civil rights in his rulings. Later, he responded positively to institutional reform litigation in other policy areas. Primarily because of his decisions on racial issues, Johnson suffered harassment, hate mail, death threats, and the bombing of his mother's home.

---

[3] Less dramatically, some other southern judges who supported civil rights in their rulings drew closer to friends who approved of their positions, seeking and obtaining reinforcement from them (Bass 1981, 115–16, 197–200).

Johnson was insulated from hostility by his social distance from the anti–civil rights establishment of Montgomery, where his court sat. He was a geographic outsider who came to his federal judgeship from northern Alabama, an area largely at odds with the prevailing political sentiments in the rest of the state. He associated with a circle of people who sympathized with his views. Further, he seemed less dependent on social approval from outside his family than are most people who achieve high office. "Instead of our being socially ostracized, we did the ostracizing, because my wife and I are just not socially inclined" (Yarbrough 1981, 60). A reporter who had observed Johnson on the bench expressed a similar idea in a different way. He recalled Johnson as

> a stern-looking man pacing up and down on the dais . . . stopping now and then to point an accusing finger at a Klan witness or a government lawyer and demand the truth. He seemed to be a judge from the Old Testament. . . . When I read, in the late sixties, that, the outrage of the local gentry over some of Johnson's decisions having turned the country club into a hostile camp, Johnson was forced to play golf at a nearby airbase, it occurred to me that an Old Testament judge must consider the location of his golf course a trifling matter indeed. (Trillin 1977, 88, 91)

To a great extent judges' responses to the challenges of the civil rights era were overdetermined, in that they reflected several strong and mutually reinforcing influences. But it is important that judges made their responses in a social context, well aware of the feelings of the people who were closest to them. Judges' recognition of how those people would react to their choices helps to explain the resistance to civil rights among federal district judges in the South, the lack of resistance from some judges, and the differences between northern and southern district judges in their school desegregation decisions.

Women's Rights

The story of judicial policy on women's rights issues is also familiar. Historically, courts showed little sympathy for challenges to laws and practices that discriminated against women, and judicial decisions strengthened legal distinctions between women and men (Johnston and Knapp 1971). Around 1970 the pattern of court policy began to change. In a relatively short time this change became fundamental, and in the past three decades judicial doctrines have supported gender equality more than inequality (see Mezey 2003).

The change in the Supreme Court was especially dramatic (C. Cushman 2001). Prior to 1970 the Court had given essentially no support to claims of sex discrimination under the Constitution. As late as 1961 the justices unanimously upheld a government practice, exempting women from the obligation to serve on juries, that sharply distinguished between men and women (*Hoyt v. Florida* 1961). In 1971 the Court's position changed abruptly. In the years that followed the Court gave life to the equal protection clause as a prohibition of sex discrimination, and it gave some broad interpretations to federal statutes that protect women's rights in employment.

Altogether, the Court's record since 1971 is mixed. Still, the extent of change in its decisions relating to women's rights is striking. As measured by case outcomes, the Court treats sex discrimination claims quite favorably.[4] The Court's doctrinal positions are also noteworthy. At least in some decisions, most justices have accepted a standard for assessing sex discrimination under equal protection that is nearly as rigorous as the strict scrutiny used in racial discrimination cases.[5] On several issues the Court has taken positions that are generally quite favorable to women's rights. One example is its decisions on sexual harassment under Title VII of the Civil Rights Act of 1964 (e.g., *Faragher v. City of Boca Raton* 1998). While these decisions are balanced by others that are less favorable (e.g., *Gebser v. Lago Vista Independent School District* 1998), there is no doubt that the Court's overall reading of the law in this field is fundamentally different from what it was up to 1970.

The change in judicial policies on sex discrimination cannot be explained by changes in court membership. The Supreme Court became more liberal on women's rights issues at the same time that new appointments made it more conservative on most other issues. It is easy to identify an alternative explanation: the changes in social thinking that accompanied the rise of the new women's movement in and after the 1960s.

There are several mechanisms by which this social change could have influenced judges, from shifts in public opinion to new litigation cam-

---

[4] This and other analyses of case outcomes in the Supreme Court are based on the Supreme Court Database, created by Harold Spaeth and archived at *http://www.as.uky.edu/polisci/ulmerproject/sctdata.htm*. In the 1971–2004 terms, the Court ruled in favor of sex discrimination claims 65 percent of the time, compared with 50 percent for all other civil rights claims. The proportions for the late Rehnquist Court (1994–2004 terms) are similar, at 71 percent and 50 percent, but there were only fourteen decisions on sex discrimination in that period. Sex discrimination cases were defined as those involving issues 283 and 284 in the database, civil rights cases as those with value 2. (Unit of analysis = 0 or 4; decision type = 1, 6, or 7.) Of course, decisional records for these two categories of cases must be compared with caution, since the cases in the two categories undoubtedly differed in other ways that affected the justices' responses to them.

[5] In some decisions, such as *United States v. Virginia* (1996), opinions using this standard have commanded a Court majority. In some other decisions, such as *Nguyen v. Immigration and Naturalization Service* (2001), the majority opinion has adopted a somewhat more lenient standard.

paigns. Undoubtedly more than one mechanism had a substantial impact, and growth in support for women's rights is another example of judicial behavior that probably was overdetermined. One key mechanism, I think, was the influence of judges' social groups.

The social changes that stemmed from the women's liberation movement of the 1960s have affected all segments of society. But that movement grew primarily from the concerns of well-educated women (Freeman 1975). From the beginning, its goals have received the greatest support from women and men of high educational status (E. Klein 1984, 107, 110–11; Reingold and Foust 1998; Sapiro and Conover 2001, 12–21; E. Cook, Jelen, and Wilcox 1992, 48–52).

Thus the opinions of people in judges' social groups, especially those of judges on higher courts, tend to favor women's rights. In this area of policy, as with sexual orientation, Justice Scalia has argued that the Court reflects elite values. In *United States v. Virginia* (1996, 567), in which the Court required that the Virginia Military Institute admit female students, Scalia said that the Court "has embarked on a course of inscribing one after another of the current preferences of the society (and in some cases only the counter majoritarian preferences of the society's law-trained elite) into our Basic Law." Although Scalia focused on lawyers, his statement suggests the importance of judges' own elite status and their associations with elite groups.

One characteristic of judges' social groups is that they are almost certain to include women. Whether judges are male or female, they may feel pressure to support rights that are important to people who are close to them. That influence is suggested by two anecdotes about the families of Supreme Court justices and the abortion issue. A friend reported that Anthony Kennedy's wife Mary Kennedy greeted the prospect of overturning *Roe* with "Don't you dare!" and this friend concluded that her influence on Kennedy's position in *Planned Parenthood v. Casey* was "very great" (Rosen 1996, 87). Harry Blackmun may have felt both specific and diffuse influence from his family in formulating his position in *Roe v. Wade*. By one account, his wife Dottie Blackmun told a law clerk sympathetic to abortion rights that "you and I are working on the same thing. Me at home and you at work" (Woodward and Armstrong 1979, 183; see S. Blackmun 2004, xviii–xix). Later statements by the two justices make the accuracy of these accounts uncertain (Rosen 1996, 87; H. Blackmun 1994–95, 198–99; see Greenhouse 2005, 83). But they symbolize the kind of impact that judges' social groups can exert on their decisions about women's issues. A report of Justice O'Connor's assurances to friends in the late 1980s that *Roe v. Wade* was not in danger (Savage 1992, 291) is another illustration of that impact. Like Elliot Richardson contemplating his reception at Harvard, Supreme Court justices hesitate to disappoint people with whom they have close ties.

PROFESSIONAL GROUPS: LAWYERS AND JUDGES

The great majority of judges, and nearly all above the lowest levels of courts, are members of the legal profession. The profession is typically an important part of their education, their backgrounds, and their work lives, and it is often important in their lives outside work. As a result, lawyers constitute a significant audience for judges.

One key segment of the profession, colleagues on the same court, was discussed in chapter 3. This section considers the legal profession from several perspectives. It begins with a general discussion of lawyers as a reference group and then turns to other segments of the profession that have particular relevance to judges. I next discuss some aspects of judicial behavior that reflect the influence of legal audiences. The final part of the section examines the relationship between judges' backgrounds and the salience of the legal profession to them.

Lawyers as a Reference Group

People within any occupation orient themselves toward others in the same occupation. This orientation rests in part on simple interaction, in part on the sense of a shared situation and shared expertise. The characteristics of some occupations make them especially important to the identities of their members (Van Maanen and Barley 1984, 298–303; Trice 1993, 26–58). In part because it is a profession, the law ranks high in these characteristics.

Thus it is important that judges share membership in an occupation—an attribute that distinguishes them from legislators and executive-branch officials—and that this occupation is the legal profession. They received the training and socialization of law school. The great majority practiced law, and for many, legal practice constituted their only pre-judicial career.

In their work lives, practicing lawyers interact frequently and intensively with other lawyers. Professional colleagues typically constitute a large part of their social circles as well. These patterns of interaction continue when lawyers reach the bench. Judges regularly deal with lawyers who practice before them, and appellate judges work most closely with their colleagues and law clerks. Judges may limit their social contacts with practicing lawyers to avoid conflicts of interest, but they continue to socialize with lawyers in settings such as meetings of bar associations. Some judges engage in these interactions with some frequency (see Shestack 2002).

For all these reasons, the legal profession is an important reference group for judges. Judges' social identities are linked—for many, linked quite strongly—with their profession.

Lawyers are the most regular and most expert critics of judges' work, a role that enhances the importance of their esteem to judges. Even in the Supreme Court a good many decisions are virtually unnoticed outside the legal community, and the proportion of such decisions is considerably higher in most other courts. Lawyers are the primary readers of judicial opinions (Schauer 1995, 1463–65; but see Tushnet 1994), and judges perceive them as the most skillful evaluators of opinions. For that reason, lawyers stand alongside the parties to cases as the primary audiences for whom opinions are written (J. Howard 1981, 152; Marvell 1978, 110–11).

As evaluators of judges' work, lawyers have more rivals at the trial level than they do at the appellate level (Posner 1996, 35–36). Trial judges write fewer opinions (especially in state courts) and interact directly with litigants and other lay participants in trials. As a result, a substantial proportion of their feedback comes from people other than lawyers. For trial judges who face elections, the salience of lay audiences in the courtroom is enhanced by their voting power. Yet trial judges also interact intensively with the lawyers who appear before them. Through direct observation and word of mouth, lawyers develop judgments about judges' decisions and courtroom conduct. Those judgments are sometimes expressed in polls conducted by local news media and the bar, polls that provide visible information about how lawyers view judges.[6]

As a consequence, judges care more about evaluations of their work by other lawyers than they do about the approval of more diffuse groups. When judges on the federal courts of appeals were asked to cite the group whose approval gave them the "greatest personal satisfaction," lawyers and judges dominated their responses (J. Howard 1981, 152). With the exception of some judges who face the electorate, what the mass public thinks of judges carries less weight than what other lawyers think of them. In this respect judges are similar to other professional groups such as medical doctors.

All lawyers specialize to some degree, many to a considerable degree. One result is that they often identify more closely with a subset of the profession than with the profession as a whole (Heinz et al. 1998; Heinz

[6] The *Almanac of the Federal Judiciary* now serves the same function for federal judges by providing samples and summaries of lawyers' evaluations of each judge. Presumably, no judge would like to read comments such as "his judicial demeanor is aloof-to-pompous," "he is a real lightweight," or "to say he is lazy would be an understatement" (Chase 2004, vol. 1, 3rd Circuit, 12; 5th Circuit, 63; 3rd Circuit, 21).

et al. 2005). Judges may carry that identification from legal practice to the bench. Moreover, many judges serve on courts or court divisions that specialize in certain kinds of cases. Regardless of their own prior legal practice, such judges are likely to orient themselves toward the legal fields on which they concentrate and toward the lawyers in those fields. This orientation can give considerable influence to those lawyers. One legal scholar has argued that the ability of a subset of bankruptcy lawyers to shape the reputations of bankruptcy judges helps move judges to favor the interests of large debtor corporations (LoPucki 2005, 23).

Segments of the Legal Profession

Specialization aside, three segments of the legal profession can be especially important to judges: lawyers who practice before them, legal academics, and fellow judges. The importance of each segment has its own bases.

LAWYERS IN COURT

Any single judge sees only a limited subset of practicing lawyers in court. Indeed, some courts are dominated by a small number of regular participants. The relationships between judges and the lawyers who practice in their courts have been described most extensively for criminal cases in trial courts (Eisenstein and Jacob 1977; Nardulli, Eisenstein, and Flemming 1988). Scholars emphasize the interdependence of lawyers and judges in those courts and the close working relationships that sometimes develop between them.

The Supreme Court is different, in that most lawyers who appear before the Court appear only once. But the two dozen lawyers in the Solicitor General's office, which represents the federal government, are regular participants in the Court (see Pacelle 2003). Other specialists in Supreme Court litigation are at least semiregular participants, and their share of the Court's work is increasing (McGuire 1993, 1995; Mauro 2004). There is greater distance between lawyers and judges in the Supreme Court than in criminal trial courts, but the Court's regulars have something of a special status in the Court. The highest status is accorded lawyers in the Solicitor General's office, a status symbolized by the provision of an office at the Court for their use.

In themselves, the working relationships between lawyers and judges make court regulars highly salient to judges. Further, regulars are the most proximate observers of judges' work, which also makes them a key source of information about that work. A judge's reputation in the legal community as a whole and in the broader community is based largely on the judgments of lawyers who practice in the judge's court. For judges on the less visible courts, hardly anyone other than these lawyers knows enough to assess the quality of their work.

Thus lawyers who appear frequently in a court are a key audience for judges within the legal profession as a whole. To the extent that they share certain values, their presence and interactions with judges may sway judges toward support of those values. This influence might be easiest to discern in courts with narrow jurisdiction. If judges in those courts orient themselves toward the specialized lawyers who appear before them, as suggested earlier, it can be posited that this orientation will be reflected in the evolution of the values they express and support in their decisions.

LEGAL ACADEMICS

As a segment of the legal profession, law schools and legal scholars are especially relevant to judges on higher courts. They interact directly with judges in conferences, judges' visits to law schools, and other settings. More important, they are prominent evaluators of judges' work. Because law professors have so much prestige, their evaluations of judges carry considerable weight.

Some evaluations by legal academics circulate by word of mouth. More tangible are articles and notes in law reviews, which constitute the most detailed and most widely circulated evaluations of judges' work. These publications typically focus on specific decisions or sets of related decisions. But in the past decade there have been several articles that rate the prestige or influence of judges on the federal courts of appeals and, in one instance, the overall quality of their work (W. Landes, Lessig, and Solimine 1998; D. Klein and Morrisroe 1999; Gulati and Sanchez 2002; Choi and Gulati 2004).

Law reviews aside, judges have other reasons to care about the opinions of legal academics. As one judge pointed out (Wald 1995, 1372), law professors control sources of judicial satisfaction such as publication of opinions in casebooks and opportunities to lecture at law schools. For some judges, these constitute significant rewards.

Judges attest directly and indirectly to the salience of legal academics as an audience. Some emphasize the importance of evaluations in law reviews. One state supreme court justice reported that his court's librarian "circulates and posts a separate sheet referencing any law review comment or note on recent decisions of our court" (Richardson 1983, 390). "You grade us," he told a group of law review editors, "and we pay attention!" (Richardson 1983, 389). More recently, a federal court of appeals judge said that "a good number of judges no doubt begin their perusal of a new [law review] issue with the case comments, anxious to see if one of their cases has been reviewed." (Ripple 2000, 441). Judge Stanley Fuld of the New York Court of Appeals exaggerated for effect, but his analysis carried a grain of truth:

> Little is more disheartening than [strong criticism from a law review]. On the other hand, it is difficult to describe the judge's bliss when he discovers a law review affirming an opinion that he wrote for the court. And nothing can be more cheering than the note that agrees with his lone dissent. . . . And so he rests content, until once more the review "reverses" another of his opinions. (Fuld 1953, 916)

Another indication of the relevance of legal academics is the volume of academic writing by judges on higher courts. In light of the heavy workloads of most judges (and of those who assist them), the widespread willingness to engage in this writing underlines its place in judges' priorities. Reasons for academic writing surely are complex and vary from judge to judge, but one important motivation for judges is an interest in their reputation in academia.

For Supreme Court justices, another indication of the salience of legal academia is the substantial number of appearances they make at law schools. Presented with a wide range of invitations, the justices collectively participate in law school programs more than in any other venue. To take an example from one of the most active justices, in 2003 Justice Scalia visited the law schools of the University of Chicago, Louisiana State University, the University of Mississippi, the University of Pennsylvania, Pepperdine University, and the University of Toledo.[7]

The justices have multiple reasons to visit law schools,[8] but the frequency with which most interact with legal academics suggests the salience of this audience to them. Indeed, the extent of this activity is one indicator of how much justices care about the approval of academics. Judges on other higher courts have fewer opportunities to visit law schools, but they are free to do legal writing. For them as well as Supreme Court justices, the volume of that writing will tend to increase with their interest in this audience.

Studies of some individual judges indicate that legal academia was an important audience for them. For instance, Benjamin Cardozo cared a great deal about how he was viewed by law professors and evaluated by law reviews (Posner 1990, 132). Learned Hand had a "hunger for

[7] This information is from Justice Scalia's financial disclosure report. Data on the justices' reimbursed appearances are presented in table 6.1.

[8] Some law school appearances are not at the school campus but at locations outside the United States where law schools have summer programs. In 2003 and 2004, according to the justices' financial disclosure reports, they participated in law school programs in such places as Oxford, Luxembourg, Paris, Florence, Barcelona, Salzburg, and Nice. It is a reasonable guess that the justices were treated fairly well at these venues.

associations with law teachers. Ever since his days at Harvard, Hand had a very high regard for legal scholars, viewing them with an awe that suggests a repression of his usual skepticism" (Gunther 1994, 413).

Cardozo and Hand did not teach in law schools prior to their judicial service, but a substantial minority of judges on higher courts do have that experience. From 1977 through 2004, about 10 percent of the people appointed to the federal courts of appeals were law professors at the time of their appointment (Goldman et al. 2005, 274). Of the federal judges who came from other positions, some (such as Anthony Kennedy and John Paul Stevens) taught part-time before reaching the bench. Some judges (such as Kennedy and Richard Posner) continue teaching in law schools during their judicial service.

Legal academics have special relevance as a reference group for judges who have held that role. Certainly this was true of Felix Frankfurter, a prominent legal scholar before his appointment to the Supreme Court (Hirsch 1981, 175). Another example is Chief Justice Harlan Fiske Stone, who had spent most of his career as professor and dean at Columbia Law School. After his appointment to the Court, Stone regularly interacted with a set of law professors whom Walter Murphy (1964, 63) characterized as a "reference group" for him (see Mason 1956). During the time that Stone was associate justice, Chief Justice William Howard Taft complained that "he hungers for the applause of the law school professors" (Post 2001, 1365). As a court of appeals judge, future Supreme Court justice Wiley Rutledge (who had taught at three law schools) consulted law professors about a few cases before him (Ferren 2004, 196–97). Court of appeals judge Calvert Magruder, a former faculty member at Harvard, consulted more regularly with legal academics. One of his law clerks said that "he not only had me to help him, he had the entire Harvard Law School faculty. And he took advantage of it" (Silber 2004, 49).

Two members of the federal court of appeals for the Second Circuit, Jerome Frank (1941–57) and Charles Clark (1939–63), were both legal scholars who taught at Yale Law School prior to their judicial service (see Schick 1970). As a judge Clark continued to live in New Haven, and "his closest attachments were at Yale" (Schick 1970, 74). For his part, Frank taught at Yale and maintained his highly active scholarly career while he served on the Second Circuit. Despite their ideological similarities, Clark and Frank engaged in a fierce rivalry on the court of appeals. The rivalry seemed to be driven largely by the aspiration of both judges to be viewed favorably at Yale. For instance, "Clark believed that Frank used his course on fact-finding at Yale to ridicule his opinions and this subject came up several times during the 1940's" (Schick 1970, 226). Judge Clark's concern is understandable: for both rivals, the Law School was a highly salient audience for their work as judges, perhaps the most important one.

Among the segments of the legal profession, almost surely the most relevant to most judges is the judges on their own court. Judges on other courts rank second in importance because they are also a peer group. Practicing lawyers and legal scholars have much in common with judges, but they are not in the same position: they lack judges' special status, and they do not do judges' work.

For these reasons, the esteem of other judges carries special weight. Moreover, judges have good opportunities to assess the work of other judges, especially because written opinions provide a basis for assessment that is readily available and widely read. Inevitably, evaluations by other judges help determine how judges feel about themselves as professionals.

Judges on different courts would constitute important audiences for each other even if they never met directly. Judges do interact a good deal. That interaction provides opportunities for judges to assess each other, and it also strengthens the relevance of fellow judges as an audience.

Sometimes this interaction grows out of preexisting ties. Some pairs of judges were in the same professional circles before either was on the bench. As law clerkships increase in number, it has become more common for one judge to have clerked with another. Frequent promotions of judges from one level to the next mean that many judges on different courts served together in the past.

Even when these ties are lacking, considerable contact occurs (Carp 1972). Judges from different levels of a court system sometimes work in the same building. One scholar noted that judges are likely to care more about the effects of their decisions on lower-court judges "when you share an elevator, parking lot, and cafeteria with at least some of those judges" (Lee 2005, 9). One formal mechanism for interaction is training and educational sessions that bring together judges from different courts (B. Cook 1971). Another is assignments of judges to serve on other courts, common in some states and the federal courts (see Brudney and Ditslear 2001). Still another is judicial conferences and meetings of groups such as the Conference of (state) Chief Justices and the National Association of Women Judges.

Not surprisingly, close relationships sometimes develop between judges on different courts (Glendon 1985, 118–27; Geracimos 1998). For instance, some Supreme Court justices have been good friends of judges on the federal court of appeals for the D.C. Circuit: Clarence Thomas with Laurence Silberman (*Legal Times* 1992), William Brennan with David Bazelon (Eisler 1993, 202–4), Hugo Black with J. Skelly Wright (Black and Black 1986, 112, 113, 132, 136, 165). In New York City, federal district judge Edward Weinfeld was close to court of appeals judges

Learned Hand and Henry Friendly (Nelson 2004). Of course, such relationships enhance the importance of fellow judges as an audience.

Even in the absence of personal ties, the judicial community would be a highly salient audience for most judges. Any judge wants to be well thought of among professional peers. As a result, judges' choices are influenced by their perceptions of the kinds of behavior that would enhance their standing among other judges.[9]

Legal Audiences and Judicial Behavior

Unlike social groups, legal audiences share certain perspectives based on their training and experience. Yet their influence on judges' decisional behavior is not homogeneous in form. In part, this is because judges differ in the kinds of regard they seek from legal audiences. For instance, a judge might simply want to be respected as a good judge. Alternatively, the judge might want to have prestige and influence (D. Klein and Morrisroe 1999)—or, put differently, fame (Posner 1990, 59)—within the judiciary and the legal profession. With such distinctions in mind, I will consider some of the more likely and more consequential effects of legal audiences.

DISOWNING YOUR OWN DECISIONS: THE IMPACT OF LAW

In October 1999, Benjamin Ratner, age 13, was in the eighth grade at Blue Ridge Middle School in Loudoun County, Virginia. On October 8, 1999, a schoolmate told Ratner that she had been suicidal the previous evening and had contemplated killing herself by slitting her wrists. She also told Ratner that she inadvertently had brought a knife to school in her binder that morning. Ratner had known her for two years, was aware of her previous suicide attempts, and feared for her safety. Thus, he took the binder from her and put it in his locker. He did not tell school authorities about the knife, but he intended to tell both his and her parents after school.

Thus began the opinion of the federal court of appeals for the Fourth Circuit in *Ratner v. Loudoun County Public Schools* (2001, 141). Anyone who has lived in the United States over the last several years can guess more or less where the story went from there. For an effort to safeguard his classmate's life,[10] Ratner was suspended from school for four months under his school district's "zero tolerance" policy concerning weapons.

---

[9] One indicator of the level of judges' concern with their standing among other judges might be their willingness to take on administrative duties within the judiciary. "A committee appointment constitutes one of the few means of status differentiation available within the judicial system" (Fish 1973, 273). That so many judges do accept these and other special duties suggests the general importance of other judges as an audience.

[10] The court of appeals opinion noted that it was taking the facts from Ratner's complaint for purposes of the appeal. Seymour (1999) describes the facts in a similar way.

Ratner sued the school district and four employees under a federal civil rights statute. The district court dismissed the case, and the court of appeals affirmed. The court's per curiam opinion noted that the school's policy may have been "harsh," but it added that "the federal courts are not properly called upon to judge the wisdom" of that policy (142). Rather, they had to decide whether the policy violated the Constitution—and, the opinion concluded, it did not. In his concurring opinion, Judge Clyde Hamilton went further:

> I write separately to express my compassion for Ratner, his family, and common sense. . . . Suffice it to say that the degree of Ratner's violation of school policy does not correlate with the degree of his punishment. Certainly, the oft repeated maxim, "there is no justice without mercy" has been defiled by the results obtained here. But alas, as the opinion for the court explains, this is not a federal constitutional problem. (143–44)

In effect, Judge Hamilton was disowning the decision he joined. Such opinions are not rare. From time to time, judges say that the decision they reach conflicts with their conception of justice or good policy but that under the law they have no choice.[11] Moreover, judges sometimes suggest that their decision produces an undesirable result and appeal to the legislature to undo that result with a new statute.

Why do judges engage in this distinctive form of self-expression? Undoubtedly, one motive is to forestall criticism from people who disagree with a decision. Indeed, judges might falsely claim to be unhappy about an unpopular outcome. But for the most part, these statements reflect the real conflict that judges feel between what they see as the dictates of the law and their preferences on other dimensions. Compelled to abandon those preferences in favor of the law, they tell the readers of their opinions that the substance of their decision does not reflect their personal values.

The persuasiveness of this interpretation depends heavily on readers' judgments about the importance of legal considerations to judicial decisions. The debate about that issue is unlikely to be resolved any time soon; the disagreements are too sharp and the evidence too limited and ambiguous.[12] However, a perspective based on judges' interest in esteem suggests the importance of judges' reading of the law to their choices.

[11] Examples can be found in *State ex rel. Schwaben v. School Employees Retirement System* (1996, 403); *United States v. Microsoft Corporation* (1999, 953, 958); *Fitzpatrick v. Cucinotta* (1999, 1149); *Adams v. Clinton* (2000, 72); *State v. Thorp* (2000, 903, 911); *Harding v. City of Philadelphia* (2001, 1252); *Shaw v. Terhune* (2003, 705–6); and *Lofton v. Secretary of the Department of Children and Family Services* (2004, 47–48). Judges sometimes express similar sentiments in delivering decisions orally; see Morley 1999, B1.

[12] For arguments and evidence in this debate, see Spaeth and Segal 1999; Whittington 2000; Gillman 2001b; Segal and Spaeth 2002; and Richards and Kritzer 2002.

Adherents to attitudinal models and most versions of strategic models believe that judges care far more about good policy than about good law. But judges seldom gain anything concrete from trying to make good law *or* good policy, and they could gain satisfaction from advancing either goal. Thus it is not self-evident that the goal of making good policy exerts more pull on judges than that of making good law (Cross n.d., 16).[13]

Nonetheless, it may be that most judges gain greater satisfaction from working on behalf of their policy goals than from working to interpret the law well. If so, one reason is that most of the audiences that are important to judges care more about policy than they do about law. For that matter, members of the legal profession are far from indifferent about the content of judicial outputs as policy. Judges can expect to receive considerable praise or blame from lawyers on the basis of the policies their decisions support, regardless of the legal merits of those decisions. Even legal academics often act as ideological partisans in analyzing issues that the courts address and in evaluating judges themselves (see Rosenberg 2000, 648).

Yet the balance of interest between law and policy in the legal community differs from that in judges' other reference groups. Because of their socialization and experience, lawyers appreciate a judge's commitment to legal reasoning and skill in interpreting the law. For this reason, judges who want the respect of practicing lawyers, legal academics, and other judges have an incentive to be perceived as committed to the law and skilled in its interpretation. "To judge is to decide with reference to the expectations of an audience that define the process of decision" (L. Carter 1979, 227). Law-oriented behavior is a powerful expectation in the legal community.

This expectation is reflected in evaluations of judicial decisions. To take one example, most people formed opinions about *Roe v. Wade* solely on the basis of their attitudes toward government policy on abortion. In contrast, some legal academics who approved of the Supreme Court's decision as public policy criticized Justice Blackmun's reasoning in his opinion for the Court. Indeed, reformulation of *Roe* to reach the same result on allegedly stronger grounds became a popular sport among law professors (e.g., Heymann and Barzelay 1973; Law 1984, 1013–28; Gins-

[13] As some scholars have emphasized (e.g., Segal and Spaeth 1993, 70), the composition of the cases decided by a court helps to determine the relative weights of legal and policy considerations in its judges' choices. Thus, the high level of legal ambiguity in the cases decided by the Supreme Court may elevate policy over law. In this discussion, I focus on judges' motivations rather than the room those motivations have to operate in particular situations. However, if the motivation to act on legal considerations is strong enough, it can have substantial impact in any court—though not necessarily in every case (Satter 1990, 63–79).

burg 1985; Koppelman 1990; Balkin 2005). Some have done the same thing with *Brown v. Board of Education* (Balkin 2001).

Of all the segments of the legal profession, the one most likely to care about a judge's quality of legal interpretation is fellow judges. After all, it is the legal element in decisions that distinguishes judges from most other decision makers in government. Skill in legal interpretation and commitment to the task of good legal interpretation are the kinds of qualities that professionals emphasize when they assess their colleagues. As a result, legal criteria are probably the most important basis for judges' assessments of other judges. This theme emerges from what judges on the federal courts of appeals say in evaluating judges on other circuits (D. Klein 2002, 93–97). The salience of colleagues on a judge's own court as an audience makes their expectations, discussed in chapter 3, especially powerful in supporting law-oriented behavior.

The aspiration to be seen as a good interpreter of the law within the legal community is consistent with the way that most judges want to see themselves: as people who "are doing their assigned job well" (Merrill 1997, 975). Central to doing that job well is demonstrating the capacity to set aside personal preferences in the service of good law (see Kleinfeld 1993–94, 11; Posner 1995, 129–34). Judges' interest in achieving this self-image and the same image in the legal community does not guarantee that they will elevate the law over other considerations. But this interest adds to the weight of the law in judicial decision making. For this reason it is not surprising that judges sometimes reach decisions that conflict with their own preferences.

THE TORT REVOLUTION: TALKING AND LISTENING TO OTHER COURTS

In 1963 the California Supreme Court decided *Greenman v. Yuba Power Products Co.* That decision began the last stage of a fundamental change in the law of liability for defective products.[14]

At the beginning of the twentieth century, two broad doctrines protected manufacturers whose defective products caused injuries. First, a plaintiff had to do more than establish that a defective product had caused an injury; it was necessary to show negligence in the manufacture of that product. Second, and even more consequential, manufacturers and sellers of products were liable only to those to whom they directly sold those products. Unless a manufacturer had dealt directly with the ultimate consumer, that consumer could not sue the manufacturer.

State supreme courts gradually modified these rules, a process that accelerated in the late 1950s. Then came *Greenman*. Following a recom-

---

[14] This discussion of tort law draws from Keeton (1969), Shapiro (1970), Canon and Baum (1981), and Baum and Canon (1982).

mendation in the pending Restatement of Torts by the American Law Institute, the California court held that a manufacturer was strictly liable to consumers for damages caused by defective products. The court fully discarded the requirements of negligence and a direct relationship between buyer and seller.

The California decision was a big step in itself, but more striking was what happened in other states. Courts quickly began to adopt the *Greenman* doctrine, and thirty-seven supreme courts fully accepted strict liability for defective products by 1976. By that time most of the other supreme courts accepted some portion of that doctrine.

This change in the law of product liability was just one part of a broader revolution in tort law. Throughout the twentieth century, and increasingly after World War II, state courts replaced doctrines that favored defendants with alternative doctrines that favored plaintiffs. Immunities of governments and charities were narrowed or eliminated. Rules that limited the liability of builders and contractors were overthrown. Procedural rules that favored defendants were changed. In the process, courts abrogated large numbers of their own precedents.

The fierce battles over tort law today are a reminder that the revolution in tort law had a strong ideological direction. In short, the law of personal injuries became substantially more liberal. Yet this revolution extended far beyond courts and states that would be considered liberal. What accounts for the sweep of this movement in the law?

A large part of the answer lies in changes in social thinking, changes that inevitably extended to judges. But much of the answer is internal to the courts. The first issue is the motivations of judges who first announce innovative doctrines, in effect acting as entrepreneurs for new interpretations of the law (McIntosh and Cates 1997). Judges who adopt and advocate new legal doctrines do so for multiple reasons. They may simply favor new interpretations of the law on their merits, and they may enjoy the intellectual process of identifying appropriate changes in the law.

Regardless of their motives, judges whose innovations attract favorable attention gain in reputation as a result. Leaving the Supreme Court aside, the judges who are innovators have the best chance to become well known and widely respected within the legal community. As a member of the New York Court of Appeals, Benjamin Cardozo strengthened his reputation with his early step to increase the liability of manufacturers for defective products (*MacPherson v. Buick Motor Co.* 1916; see Posner 1990). California Supreme Court justice Roger Traynor spoke only for himself when he advocated strict liability for defective products in *Escola v. Coca Cola Bottling Company* (1944), but the subsequent national movement toward his position enhanced his own considerable reputation.

For at least some judges, this consequence is also a powerful motivation. As Judge Posner (1990, 59) put it,

> People derive utility from being famous in their lifetime and from the expectation that they will be famous (even if only within a small circle—and they may prefer fame in that circle to a broader but less discriminating regard) after they are dead.

And without boldness in interpreting the law, a judge has little chance of becoming famous.[15]

The second issue is why so many courts accept some innovative doctrines after the first court adopts them. Judges have no obligation to follow the lead of courts that do not stand above them in the judicial hierarchy. Yet they give considerable attention to the decisions of other courts. For instance, state supreme courts frequently cite the decisions of courts in other states, courts that are part of separate legal systems (Merryman 1977; Caldeira 1985, 1988).

Citation does not necessarily mean influence, but judges do respond to individual decisions and decisional trends in other courts that are parallel to their own. Certainly this is true of state supreme court justices (Shapiro 1970; Canon and Baum 1981). It appears that several motivations contribute to this behavior (Shapiro 1970, 51; D. Klein 2002, 27–28). As with the establishment of new doctrines, one of those motives is judges' interest in their professional reputations. Judges want to be perceived as participants in the collective development of the law because that is a norm of judging. "Failure to listen and adapt to other judges' views is considered unprofessional and is punished by withdrawal of professional esteem" (Shapiro 1970, 52).

This motivation helps to explain the growing citation of court decisions and other legal materials from outside the United States in Supreme Court opinions, a trend that continues despite considerable criticism within and outside the Court.[16] Several justices have cited these materials and treated

---

[15] This discussion raises the question of whether legal considerations as I have described them exert less impact on judges who are interested in standing out than on other judges. This is likely to be true to a limited degree. To innovate and make a mark, judges usually must depart from the existing legal rules. But judges probably would weaken their standing in the legal community if they did not demonstrate that they are willing and able to follow existing rules the great majority of the time.

[16] This trend has drawn strong protests from Justice Antonin Scalia in some opinions, and Scalia and Justice Stephen Breyer engaged in an unusual public debate about its desirability (*AU News* 2005). Other protests have come from Congress, most notably in a proposed resolution that was cosponsored by seventy-four Republican members of the House and considered in a committee hearing (H. Res. 568, 108th Congress, 2d Session, 2004; see also S. Res. 92, 109th Congress, 1st Session, 2005). The resolution quoted the passage in the Declaration of Independence complaining that King George III had "combined [with

them as significant in constitutional cases on civil liberties issues (e.g., *Atkins v. Virginia* 2002, 316; *Grutter v. Bollinger* 2003, 344; *Lawrence v. Texas* 2003, 572–73; *Roper v. Simmons* 2005, 43–49). One reason for these citations is the interactions of some justices with their counterparts from other nations in conferences and other forums (e.g., Badinter and Breyer 2004) and their desire to be seen as active participants in an international process of legal development (Curriden 2004; Slaughter 2004, ch. 2). Indeed, a commentator has suggested that for Sandra Day O'Connor and Anthony Kennedy, one motivation for taking foreign law into account is an interest in gaining greater respect from the judges of other countries with whom they interact (Mauro 2003). The same is likely true of other justices who cite these legal materials (see G. Taylor and Baillot 2004).

If judges pay attention to doctrinal developments in other courts, the result should be an element of momentum in the evolution of legal doctrine. As a trend develops on an issue, judges feel some pressure to follow the trend rather than be left behind. Indeed, David Klein (2002, 71–79, 88–91) found that decisions by federal courts of appeals on a legal issue were affected by the lineup of other circuits on the issue and that many judges attested to this influence.

All this helps to explain the revolution in tort law. The succession of new doctrines favoring plaintiffs gained the status of a trend, and the influence of these doctrines grew with the number of supreme courts that adopted them. Opinions regularly cited the weight of authority behind the new doctrines, and judges who rejected new doctrines often felt compelled to defend their choices against the implicit rebuke of their counterparts in other states. In this way the revolution pulled along courts that would have seemed disinclined to join in. For many state judges, the desire to keep up with the judicial community outweighed any doubts about the wisdom of shifting the balance between tort plaintiffs and defendants.

NINTH CIRCUIT REBELLION: THE AMBIGUITY OF JUDICIAL HIERARCHY

For the most part, the federal courts of appeals labor in obscurity. Except for the occasional major decision, information about these courts seldom travels very far. Perhaps the outstanding exception is the record of the Ninth Circuit on the West Coast. The court's relative liberalism and the willingness of its judges to take bold positions receive attention even outside the legal system (e.g., Kasindorf 2003), and proposals to divide the circuit stem in part from conservatives' unhappiness with those two traits. Both traits were reflected in the court's widely noticed decision in *New-*

---

others] to subject us to a jurisdiction foreign to our constitution and unacknowledged by our laws." (The bracketed words are in the Declaration but not the resolution.)

dow v. United States Congress (2002), holding that the inclusion of "under God" in the Pledge of Allegiance was unconstitutional. Along with all its other effects, the *Newdow* decision enhanced the Ninth Circuit's reputation as a maverick court.

The ideological distance between the Ninth Circuit and the Supreme Court is compounded by the way that many of the court's judges use Supreme Court authority.

> The 9th Circuit, while willing to bind itself by existing Supreme Court precedent, is not interested in playing the game played by other courts of appeals—namely, trying to predict how the high court might rule in cases of first impression. (Lithwick 2003a)

Indeed, some of the Ninth Circuit's judges seem to harbor a rebellious attitude toward the Supreme Court. This attitude was reflected in a 2003 panel opinion that cited *Bush v. Gore* as the authority for a decision postponing a recall election for governor. By doing so the opinion twitted the Supreme Court not very subtly for its effort to warn judges away from applying the rationale in *Bush v. Gore* to other cases.[17] This approach makes a court susceptible to reversal, and the Ninth Circuit gets reversed with unusual frequency. The circuit's reversal rate stands out even when its large volume of decisions is taken into account (Scott 2004; see Herald 1998).

This reversal rate represents a challenge for students of judicial behavior. It seems inconsistent with the conception that judges avoid reversal as a means to advance their policy goals (Songer, Segal, and Cameron 1994; Cross and Tiller 1998; see Cameron, Segal, and Songer 2000), although it could be consistent with a more complex strategy. More important for the current discussion, this reversal rate raises questions about the importance of the legal community as a judicial audience. After all, reversal is widely regarded as a sign that judges have failed to get the law right. Moreover, the Supreme Court has chastised the Ninth Circuit for its positions, both formally (*In re Blodgett* 1992; *Calderon v. Thompson* 1998) and informally (Carrizosa 1992). Meanwhile, the circuit's reputation among judges in other circuits has suffered (D. Klein 2002, 92–93). If judges care about what other judges and lawyers think of them, why do the judges of the Ninth Circuit take a path that leads to a high reversal rate?

---

[17] Lithwick (2003a) subtitled her analysis of this decision, "The 9th Circuit Moons the Supreme Court." The decision was *Southwest Voter Registration Education Project v. Shelley* (2003). Shortly afterwards, an en banc ruling by the Ninth Circuit under the same title overturned the panel decision, thus allowing the recall election to go forward. This was the election in which Arnold Schwarzenegger became governor.

This question can be addressed on two levels. On the first level, the norm of obedience to higher courts is only one of many forces that shape judicial behavior, and it can be outweighed by other forces. Even if a judge cares only about standing in the legal community, that consideration may be consistent with rebellion. The southern federal district judges who resisted desegregation received considerable reinforcement from lawyers and judges in their region despite reversals by the Fifth Circuit. Judges who seek prestige may calculate that reversals are the necessary price for positions that enhance their standing in some segments of the legal community, both at present and in the future.

Moreover, judges have other audiences. Alabama Chief Justice Roy Moore maintained his display of the Ten Commandments even though his defiance of a federal court decision on the display led to the extraordinary sanction of removal from his position. Apparently he did so because his personal convictions and the strong approval of nonjudicial audiences (approval that had made him chief justice in the first place) gave him strong incentives to adhere to his position (Gettleman 2003; *In the Matter of Roy S. Moore* 2003; Moore and Perry 2005).

The record of the Ninth Circuit is not difficult to understand in this light. The geographic areas in which many Ninth Circuit judges live and work have an abundant supply of people who applaud judges for liberal stands on civil liberties issues. That applause may be sufficient to outweigh any damage to judges' reputations from other quarters. The Ninth Circuit's most prominent liberal, Judge Stephen Reinhardt, has said, "I follow the law the way it used to be, before the Supreme Court began rolling back a lot of people's rights" (Carlsen 1996, 5). That stance has earned Reinhardt a number of reversals, but it also wins him admiration from lawyers and others who share his views.[18]

On the second level, the Ninth Circuit's rebellion attracts attention because it is an anomaly.[19] Although other courts have also rebelled to one degree or another (see Liptak and Blumenthal 2004), by and large, judges follow the Supreme Court's lead. The overall level of judicial compliance with the Court's precedents appears to be very high. Moreover, ideological trends in the Court have considerable impact on the trends in lower courts.[20] For that matter, even the Ninth Circuit's rebellion is limited.

[18] It may be worth noting that Judge Reinhardt is married to Ramona Ripston, executive director of the American Civil Liberties Union chapter in Southern California.

[19] One might be tempted to say that the Ninth Circuit is the exception that proves the rule. But one would want to avoid the controversy, occasionally quite heated, over the meaning of that aphorism (C. Adams 2001).

[20] For a sampling of the research on hierarchical relationships in the courts, see Peltason 1971; Tarr 1977; C. Johnson 1987; Songer 1987; Songer and Sheehan 1990; Songer, Segal, and Cameron 1994; Sanders 1995; Reddick and Benesh 2000; and D. Klein 2002, ch. 6. The research is summarized in Canon and Johnson 1999, ch. 2.

Only a subset of the court's judges frequently take positions that are likely to evoke reversals, and even they generally do so on issues that the Supreme Court has not yet addressed directly. Implicit or explicit defiance of the Court's precedents is uncommon (see *Wallace v. Castro* 2003).

The high level of lower-court obedience to the Supreme Court is part of a broader pattern of acceptance of hierarchical authority within the judiciary. This pattern is noteworthy because the powers of higher courts are so limited. Even in organizations in which superiors have more impressive powers, hierarchical control is typically quite imperfect (Brehm and Gates 1997).

Lower-court obedience might be read as the product of either policy-oriented strategy or the strength of judges' interest in following legal norms. A brief discussion cannot adequately analyze the strengths and weaknesses of these alternative explanations. However, it seems clear that strategy can provide only a partial explanation. A court of appeals strategy of avoiding Supreme Court reversals is not fully parallel with a Supreme Court strategy of avoiding congressional overrides, and on the whole, avoidance of reversal is a more attractive strategy.[21] But some of the same considerations work against the two forms of strategy. In particular, deciding a case as the Supreme Court is predicted to decide it in order to avoid reversal requires judges to take a position that conflicts with their own conceptions of good legal policy. Thus they lose the satisfaction of taking what they (and perhaps some important audiences) perceive as the right position. The judges who have to worry the most about reversal, the ones whose preferences are distant from those of the Supreme Court, would give up this satisfaction regularly. That is a high price to pay.

Legal norms seem to provide a larger part of the explanation. Judges are socialized in those norms, and lawyers and other judges are important audiences. Thus judges want to see themselves as people who follow their duties under the law, and they want others to see them in the same way. Following the lead of higher courts, an important norm, is one means to maintain this image and self-image. To the extent that the prospect of reversal affects judges' choices (see D. Klein and Hume 2003), a key to that impact is its status as a visible indicator that a judge has erred as a professional. From this vantage point it is understandable that some judges keep track of their reversals (Schick 1970, 145) and that high reversal rates raise questions about a judge's competence.

The dominance of centripetal forces over centrifugal forces is one of the most striking features of the judiciary. Serious rebellion is exceptional,

---

[21] One difference is that reversals are probably more predictable than congressional overrides. Another is that reversals can give wider geographic scope to what a judge regards as bad policy: instead of that policy prevailing in a single federal circuit, for instance, it becomes national law.

obedience typical. To a considerable degree this reality reflects the salience of the legal community as a judicial audience.

The Impact of Judicial Backgrounds

In chapter 3, I posited that the relevance of the general public as a judicial audience varies with the extent of judges' past involvement in electoral politics. By the same token, judges with greater involvement in the legal profession could be expected to develop a stronger orientation toward the profession and its norms. At one end of the spectrum, some future judges devote themselves to the private practice of law, with limited participation in politics and public affairs until they become judges. At the other end, some never engage in legal practice, moving directly from law school to the political world and from there to a judgeship. For the "political" lawyer who becomes a judge, the legal profession and its ways of thinking may be quite peripheral and reputation among lawyers a matter of little concern.[22] For the judge who was immersed in the law as a profession, the values of the bar have much greater relevance (see Grossman 1965, 206–7).

To take two familiar examples, Earl Warren and Lewis Powell brought quite different orientations to the Supreme Court. Powell, a practicing lawyer until his appointment to the Court, was an active participant in the organized bar who served as president of the American Bar Association (Jeffries 1994, 193–204). In contrast, Warren spent nearly his entire pre-Court career in government positions, the preponderance of that time in elected office. He did not feel a strong bond with the organized bar, and as chief justice he became involved in conflicts with the ABA that culminated with his resignation from the organization (B. Schwartz 1983, 282–86; Cray 1997, 340–41).

The strength of judges' orientation toward the legal profession could affect several aspects of their behavior. One example is the publication of opinions. On most courts, judges have a choice whether to publish opinions (and sometimes whether to write them) in specific cases. Studies of decisions whether to publish show that these decisions reflect a range of considerations and that judges differ in their propensities to publish (Songer 1990; Merritt and Brudney 2001; Swenson 2004; Taha 2004; Morriss, Heise, and Sisk 2005).

Published opinions are a means to demonstrate legal skill and creativity to the legal community. All else being equal, judges' use of opportunities

---

[22] No matter how political a judge's orientation, legal considerations have some impact. In a case in which the lawyers on both sides were well connected politically, one Chicago judge announced that "where the clout is equal, the law must prevail" (Slovak 1979, 470).

to publish could be expected to increase with the level of their interest in the esteem of lawyers and other judges. Existing studies provide some suggestive evidence by testing the relationship between characteristics of judges' career experience and publication decisions; overall, the findings do not have clear implications. A study of decisions on one legal issue did find that judges who received higher ratings from the American Bar Association when nominated were more likely to publish (Taha 2004, 18–19). On the whole, it appears that nominees who are more fully integrated into the legal system receive higher ABA ratings (see Haire 2001). In conjunction, these two pieces of evidence suggest that the salience of the legal profession does affect judges' publication decisions, though this relationship remains uncertain.

More consequential are the criteria by which judges decide cases. If an orientation toward the legal profession strengthens the legal element in judges' thinking about cases, there could be a relationship between the balance of law and politics in judges' backgrounds and the impact of legal considerations on their decision making. In the context of this hypothesis, the changes that have occurred in recruitment paths to the Supreme Court are noteworthy. Table 3.1 summarized the rise of lower-court judgeships in the justices' backgrounds. In none of the three eras between 1861 and 1968 did half of the Supreme Court appointees come directly from lower courts, and the proportion in 1933–68 was only 29 percent. In the 1969–2005 period, in contrast, 85 percent of the new justices came from lower courts. Even more relevant to this hypothesis are the increasing portions of their careers that justices typically spend in the legal system. Among the justices appointed in 1933–68, the median proportion was 67 percent; among those appointed in 1969–2005, the median was 89 percent.[23] Thus the careers of justices in the current era link them more closely to the legal community than was true of their predecessors.

A similar but less dramatic trend has occurred in the lower federal courts (Goldman 1997, 348–50, 354–56; Goldman et al. 2005, 269, 274). Since the 1930s there has been a decline in the proportion of judges who came to these courts from nonlegal positions in government and politics and an increase in the proportion coming from other judgeships or private law practice. For this reason, a corollary of the hypothesis about the im-

---

[23] These proportions are not shown in table 3.1. For calculation of the proportions, private legal practice, corporate practice, positions in law schools, judicial clerkships, and judgeships were treated as positions in the legal system; legal positions in government were not. The number of years in a career was calculated from the time that legal training was completed, except that time in the military was excluded. There were some ambiguities, primarily when future justices served simultaneously in two positions. In that situation, the position in which the person seemed to be spending more time was used. Biographical data were taken from the Federal Judges Biographical Database (Federal Judicial Center 2005).

pact of judges' backgrounds is that federal judges as a group give greater weight to legal audiences and thus to legal considerations than they did in earlier eras.

There is considerable reason for skepticism about this corollary. The scholarship on judicial behavior has amply documented the ideological dimensions that exist in the decisional behavior of federal judges in the current era. Moreover, the most visible actions by federal judges today, both on and off the bench, underscore the interest that many of them clearly have in achieving good policy as they see it.

In light of this evidence, one possibility is that the changes in the career patterns of federal judges have had no impact on their orientations toward decision making. Another is that these changes have been counterbalanced or even outweighed by forces operating in the other direction. One such force could be the growth in ideological polarization among political elites; the impact of this development on judges is discussed in the next chapter.

But the possibility that federal judges as a group give greater weight to legal considerations today than in the past should not be dismissed out of hand. Evidence of a strong judicial interest in making good public policy is abundant in past eras as well as the current one. Whatever actually is the balance between legal and policy considerations in the behavior of current federal judges, today's judges as a group may be more legally oriented than their counterparts in past eras.

Thus this corollary merits consideration. More broadly, there is good reason to probe the relationship between judges' career experiences and the balance of considerations in their choices as decision makers. As I have argued, one reason to expect such a relationship is the impact of judges' careers on their constellations of personal audiences.

CONCLUSIONS

Judges' social groups and the legal profession are quite different audiences in some respects. Perhaps most important, fellow lawyers are closely connected with judges' work, while members of judges' social groups who are not lawyers stand apart from that work. In a broad sense, however, these two audiences have much in common. Only on occasion does their approval do much to advance judges' concrete self-interest. Further, the esteem of other lawyers can advance judges' policy goals only to a limited degree, the esteem of social groups hardly at all. For these reasons the dominant models of judicial behavior take no account of judges' social groups. For the same reasons, these models leave aside potential influence on judges from the legal profession, except for interactions within appellate courts and relations between higher and lower courts.

Once we step outside the dominant models, it seems quite short-sighted to ignore the potential impact of these two audiences. Judges spend most of their time interacting with members of their profession and their social groups. In part for that reason, these are usually their most salient audiences. Their self-esteem depends heavily on their perceptions of what these audiences think of them. In light of those realities, it is difficult to imagine that social and professional groups have no impact on judges' choices as decision makers. Indeed, to the extent that judges' interest in the approval of these audiences can be separated from their interest in good legal policy, there is no good reason to assume that the latter carries more weight than the former. Why would judges elevate an abstract concern with the state of legal policy over their standing with family, friends, and fellow lawyers?

Of course, these two interests are not entirely separate. Judges' relationships with social and professional groups are linked with their thinking about law and policy and with their efforts to make good legal policy. The discussions of other personal audiences in chapter 5 probe additional linkages between policy goals and judges' interest in approval, linkages that underline the value of taking judicial audiences into account.

Chapter 5

POLICY GROUPS, THE NEWS MEDIA,

AND THE GREENHOUSE EFFECT

OF ALL THE TYPES of personal audiences, social groups and the legal community have the greatest impact on the choices of most judges. But other kinds of groups may be highly salient to certain judges. This chapter considers two quite different kinds of groups, policy groups and the news media. It concludes by probing the hypothesis that a "Greenhouse effect" has moved some Supreme Court justices in a liberal direction, a hypothesis based on the perceived impact of several personal audiences.

POLICY GROUPS

Policy groups can be defined as sets of people who share particular policy positions or ideological orientations. Some policy groups are embodied in concrete organizations such as interest groups, but many are informal and less clearly defined.

This section begins by considering policy groups in general and then turns to several specific topics. The Federalist Society exemplifies organized policy groups, and it illuminates how policy groups can function as reference groups for judges. The two subsections that follow consider judicial partisanship and polarization as they relate to policy groups. Finally, I discuss Justice Clarence Thomas as a judge for whom policy groups appear to be highly salient.

The Roles of Policy Groups

Policy groups can be important to judges for instrumental reasons, chiefly when they affect the achievement of career goals. Judges who face elections, for instance, benefit from the campaign spending of interest groups. As campaign costs rise and elections become more competitive in some states (Glaberson 2000; D. Goldberg, Holman, and Sanchez 2002), the value of contributions to judicial candidates and independent spending on their behalf has grown. Support from groups can also assist judges in winning appointments to higher courts. Thus career-minded judges may have good reason to keep policy groups in mind when they make their choices on the bench.

But at least for judges with secure tenure, the potential influence of policy groups derives chiefly from judges' personal identification with them. If people who share a point of view about legal policy function as a reference group for a judge, the judge has an incentive to take actions that those people approve. That is especially true when their approval would counterbalance criticism from other sources. Certain judges "may lack for respect among their colleagues, but receive the adoration of fellow ideologues in the political world that they care about" (McGarity 1995, 1105).

Judges often have personal links with formal and informal groups that can be characterized as policy groups. Some judges developed close relationships with political interest groups in their pre-judicial careers. Much of Ruth Bader Ginsburg's professional work was for the Women's Rights Project of the ACLU. For most of his years as a lawyer, all of Thurgood Marshall's work was for the Legal Defense Fund of the NAACP. The careers of other people who become judges link them with groups that have a distinct point of view on policy issues: the law enforcement community for prosecutors, the business community for lawyers in large firms. Outside their work, future judges also join and identify with political parties and other policy groups.

Identifications with these groups do not disappear automatically when a lawyer becomes a judge, and strong identifications are especially likely to persist. We would hardly expect Justice Ginsburg to disengage emotionally from the feminist movement (see Biskupic 1995b) or Justice Marshall from the civil rights movement. Harold Burton maintained a strong orientation toward the American Legion after his appointment to the Supreme Court (Danelski 1970, 129–30). On occasion, judges develop new identifications with policy groups after reaching the bench. As I suggest later, this likely was true of Harry Blackmun during his Supreme Court service.

Moreover, judges often interact with policy groups. They make speeches or accept awards at meetings of groups such as the Freedoms Foundation (*Washington Post* 1982), the American Trial Lawyers Association (Kemerer 1991, 79), and the NAACP Legal Defense Fund (Greenberg 1994, 367; see *Legal Times* 2003). Justice Ginsburg appeared at a lecture series, named in her honor, that was cosponsored by the NOW Legal Defense and Education Fund (now renamed Legal Momentum).[1]

---

[1] In response to the criticism of Justice Scalia for his duck-hunting trip with Vice President Cheney, discussed in chapter 3, conservatives argued that Ginsburg's relationship with the NOW Fund required that she recuse herself in any case in which the group took a position,

Some federal judges have served on the board of the Foundation for Research in Economics and Environment (FREE), a conservative group that conducts seminars on policy issues for federal judges (Leonnig 2004).[2]

Even when judges have strong ties to policy groups, those ties do not necessarily produce influence. The potential influence of policy groups on judges' choices requires some consideration.

The influence of policy groups that serve as instrumental audiences can be explored from the vantage point of a state judge who hopes for an interest group's financial support for a reelection campaign. Commentators have expressed concern that groups essentially buy favorable policies from judges through their campaign contributions. Specifically, they fear that judges take certain positions in order to elicit future group support or to reward past support (e.g., Kaplan 1987; Kaplan and Davidson 1998; Texans for Public Justice 2001; Committee for Economic Development 2002, 22–23; D. Goldberg 2003).

The extent of such behavior is highly uncertain, in part because it is so difficult to determine the causal relationship between campaign contributions and judicial decisions.[3] But some of the concern about the impact of contributions seems misplaced. For interest groups it is a far better strategy to seek out candidates and judges who are already sympathetic toward the group's positions than to try to convert people to their positions with monetary contributions. For judges it is unattractive to depart radically from personal preferences in order to cultivate group support for reelection. It would exact a heavy personal cost for a judge whose own inclinations are proconsumer to establish a probusiness record. Liberal judges can avoid those costs by obtaining support from groups whose positions are also liberal.

In practice, this is what generally happens: judges and groups sort each other out on an ideological basis. Groups such as trial lawyers and the Chamber of Commerce enter campaigns primarily to elect judges whose

---

and some commentators raised questions about her ties with the group (Serrano and Savage 2004; *Los Angeles Times* 2004).

[2] After formal ethics complaints were brought against the four judges on the FREE board, three resigned from the board (Leonnig 2005a). The complaint against the fourth judge was dismissed by the judge who was designated to consider it (Leonnig 2005b). Critics of the seminars conducted by this group and other conservative groups argue that because these seminars are typically held in attractive locations and often include considerable leisure time, they create a sense of obligation on the part of the judges who attend them (Marcus 1998; Kendall and Rylander 2004). It might be, however, that if these seminars have an impact, it is primarily to create or strengthen some judges' identifications with the sponsoring groups and their point of view.

[3] For studies of this relationship, see Ware 1999; Waltenburg and Lopeman 2000; and McCall 2001, 2003. Research on the impact of campaign contributions on legislators is more abundant; see Wright 1996; and Bronars and Lott 1997.

preferences favor the group's interests rather than to draw judges away from their preferences. For their part, judges who work to gain the support of interest groups concentrate on groups whose viewpoint is similar to their own.

Still, there is room for interest groups to influence the choices of judges whom they support. They can do so by reinforcing judges' preexisting tendencies, so that judges support a group's interests more consistently than they would otherwise. Liberal judges, for instance, might take positions that are even more favorable to labor than their personal preferences would dictate in order to cultivate and maintain the support of labor unions.

A similar process can occur when judges' career goals depend on appointment rather than election. One example is a conservative federal judge who hopes for promotion. That judge might adhere more strongly to conservative positions in order to win support from groups that influence judicial nominations in Republican administrations.

This kind of behavior could be reflected in temporal patterns: a judge's decisions become more favorable to a like-minded interest group as the need for its support increases. One example is when an unusually competitive election looms. Another possibility is that a judge's decisions are most favorable to a supportive group in the cases of greatest salience to that group.

Under some circumstances career-minded judges can be influenced by policy groups with which they strongly disagree. The most likely situation is one in which liberal judges curb their support for criminal defendants in order to avoid opposition from law-and-order groups (see M. Hall 1987, 1992). In criminal justice, unlike the economic arena, judges cannot choose from groups on both sides of the issue. Ordinarily, however, groups that affect judges' career prospects reinforce their existing ideological tendencies rather than creating new ones.

To a considerable degree, policy groups that serve as personal audiences for judges can be expected to exert their influence in an analogous way. This mechanism of influence relates to an argument discussed in chapter 2. According to that argument, judges' personal audiences have little impact on their behavior because judges choose audiences who share their preferences. That argument is most applicable to policy groups. For one thing, these groups are located throughout the ideological spectrum, so judges can easily find groups of people whose point of view is similar to their own. Further, people are especially prone to choose policy groups on the basis of their own policy views. Judges may identify with friends or professional colleagues despite basic disagreements about policy issues. Seldom do they identify with policy groups whose views conflict with their own.

This reality does not preclude an influence for policy groups with which judges identify. Those groups, like groups that serve judges' career goals, can exert an impact by reinforcing preexisting tendencies in judicial behavior. Judges' interest in the approval of certain groups may move them to take positions that accord more fully or more consistently with the groups' policy positions.

This influence may help to account for the strength of the ideological dimensions that scholars have identified in the votes of federal judges on case outcomes. Like legislators who adhere to their voting history on an issue (Asher and Weisberg 1978; Fenno 1978; Bianco 1994; Meinke 2005), judges might act consciously or unconsciously to maintain consistency in their positions as a way to please audiences that favor those positions. This is especially true of audiences that constitute the equivalent of core constituencies for them. For example, liberal judges who identify with liberal policy groups may hesitate to disappoint those groups by taking conservative positions in particular cases to which their audiences are attentive. They will be more hesitant to do so when colleagues who are also identified as liberal take liberal positions. The result would be to reduce deviations from unidimensional voting patterns in particular policy areas.[4]

One possible illustration of this effect is the complicated sequence of Supreme Court decisions that culminated in the executions of Julius and Ethel Rosenberg (see *Rosenberg v. United States* 1953). During most of this sequence Justice William O. Douglas voted against the Rosenbergs' claims even as some colleagues supported them, but later on he unexpectedly issued a stay of execution. Two of Douglas's colleagues believed that he was departing from his earlier positions "to play to his liberal constituency" (Simon 1980, 299). If so, Douglas may have been especially concerned that some other justices had appeared to be more favorable to civil liberties than he was.

If audiences of policy groups move judges toward greater ideological consistency in their choices, these audiences can affect the incidence of strategic voting. Judges might calculate that deviation from their preferred positions in particular cases would advance their policy goals in the long run. When members of a policy group recognize and appreciate strategic behavior, a judge can deviate without jeopardizing their support. Justice William Brennan built a reputation for effective strategy, one that appealed to at least some of his admirers (see Clark 1995).

[4] In contrast, a judge who seeks the regard of a legal audience may be drawn to just the opposite behavior—a pattern of voting that is ideologically inconsistent—as a way of demonstrating fealty to legal considerations. Some judges who are difficult to characterize ideologically are simply moderates, but others may be responding to audiences that favor nonideological judging.

But the appearance of stubborn adherence to principle, a trait associated with Brennan's colleagues William O. Douglas and Antonin Scalia, is usually more attractive to an audience that cares about policy. A group's disappointment with a judge's deviation from its position is immediate, while the effects of strategic choices are less immediate and uncertain. Thus, just as concern about constituents can limit strategic voting by legislators (Denzau, Riker, and Shepsle 1985; Wilkerson 1990; Austen-Smith 1992), links with policy groups may work against strategic action by judges.

The impact of policy groups in moving judges toward greater ideological consistency may be reinforced by the sense of competition between groups that is an element of social identities. Unlike other kinds of personal groups, policy groups always have counterparts with opposing viewpoints. Judges who identify strongly with certain groups are likely to have negative feelings toward groups on the other side, and they will hesitate to give aid and comfort to the opposition.

The influence of policy groups can go considerably deeper, providing some of the motivation for judges' commitment to certain policy goals. As suggested in chapter 2, personal audiences help induce judges to pursue good policy as a judge and an audience define it. Policy groups seldom are as integral to judges' social identities as social groups and the legal profession, but by definition their members feel strongly about public policy. For that reason they may be especially important in motivating policy-oriented judging.

Organized Policy Groups: The Federalist Society

For the most part, the policy groups with which judges identify are informal. But judges attach themselves to some organized policy groups, and the most prominent today is the Federalist Society for Law and Public Policy Studies. The Federalist Society was organized in 1982 by conservatives in law schools who sought to counterbalance what they saw as the liberal orthodoxy of the legal academy. It has become a large organization whose membership continues to grow rapidly (N. Lewis 1991; Bossert 1997; Mahler 1998; T. Carter 2001; Federalist Society 2003; Baldas 2004). In recent years the society and its members have wielded considerable influence in government, and many people—especially its ideological opponents—depict it as a very powerful group (Gerchik 2000; Landay 2000; Edsall 2001; N. Lewis 2001a; T. Carter 2001; Radelat 2004b).

As the society grew in membership, it began to function as a career network. A perception developed that membership and activity in the society facilitated clerkships with conservative judges, legal positions in

Republican administrations, and judicial appointments by Republican chief executives. As one commentator put it, the Federalist Society

> has evolved into not only a power broker in Republican circles—its members honeycomb the Bush administration—but also a sort of judicial hatchery, spawning and cultivating reliably conservative judges and their reliably conservative law clerks the way state-of-the-art fish farms produce salmon, leaving little to the maddening caprices of nature. (Margolick 2003, 150)

Career considerations have contributed to growth in the Federalist Society, but professional opportunities account only in part for its popularity among law students and lawyers. It functions as an organization in which people with conservative views can feel comfortable, because other members share their goals and perspectives (see *Legal Times* 1992; Federalist Society 1998; Landay 2000). A sense of efficacy strengthens members' ties to the society, yet the organization continues to draw on conservatives' belief that they are a beleaguered minority in the legal community (see A. Cohen 2002). Indeed, the Federalist Society collectively frames its work as an effort to counteract the effects of liberalism on law and policy. The society's self-descriptions and transcripts of talks at its events provide clear evidence of the "we-they" thinking that helps bind people to particular groups (Brewer 1991, 2003).

The membership of the society includes a good many judges. By one count, in 1998 at least twenty-two federal judges were members (Gerchik 2000, 2), and fifteen of George W. Bush's first forty-one appointees to the courts of appeals identified themselves as members (DeParle 2005). Five of the seven Michigan Supreme Court justices in 2000 (Landay 2000, 23) and four of the eight Alabama justices in 2004 (Radelat 2004a) were members.

Both liberal and conservative judges participate in the society's programs. Naturally, the judges who belong to the society or have close relationships with it are conservative. In the view of one observer, "a number of Republican judicial appointees have more or less actively continued their old ideological links through support or membership in the Federalist Society" (L. Walsh 1998, 1389). Antonin Scalia was an early organizer of the society as a faculty member at the University of Chicago (Canellos 2003), and Scalia and Clarence Thomas participate frequently in its events.[5]

---

[5] In a 2004 talk at the society, Justice Scalia said that during that year's presidential campaign he had received a fund-raising flyer with the headline, "What Would You Think of CHIEF JUSTICE Scalia?" According to a reporter, "the audience erupted into sustained and thunderous cheers and applause" (Richey 2004, 1). Like the episode in which Justice Blackmun mused about his possible retirement, described at the beginning of chapter 1, this remark is a reminder that judges enjoy evidence that they are appreciated.

The society's gatherings are a forum at which conservative judges can express themselves freely to people who share their point of view. An example is federal court of appeals judge Laurence Silberman. Judge Silberman used one talk before the society to advise Republican nominees to the federal courts on how to handle confirmation hearings (Groner 2002a). In another he made a wide-ranging attack on judges who opposed the confirmation of Clarence Thomas to the Supreme Court, on other out-of-court activities by judges, and on the ideological orientations of law schools and the news media (*Legal Times* 1992). Expressions by some conservative judges indicate that the society remained a significant reference group for them after they reached the bench. This is true of Justice Thomas, for instance (C. Thomas 1999; see R. Winter 1992).

Judges' career goals create a potential source of influence for the Federalist Society. For judges who seek promotions from Republican presidents, the networks to which the society is connected strengthen the incentive to adhere to conservative positions. But the society's function as a personal audience is probably a more potent source of influence. Judges who identify with the society and participate in its activities have an attentive audience that applauds certain kinds of decisions and doctrines. In this way the organization makes more concrete and thus more salient the ideological reference groups of conservative judges. One result is to provide additional reinforcement for the kinds of conservative positions that members of the society favor.

One indication of the group's importance is the efforts of liberals to create a counterpart organization of their own (Hines 2001). The organization that resulted from these efforts is the American Constitution Society, founded in 2001 (Wohl 2003; Baldas 2004; American Constitution Society 2005). It is strikingly similar in form to the Federalist Society. One similarity is the participation of judges who share its basic point of view (though, like the Federalist Society, it includes other judges in its programs).

Like the Federalist Society, the American Constitution Society provides a forum in which judges can speak more freely than they ordinarily do. An incident at the society's 2004 convention is illuminating (Gerstein 2004; Preston 2004; *In re Charges of Judicial Misconduct* 2005). Judge Guido Calabresi of the federal court of appeals for the Second Circuit, speaking impromptu, likened the presidential accession of George W. Bush to the accessions of Mussolini and Hitler and indicated that it was necessary to deny Bush reelection for the good of the democratic system.

When John Roberts was nominated to the Supreme Court in 2005, the extent of his involvement in the society was the subject of some disagreement. Members of President Bush's staff sought to minimize that involvement, apparently because they wanted to avoid inferences that Roberts shared the society's conservatism (Lane 2005).

Clearly, Judge Calabresi (who later apologized for his remarks and was admonished by his chief judge) felt sufficiently comfortable among ideological allies to say things that he would not have said in other public settings. According to one observer's report, the remarks by a panel of judges at the society's 2003 convention were another example of judicial candor (Bashman 2003).

The existence of the Federalist Society and the American Constitution Society makes the policy groups they encompass more concrete for the judges who identify with them. In a sense, however, they simply formalize what some judges always have done: maintain and build on networks of people with whom they share policy views. These networks can include a wide range of participants, from officials in the executive branch to academics to judges on other courts. There were strong links between some of Franklin Roosevelt's Supreme Court appointees and other liberals in the New Deal era (Lash 1975; Newman 1997; R. H. Jackson 2003). Liberal justices on the Court and the federal courts of appeals for the District of Columbia interacted with each other and with like-minded people who held other positions in the 1960s and 1970s. Indeed, the dining room of a liquor warehouse in Washington served as something of a "salon" for liberals in and out of the judiciary during that era (Barbash 1981; see Clines and Weaver 1982). And current judges who choose not to participate in organized liberal and conservative groups may still identify with informal groups that have strong ideological orientations.

Judicial Partisanship

For political elites policy and political parties are intertwined, in that ideological positions are highly correlated with party identifications. As a result, policy groups typically have a strong partisan coloration. Undoubtedly, the membership of the Federalist Society is overwhelmingly Republican.

Moreover, the parties constitute important reference groups in themselves. A substantial proportion of judges were active in political party organizations. Whether or not they were active, surely most judges have the strong emotional attachments to a party that are abundant in the general population (Green, Palmquist, and Schickler 2002, ch. 2). Like other group memberships, identifications with parties can reinforce the ideological element in judges' behavior, what Howard Gillman (2001a, 7) called "high" politics. Partisan ties also can foster what Gillman labeled "low" politics, "partisan favoritism."

Judges in some states have reputations for partisan favoritism in cases such as election disputes. These reputations are fostered by decisions such as the rulings on legislative redistricting by the Colorado and North Carolina supreme courts in 2003. In both cases all the justices supported their own parties' interests.[6] Such behavior reflects some combination of several relevant motives, including judges' gratitude for the parties' assistance in their winning judgeships, a desire to maintain party support for a new term of office or another position, and identification with a party's fortunes.

Federal judges also exhibit partisan favoritism. Two studies of legislative districting indicate that district judges are inclined to support their party's interests (Lloyd 1995; McKenzie 2004). Occasional appellate decisions indicate that partisanship can outweigh ideology. In the criminal appeals of Oliver North and of Lyn Nofziger, both connected to the Reagan administration, Republican conservatives overturned convictions while Democratic liberals dissented (*United States v. North* 1990; *United States v. Nofziger* 1989). The motives that operate in state courts are relevant to federal judges, but their secure tenure in office reduces the salience of career considerations. Identification with one of the parties is probably the key factor.

Because career considerations are irrelevant to the great majority of Supreme Court justices, their behavior is of particular interest. The anecdotal evidence on partisan favoritism on the Court is mixed. The justices voted unanimously in *United States v. Nixon* (1974) and in *Clinton v. Jones* (1997), the decision that led ultimately to President Clinton's impeachment. On the other hand, the two Democratic justices dissented when the Court decided not to hear two other cases involving investigations of Clinton's activities (*Office of the President v. Office of Independent Counsel* 1998; *Rubin v. United States* 1998). Legislative redistricting cases, which often pit the parties' interests against each other, have not been analyzed systematically. However, in cases involving race and redistricting, the justices often diverge from the interests of the party that they presumably favor. As political scientist David Canon said after one decision, "race trumps party on this issue" (Clymer 2003, A18).

This brings us to *Bush v. Gore*. Strictly speaking, the justices did not split along partisan lines; the Republicans John Paul Stevens and David Souter voted in favor of Al Gore. But Stevens and Souter were on the ideological left side of the Court. The partisan element in the justices' voting was highlighted by the fact that the justices who fully supported

[6] The Colorado decision in *People ex rel. Salazar v. Davidson* is discussed in Hughes 2003. The North Carolina decision in *Stephenson v. Bartlett* is discussed in *Charlotte Observer* 2003.

George W. Bush's equal protection claim were those who generally gave the least support to such claims (Gillman 2001a, ch. 6).[7]

A justice might have favored Bush or Gore with retirement in mind. Perhaps some associate justices sought to preserve their chances for promotion to chief justice. Posner (2001, 175–76, 180–81) discusses the justices' interest in the future composition of the Court as a possible motive for their votes.

But in all likelihood, the most powerful force was the justices' own rooting interests. When he later acknowledged the possible impact of partisan thinking on his position in this case, Justice Breyer pointed to the role of these rooting interests: "I had to ask myself, would I vote the same way if the names were reversed. I said 'yes.' But I'll never know for sure—because people are great self-kidders" (Levey 2004).

The rooting interests of some justices undoubtedly were reinforced by their ties with political groups other than the parties. The groups with which Justice Ginsburg identifies would not have reacted to a vote for Governor Bush with equanimity. For their part, if Justice Scalia and Justice Thomas had taken a position that helped Al Gore become president, they would have been greeted with somewhat less warmth at the next gathering of the Federalist Society. And as one scholar speculated, Justice Kennedy may have perceived that if he sided with Gore, he would "be forever seen as a traitor to Republican conservatives," a prospect that could have influenced his position (Cross 2004). The "low politics" of *Bush v. Gore* may have been conscious or unconscious, but in either case identifications with political groups had at least a subtle impact on the positions that justices took.

Polarization in the Courts?

Political scientists have amply documented a growth in polarization between the political parties at the elite level.[8] Party polarization involves a "disappearance of moderation" (McCarty, Poole, and Rosenthal 1997, 3), which produces an increased homogeneity of views within each party and a concomitant increase in ideological differences between the parties.

---

[7] The same lineup appeared in *Department of Commerce v. U.S. House of Representatives* (1999), a case that involved the use of sampling methods in the federal census for allocation of seats in the House of Representatives. On that issue it is very difficult to discern an ideological element. Nonetheless, the four most liberal justices supported the interests of the Democratic Party, while their five colleagues supported Republican interests.

[8] See Fleisher and Bond 1996, 2004; McCarty, Poole, and Rosenthal 1997; Abramowitz and Saunders 1998; Bond and Fleisher 2000; Hetherington 2001; Layman and Carsey 2002; and Jacobson 2004. Whether the mass public has become more polarized in its opinions, partisan divisions aside, is less certain (Fiorina, Abrams, and Pope 2005).

These developments have helped to produce greater partisan conflict and a decline in civility (Uslaner 1993). At the perceptual level people in politics are now more inclined to view those who have different views with suspicion or stronger emotions. Put differently, there has been a growth in positive affect toward some political reference groups and in negative affect toward others.

Judges could not be fully insulated from these changes. Undoubtedly their own political attitudes have become more polarized, especially if they identify strongly with parties or other policy groups. Compared with the past, we might expect judges to think in more partisan and ideological terms, to gravitate more toward like-minded people in and out of the courts, and to harbor more negative feelings about judges and others with whom they differ.

Direct evidence on these changes is very difficult to gather, and the evidence we do have is ambiguous. In a sense it is striking that some judges participate actively in groups that have ideological agendas, but those judges are a small minority even of those on higher courts. Moreover, if the Federalist Society and American Constitution Society had existed in the 1960s, judges might well have involved themselves with those groups at the same rates that they do today.

If polarization has occurred, it might be reflected in a decline in comity within courts similar to the decline in Congress. Recent conflicts such as those in the federal court of appeals for the Sixth Circuit are noteworthy (see *In re Byrd* 2001, *Grutter v. Bollinger* 2002, and *In re Williams* 2004), but such conflicts are hardly unique to the current era. Perhaps opinions that attack colleagues' positions in strong terms have become more common, but no study has investigated that issue.

As with most other issues, we know the most about the Supreme Court. Patterns of decisional behavior in the Court do not indicate increased polarization: rates of dissenting and concurring opinions and proportions of close decisions have not increased in the past decade or so.[9] It is possible that the Court's decision *processes*, like those in Congress, have changed. Meaningful analysis of those processes must await data on recent years from the justices' papers, but it is doubtful that the level of interpersonal conflict on the Court exceeds that in some earlier periods (see P. Cooper 1995).

One piece of systematic evidence that we do have is intriguing.[10] In the 1970s it became the standard practice for justices to hire law clerks who

[9] Since the 1960s, the proportions of decisions with dissenting or concurring opinions have remained stable. The proportions of cases decided by one vote increased, but that growth was completed by the 1980s. These conclusions are based on data in Epstein et al. 2003, 211–25.

[10] This discussion of law clerk selection is based heavily on Ditslear and Baum 2001.

TABLE 5.1
Percentages of Supreme Court Law Clerks Drawn from
Democratic-Appointed Judges, by Time Period

Terms	Highest Percentages	Lowest Percentages	Standard Deviation
1975–1980	Stewart (75.0) Brennan (69.6) White (68.4)	Rehnquist (37.5) Stevens (46.2) Powell (50.0)	12.4
1981–1985	Blackmun (75.0) Brennan (73.7) Marshall (70.0)	Burger (40.0) Rehnquist (40.0) O'Connor (55.6)	13.1
1986–1992	Blackmun (82.1) Brennan (81.3) Stevens (77.8)	Kennedy (10.5) Scalia (16.7) Rehnquist (38.1)	27.0
1993–1998	Souter (83.3) Stevens (77.8) Ginsburg (68.4)	Thomas (0.0) Scalia (4.2) Rehnquist (5.6)	34.0
1999–2004	Stevens (90.5) Breyer (66.7) Ginsburg (66.7)	Kennedy (0.0) Thomas (0.0) Scalia (4.2)	34.5

Sources: Data are taken from the research for Ditslear and Baum 2001, updated. The original sources for all data are the annual information sheets on the law clerks, "Law Clerks—October [various years]; Law Schools and Prior Clerkships" and the information sheets, "Law Clerk Report by Justice," both provided by the Public Information Office of the U.S. Supreme Court.

Note: Clerks without lower-court service are excluded from the calculations of percentages. Only justices in active service during most terms of the period are included. The standard deviation is for all the justices who qualified for inclusion, nine in each period.

had served in lower courts. Since that time justices increasingly have drawn clerks from court of appeals judges who are ideologically similar to themselves. The sharpest change occurred in the late 1980s and early 1990s, when the level of ideological affinity between justices and the judges from whom they drew clerks strengthened considerably. This development can be charted in terms of the party of judges' appointing presidents, and it is summarized by that measure in table 5.1.

This trend results in part from changes in the practices of some justices during their tenure on the Court, in part from the strong tendency of some justices appointed in the late 1980s and early 1990s to hire clerks who had worked with ideological kin in the courts of appeals. Both liberal and conservative justices now turn primarily to like-minded judges in the lower courts. Throughout the period since the mid-1980s a majority of active court of appeals judges have been Republican appointees, so the deviation of liberal justices from an ideologically random selection of clerks is greater than the table suggests. But the choices of four conservative justices are striking: through the 2004 term Antonin Scalia and Anthony Kennedy had taken more than 90 percent of their clerks from Republican appointees during their tenure on the Court, William Rehnquist about 95 percent since the 1992 term. And Clarence Thomas had never chosen a law clerk who had served with a Democratic appointee.[11]

This pattern in the selection of law clerks provides a window into the thinking of the justices. It may be that justices think explicitly in ideological terms more than they did a quarter century ago. Although the policy preferences of Supreme Court clerks do not necessarily match those of the judges for whom they served in the courts of appeals, at the least justices feel more comfortable with clerks who have been certified by ideologically similar judges.

The selection of law clerks also suggests the possibility of a change in the associations of Supreme Court justices. Justices often draw their clerks from judges with whom they are acquainted. Perhaps more than in the past, justices associate with other judges who share their conceptions of good policy. If this change has occurred, in all probability it reflects broader changes in the justices' thinking and extends beyond the members of one court.

Despite the evidence about selection of law clerks, it is quite uncertain that polarization in the courts has actually increased. Perhaps the tendency toward greater polarization in government has been neutralized in the courts by a strengthening of judges' legal orientations, considered in chapter 4. Nor is there concrete evidence that any growth in polarization has changed the behavior of Supreme Court justices as decision makers, let alone the choices of lower-court judges. Yet a major change in elite political attitudes inevitably affects judges. At the least, judges who orient themselves toward policy groups feel greater pressure to adhere to their usual side. More than in the past, to cross ideological lines in a highly salient case would disappoint a judge's allies and bring comfort to those on the other side. Those costs certainly do not rule out such line-crossing, but they may deter it.

---

[11] The proportion for Kennedy is interesting, because he has greatly disappointed conservatives with his relative moderation. Miguel Estrada, a clerk for Kennedy in his first term (Estrada's nomination for a court of appeals judgeship failed in 2002), helped to screen candidates for clerkships in later terms. According to some reports, Estrada aggressively screened out candidates with liberal views (Groner 2002b; Newfield 2002).

Clarence Thomas

If policy groups reinforce any judge's ideological tendencies, one of the most likely candidates is Justice Clarence Thomas.[12] Justice Thomas is a very good example of a judge who identifies with groups that are defined by ideology. Political conservatives function as a positive reference group for Thomas, liberals as a negative reference group that is at least equally important to his thinking.

This negative side is connected with the heavy criticism that Thomas has received from liberals during his public career. That criticism was expressed when President Reagan nominated him to chair the Equal Employment Opportunity Commission in 1982 and, even more, when President George Bush nominated him to a court of appeals judgeship in 1990. Thomas's 1991 nomination to the Supreme Court elicited strong opposition well before Professor Anita Hill's charge of sexual harassment.

The hearings on that charge changed few votes in the Senate, but they increased the level of hostility toward Thomas at the time he joined the Court. This hostility grew when Thomas's early record indicated the strength of his conservatism on civil rights and other issues, conservatism that he had downplayed at his confirmation hearings (C. Smith and Baugh 2000). Some African-American leaders and groups that supported Thomas's confirmation or at least refrained from opposing it later criticized him in strong and bitter terms. Early in his Supreme Court tenure Thomas was unwelcome in some forums in which people ordinarily would be pleased to host a Supreme Court justice, and he faced the prospect of demonstrations and other negative reactions elsewhere.[13]

Anyone would find this kind of opposition unpleasant, and Thomas certainly did. "It pains me . . . more deeply than any of you can imagine, to be perceived by so many members of my race as doing them harm" (Biskupic 1998b, A1; see Foskett 2004, 4, 260). Understandably, the confirmation process for the Supreme Court was especially traumatic for Thomas. According to the account by his friend Senator John Danforth, Thomas believed that his opponents in the confirmation battle were trying to kill him figuratively and—it appears—literally (Danforth 1994, 10, 11, 50). A friend reported in 2004 that Thomas continues to keep track of his supporters and opponents in that battle (Merida and Fletcher 2004a, A18). And Thomas is affected by the criticism of his work on the Court,

---

[12] This discussion is based on a number of sources about Thomas's career and his off-the-bench activities. Especially useful were Toobin 1993; M. Fisher 1995; A. Thomas 2001; Foskett 2001a, 2004; and Merida and Fletcher 2004a. Material is also drawn from Phelps and Winternitz 1992; Danforth 1994; and J. Mayer and Abramson 1994.

[13] Negative reactions to Thomas's appearances have continued (Mauro 2002; McCarthy 2002; A. Jones 2003), though those reactions have died down somewhat.

criticism that includes considerable questioning of his abilities and asser-
tions that he follows one colleague's lead. Asked in 2000 whether he
wrote all his own opinions, Thomas responded, "No, Justice Scalia does"
(Foskett 2001b, 1A).

Thomas expresses considerable enmity toward his critics. In the 1991
confirmation episode, he described his opponents as embodiments of evil
(Danforth 1994, 89, 130). In public statements, Thomas sometimes expresses a strong aversion toward political liberals. Since 1991 he has
sometimes returned to the theme he adopted at the phase of his confirmation hearings dealing with the sexual harassment charge: he and others
who hold his values are the targets of attacks because, among other
things, they "dare to disagree with the latest ideological fad" (Toobin
1993, 39; see Page 1998). "They think they can bully me. They've got the
wrong guy. I will not be bullied" (Biskupic 2001).

Thomas's negative view of political liberals is matched by a strong identification with political conservatives. Prior to his appointment as a federal judge, he spent the preponderance of his career in government. He
worked exclusively for Republican officials and administrations, and he
developed friendships and associations with people who held conservative
views on politics and policy. To a degree, the conservatism that he brought
to the bench reflected his interactions with conservatives in his work and
elsewhere. Thus conservatives would have served as a reference group
even in the absence of hostility between Thomas and his liberal critics.
But his identification with conservatives is strongly reinforced by his continued antipathy toward liberals whose values he rejects and whom he
blames for unfair attacks on him.

During his tenure on the Supreme Court, Thomas has largely avoided
people who are unfavorable to him. As one reporter put it in 1995, he
"has constructed a world apart from his critics" (M. Fisher 1995, B1).
During and after the battle over his confirmation, he reportedly stopped
reading newspapers altogether (Mauro 1992, 10). In any event he appears
to pay limited attention to the news media, except for those with a distinctly conservative orientation (Roderick 1994, 369–70). He generally
turns down opportunities to appear in forums where negative reactions
are likely. In discussing his prospective memoir with publishers, he indicated that he would avoid interviews about the book with people he saw
as unsympathetic toward him (Kirkpatrick and Greenhouse 2003).

The people with whom Thomas does associate tend to share a conservative point of view. His wife Virginia Lamp Thomas is a strong and active
conservative. His social circle has included a number of prominent conservatives such as former House majority leader Dick Armey (for whom
Virginia Lamp Thomas worked), former solicitor general Theodore
Olson, and radio commentator Rush Limbaugh (at whose wedding he

officiated). His associations with conservatives and their admiration for him have allowed him to act as a power broker behind the scenes. In that role he helped to win confirmation for two African-Americans who were nominated by Bill Clinton to federal judgeships after Republicans became the majority party in the Senate (Merida and Fletcher 2004a, A18; 2004b; Turley 2004).

Many of Thomas's public appearances are before conservative political groups such as the Federalist Society, the American Enterprise Institute, the Heritage Foundation, and the Eagle Forum. Early in his tenure on the Supreme Court the universities and law schools that he visited were disproportionately those with conservative orientations. In speeches and remarks at these forums, Thomas has expressed a personal identification with conservative groups. He has also expressed gratitude to the conservatives who supported him in his confirmation battle.

In his speeches Thomas frequently supports conservative positions on social and political issues. He has criticized the "rights revolution," "the legal revolution of the past 30 or so years in creating and expanding individual rights" (*Legal Times* 1994, 23). He has expressed concern about "the transformation of our society into one based upon victims rather than heroes" (*Legal Times* 1995, 10; see also C. Thomas 1999–2000). In a speech accepting an award from the American Enterprise Institute in 2001, he urged conservatives to participate vigorously in what he characterized as a cultural war despite the risk of the kinds of attacks that he had suffered for expressing his views (C. Thomas 2001; see N. Lewis 2001b).

How much do Thomas's political reference groups actually affect his choices as a justice? Had he paid no attention to the world outside the Court, he still would have established a conservative record. Indeed, it can be argued that his record would be exactly the same.

But it is unlikely that these audiences have no effect on Thomas's positions. He has strong identifications and relationships with people and groups whose views are distinctly conservative.[14] On judicial issues that divide the left and right, departures from a conservative path would disappoint a set of friends and associates whose support and respect is important to Thomas.

---

[14] Thomas's selection of law clerks is interesting. As noted earlier, he has never chosen a clerk who served an appointee of a Democratic president. The judges from whom he has taken the most clerks are J. Michael Luttig of the Fourth Circuit and Laurence Silberman of the D.C. Circuit, both strong conservatives whom Thomas knows personally. He reportedly supervises a careful "ideological vetting" of prospective clerks themselves (A. Thomas 2001, 465). Asked to explain why he recruits clerks from judges who share his judicial philosophy, Thomas said that choosing clerks is like "selecting mates in a foxhole" (Ditslear and Baum 2001, 883).

Just as important, departures from conservatism would give comfort to the political liberals for whom Thomas feels animosity. This animosity may affect some of his choices as a justice. As one commentator said about his dissent in a prisoner rights case (*Hudson v. McMillian* 1992), some of his opinions read "like a deliberate provocation—a thumb in the eye of the liberal establishment" (Toobin 1993, 47). The perceptions of Thomas's friends, reported by a biographer (A. Thomas 2001, 468–70), are similar. Many of those friends believe that the confirmation process had increased Thomas's conservatism. According to one friend, "I think much of what he does now is not a payback, that's too crass, but is just a natural reaction to the pain they put him through" (A. Thomas 2001, 469).[15]

Thomas himself has given credence to the perception that he is motivated by hostility toward political liberals. A law clerk reported that in 1992, Thomas said he would serve on the Court until 2034: "The liberals made my life miserable for 43 years, and I'm going to make their lives miserable for 43 years" (N. Lewis 1993). He perceives a liberal establishment that praises conservative justices who "evolve" and move toward the ideological center; early in his career, Thomas would tell his law clerks, "I ain't evolving!" (Barrett 1993, A6). There is no reason to doubt his prediction: to evolve would run contrary to his way of thinking about himself. In this respect Justice Thomas exemplifies the impact of social identities on judicial behavior.

THE NEWS MEDIA

The news media differ from the personal audiences that have been discussed so far, in that few if any judges identify closely with reporters or the organizations for which they work. Moreover, judges typically have more limited relationships with the news media than do policymakers in the other branches of government (T. Cook 1998, 120–63; D. Graber 2002, 271–320). With the exception of criminal trials the courts receive less coverage, and judges interact with reporters less frequently.

Yet the news media may be important to the judges on two levels. First, the media act as intermediaries between judges and other audiences they care about. Most people's impressions of judges are based heavily on what

---

[15] Also of interest is the article in *People* magazine by Virginia Lamp Thomas shortly after Thomas's confirmation to the Court. The article, undoubtedly intended to help rehabilitate Justice Thomas's reputation, also contained a striking statement: "Clarence will give everyone a fair day in court. But I feel he doesn't owe any of the groups who opposed him anything" (V. Thomas 1991, 112).

they learn from the media. Judges who seek public approval are especially dependent on coverage of their activities and themselves in the media.

Second, what the news media say can be important to judges in itself, so that the media constitute a distinct judicial audience. The information that the media print and broadcast about judges is a tangible description and evaluation of their work that takes on a life of its own. Judges prefer to see positive reviews of their work in the media, whether or not those reviews affect the judgments of other audiences.

In practice, these two levels can be difficult to distinguish. Judges who care about their reputations are likely to seek favorable coverage in the media for its own sake as well as for its impact on other audiences. For judges who are concerned about reelection, however, the function of the news media as an intermediary is dominant. Trial judges who serve areas with small populations interact with a substantial proportion of their constituents, and many voters' impressions of those judges are shaped by direct observation and word of mouth (Raymond and Paluch 1994). But in large constituencies served by multiple judges, the direct information flow between judges and the general public is weak. As a result, what voters know about judges, at least in between campaigns, comes chiefly from the mass media. If enough voters gain a negative impression of a judge to threaten the judge's reelection, generally that impression results from information in the media.

Not surprisingly, elected judges sometimes try to influence coverage of their decisions in the media. Most often, they seek to deflect blame when their actions have been criticized or they fear criticism. This is especially true in criminal justice, the area of judicial activity in which criticism is most likely to have electoral consequences (e.g., Shatzkin 1997). For instance, after the Ohio Supreme Court unanimously overturned a murder conviction in 2004, the chief justice (who authored the opinion) gave several interviews to explain the decision.[16] In 2003 an organization of trial judges in New York State hired a public relations firm to counter a long series of editorials criticizing elected judges in the *New York Daily News* (Wise 2003). Similarly, elected judges may jump at opportunities to secure favorable media coverage.

But even judges who have no fear of electoral defeat may take steps to influence how they are portrayed in the media. Some judges who allow trials to be televised are motivated by what they see as an opportunity to gain favorable publicity. (As illustrated by Judge Lance Ito's experience

---

[16] Two colleagues took the unusual step of writing a letter to relatives of the murder victims, who had criticized the decision, to defend their action (Welsh-Huggins 2005). The opening passage of the court's opinion in the case was aimed at limiting criticism of the justices (*State v. Yarbrough* 2004, 848–49).

in the trial of O. J. Simpson, they do not always make good use of that opportunity.) Minnesota judges face little electoral competition, but a study found that they cooperated with reporters a good deal. Their cooperation was partly a means to explain their actions and to avoid what they saw as inaccuracies in reporting (Drechsel 1983, 96–134; see Stanga 1971, 281–84). Some judges, elected or appointed, talk with reporters about cases that are currently before them (Auletta 2001a, 2001b; Solomon 2004).

Supreme Court justices show considerable interest in news coverage of the Court. Justices Black and Frankfurter made annotations on negative articles (B. Schwartz 1983, 251, 256). Examining the files of three recent justices, Epstein and Knight (1998, 145) "came across many clippings of newspaper stories and editorials about specific cases," some of which justices circulated to colleagues. Richard Davis (1994, 17, 38–39) found evidence of the same practices, and he reported that the Court's public information officer kept the justices informed of press coverage about the Court and about them personally (Davis 1994, 56–57). Justice Blackmun was aware of journalists' criticisms of him (H. Blackmun 1994–95, 347, 493), and Justice Thomas's "near-photographic memory" allows him to remember the dates of negative articles about him and the names of their authors (Foskett 2004, 18).

Some justices do nothing to influence coverage of themselves in the news media, and overall the efforts of the justices pale in comparison with policymakers in the other branches and even, it appears, judges on lower courts (Grey 1968). But justices have taken action to combat negative portrayals of themselves or to secure positive coverage.[17] On occasion a justice contacts reporters or editors to express unhappiness with criticism (*Wall Street Journal* 1968; Jeffries 1994, 272–81). In one instance Justice Scalia wrote to a legal newspaper to refute a story about his position on outside income limits for federal judges. One of the authors was Tony Mauro, and Scalia referred to the story as "characteristically Mauronic" (*Legal Times* 2000).

Some justices interact with reporters, sometimes in an effort to win favorable coverage (W. Murphy 1964, 128–29; Davis 1994, 102–31). Some justices in the current era speak to reporters on the record, and background interviews are common. Warren Burger, who strongly discouraged justices and clerks from talking with reporters, nonetheless mailed copies of his speeches to reporters and made phone calls to columnists (Greenhouse 1995, C10; see Goulden 1974, 253). Burger's predecessor Earl Warren socialized with reporters (Cray 1997, 396). During at

---

[17] Some observers perceive that the Court uses the media to enhance its collective image (Davis 1994; B. Perry 1999; but see Greenhouse 1996).

least part of his tenure, William Rehnquist "liked to go out for lunch with law clerks and reporters" (Savage 1992, 150). Four justices attended a party to celebrate the book on Harry Blackmun by *New York Times* reporter Linda Greenhouse (Leiby 2005). According to Davis (1994, 106), several reporters mentioned "a close personal relationship" with Blackmun, and Daniel Schorr (*All Things Considered* 1994) referred to Blackmun as a friend. In an earlier era, a close relationship developed between Chief Justice Salmon P. Chase and writer-scholar Henry Adams, a journalist at the time. As Adams (1918, 250) described it, "the Chief Justice was very willing to win an ally in the press who would tell his story as he wished it to be read."

Like their counterparts in the other branches, justices are sometimes successful in shaping news coverage. When Jo Powell was asked why the media were so nice to her husband Lewis Powell, she responded, "Because he is so nice to them" (Jeffries 1994, 273). Blackmun's close relationships with reporters help to account for the favorable coverage he received in his later years on the Court. On the other hand, Burger's efforts to influence news coverage were outweighed by reporters' awareness of his general hostility toward the news media. One reporter concluded that much of the writing about the Burger Court "was tinged with antagonism toward him because of his disdain for us" and because of "the cult of secrecy that he fostered at the court" (Mauro 1998b, 219).

Efforts at image building might stand apart from judges' choices in deciding cases. Yet judges who care about their portrayal in the media could act on that interest, consciously or unconsciously, in making decisions. The most obvious possibilities are avoiding positions that might be criticized by the media and retreating from positions that already were criticized. Hugo Black was one of the Supreme Court justices who shifted position in the 1940s on requirements that public school students salute the flag. His colleague Felix Frankfurter reported the following conversation with Justice William O. Douglas a few months after the first decision (Hirsch 1981, 152).

> **Douglas:** Hugo tells me that now he wouldn't go with you in the Gobitis case.
> **FF:** Has Hugo been re-reading the Constitution during the summer.
> **Douglas:** No—he has been reading the papers.

Judges who care about their portrayals in the media might be especially wary of taking positions that adversely affect the interests of the media themselves.[18] The strong media criticism of *Gannett v. De Pasquale*

---

[18] Justice Byron White, whose hostility to the press predated his Supreme Court service, was a prominent exception (see Hutchinson 1998).

(1979), the Supreme Court decision allowing trial judges to bar the public (and reporters) from at least some criminal proceedings, may account for the Court's finding a way to negate the effects of *Gannett* the next year in *Richmond Newspapers v. Virginia* (1980) (A. Lewis 1981). It is noteworthy that four justices had made public statements about the meaning of *Gannett*, indicating their awareness of the criticism, and that the Court decided *Richmond Newspapers* so soon after *Gannett*.

The federal court of appeals for the District of Columbia responded to negative reactions even more quickly in 1994. After deciding that book reviews had no special protection from libel suits, a panel of the court was heavily criticized in the media. Ten weeks later, the two judges in the original majority reversed their positions in the case (*Moldea v. New York Times Company* 1994; see Biskupic 1994b).

In such instances, the news media have an impact that is independent of other sources. More often, however, the media's influence is intertwined with that of audiences such as the general public and political groups. This intertwining magnifies the impact of judges' concern with their portrayals in the media. It also increases the difficulty of isolating media influence on judges' choices.

A Greenhouse Effect?

Savvy federal appellate court Judge Laurence H. Silberman once said his experience was that judges are swayed by a desire for praise. Nowhere has that judicial vanity been flattered more than in The New York Times, and no one laps it up more than Harry Blackmun. This whole phenomenon can be called the Greenhouse effect, in honor of Linda Greenhouse, its most prominent practitioner. (Sowell 1994)

[T]he American working press has, to a man and woman, accepted and embraced the tenets of judicial activism. . . . It seems that the primary objective of the [New York] *Times*' legal reporters is to put activist heat on recently appointed Supreme Court justices. Tom Sowell has described this technique as the "Greenhouse effect," after the *Times*' leading court reporter. . . .

I do not think I fully appreciated until I became a judge, however, how much impact press coverage can have on judges. . . . So I understand better today the reason for the evolution of some judges. More often than not, it is attributable to their paying close attention to newspaper accounts of their opinions. (Laurence Silberman, in *Legal Times* 1992, 16–17)

The Warren Court's expansions of civil liberties aroused strong opposition from political conservatives, and that opposition was a theme of Richard Nixon's successful 1968 campaign for president (Stephenson 1999,

179–82). Between 1969 and 1991, all of the ten new Supreme Court justices were appointed by Nixon and later Republican presidents. During that period the Court became increasingly conservative in its doctrinal positions, but not as quickly or as fully as most students of the Court would have expected (Simon 1995; B. Schwartz 1998). Bill Clinton's appointments of Ruth Bader Ginsburg and Stephen Breyer left the Court's ideological composition pretty much as it had been prior to his presidency.

The Court's relative moderation reflected the positions of several Republican appointees. Of the ten justices appointed by Presidents Nixon, Ford, Reagan, and George Bush, as many as six developed more liberal positions on civil liberties issues than strong conservatives had hoped. This outcome was highlighted by some of the Court's major decisions. In *Planned Parenthood v. Casey* (1992), a decision that provoked particular unhappiness among conservatives (e.g., Bork 1992), the five justices who voted to maintain *Roe v. Wade* wholly or in most respects were all Republican appointees. With no more than two Democrats on the Court since 1990, Republican appointees have provided most of the votes for each of the Court's noteworthy liberal decisions. Among them are the rulings that upheld affirmative action in university admissions (*Grutter v. Bollinger* 2003), that struck down state laws against sodomy (*Lawrence v. Texas* 2003), and that ruled out the death penalty for crimes committed by people who were not yet eighteen years old (*Roper v. Simmons* 2005).

As the quotations from Dr. Sowell and Judge Silberman indicate, some conservative commentators have an explanation for the unexpected moderation of certain Republican appointees.[19] In their view, Supreme Court justices work in a social environment that is dominated by liberal influences. Most reporters who cover the Court are liberals who lavish praise on justices who take liberal positions, especially those who have moved to the left. Further, elite segments of the legal profession, including the law schools and their law reviews, are highly liberal in their preferences. According to one conservative federal judge, focusing on academia,

> Any judge knows that if he or she cares to be famous, widely praised in universities, the object of adulation among the greatest number of law clerk applicants, and invited to speak at the largest number of universities, the most efficient means is a novel and creative opinion favoring the interests of those groups that are now politically favored in universities. (Kleinfeld 1993–94, 18)

[19] Other statements of this explanation include Bryden 1992; Eastland 1993; Fein 1993; Kleinfeld 1993–94; Glendon 1994, 149–50; *Human Events* 1996; Boot 1998, 119–20; S. Taylor 2003; *Wall Street Journal* 2004; Barone 2005; and Mark Levin 2005, 61. See also Kozlowski 2003, 13–31.

The same is true of the Washington social circles in which justices mingle. The cumulative impact is that conservatives appointed to the Court have strong reasons to move to more liberal positions.

> [A]ll the influences and incentives are to move leftward. That is how you get the applause of the American Bar Association, good ink in the liberal press, acclaim in the elite law schools and invitations to tony Georgetown parties. (Sowell 2003)

Public discussion of the Greenhouse effect began in the early 1990s. But two decades earlier, President Nixon expressed concern about the social environment in Washington. Nixon thought that Justice Potter Stewart was a "weak [expletive deleted]" who had been "overwhelmed by the Washington-Georgetown social set" (Reeves 2001, 338). He asked whether one prospective Supreme Court nominee had "a social wife" who might get involved with "that [expletive deleted] Georgetown set" (Dean 2001, 171). He asked Harry Blackmun a similar question about his wife (H. Blackmun 1994–95, 148) and raised his concern about Blackmun himself:

> [T]he "Georgetown crowd" will do their best to elbow in on you. You will be wined and dined and approached. I suspect that two of the Justices have fallen victim to this kind of thing. Can you resist the Washington cocktail party circuit? (Greenhouse 2005, 48)

For his part, Republican Senator Orrin Hatch worried in 1986 that the Washington social establishment and the *Washington Post* and *New York Times* were moving Justice O'Connor in a liberal direction (Roderick 1994, 247).

Considering the Greenhouse Effect

Scholars have largely ignored conservative claims about the impact of the justices' social environment (but see Baum 1998, 178; Schauer 2000, 625–30).[20] This reaction is understandable. The idea of a Greenhouse effect has the ring of a search for a scapegoat by unhappy political partisans. More important, it does not fit into the dominant theories of judicial behavior.

But a Greenhouse effect is consistent with the perspective presented in this book. For commentators such as Sowell and Silberman, the basic premise is that Supreme Court justices want to be liked and respected, that they care about their reputations. As I have argued, it would be surprising if this premise were not valid. Indeed, two of the episodes described at the beginning of chapter 1 suggest that one justice named by

---

[20] A few scholars (Rosenberg 2000, 646–47; Tushnet 2005, 60–61, 177) have expressed doubts about aspects of the Greenhouse effect.

those who posit the Greenhouse effect (Kennedy) seeks favorable treatment by the news media (see also Rosen 1996) and that another (Blackmun) enjoyed positive reactions from liberal policy groups.

Thus, if a judge's most salient audiences are primarily liberal in their views on judicial issues, it is reasonable to posit that the judge's interest in their approval would work subtly to move the judge to the left. The claim of a Greenhouse effect is especially intriguing because it can encompass all four categories of personal audiences discussed in this chapter and the preceding one: social groups, the legal profession, the mass media, and—less directly—policy groups.

There is some basis for conservatives' portrayal of certain Court audiences as liberal. A survey of law professors who began their careers after 1986 found that 75 percent thought of themselves as liberal, 10 percent as conservative (Merritt 1998, 780 n. 54; see Sisk, Heise, and Morriss 1998, 1463; McGinnis and Schwartz 2003).[21] While the community of journalists may not be as liberal as it is sometimes viewed, the elite segments of the profession that are most relevant to the justices appear to be more liberal than conservative (Rothman and Lichter 1985; Weaver and Wilhoit 1991, 25–32; see Hess 1981, 87–90).

It might be that approval of left-leaning audiences simply makes judges feel better about doing what they would have done anyway (see Bork 1992).[22] Yet what we know about social identities should caution against dismissing the possibility that these audiences exert an impact. Thus the hypothesis of a Greenhouse effect merits exploration.

Measuring the Greenhouse Effect

The first step in that exploration is to determine whether conservative commentators are correct in their perceptions of the justices' behavior. Change is central to the hypothesis of a Greenhouse effect. If the social environment of the Supreme Court pushes justices leftward, that push will be reflected in movement over time. The question, then is whether

[21] The liberalism of legal academics (and of other surveyed groups) may be reflected in their ratings of Supreme Court justices (Ross 1996, 405–11). Arguably, in the current era, leaders of the organized bar also tend to be liberal. Their perceived liberalism is reflected in conservatives' complaints about evaluations of federal judicial nominees by the American Bar Association, complaints that led the George W. Bush administration to cut the ABA out of the nomination process (Bilodeau and Ringel 2001).

[22] This judgment aside, Judge Bork (1992) offered an interesting view of the justices' relevant audiences when he argued that the prevailing opinion in *Planned Parenthood v. Casey* "is intensely popular with just about everybody Justices care about: The New York Times, The Washington Post, the three network news programs, law school faculties and at least 90 percent of the people Justices may meet at Washington dinner parties."

justices who have been portrayed as susceptible to a liberal social environment actually became more liberal during their tenure.

Because the hypothesis of a Greenhouse effect is based on actual observation of justices' behavior, analysis of the same behavior is not a truly independent test of the hypothesis (Mock and Weisberg 1992, 1024–25). But this does not mean that the observations of conservative commentators are necessarily accurate. For one thing, their perceptions may be colored by their disappointment with the Court. Further, observers such as Professor Sowell and Judge Silberman—like people in general—are drawn to vivid, unexpected events such as Justice Kennedy's positions in *Planned Parenthood v. Casey* and *Lawrence v. Texas* (Nisbett and Ross 1980, 43–62). Such decisions can give a misleading picture of a justice's behavior, especially behavior that occurs over a long period of time. Finally, these observers cannot go beneath the surface of observed behavior—to determine, for instance, whether change in a justice's voting record results from change in the justice's policy positions or from change in the issues that the Court addresses.

In determining whether justices have moved to the left in their decisional behavior, several choices need to be made. (Methodological details of the analyses are presented in the appendix to this chapter.) The first question is how to measure that behavior. I follow the conventional path of using the justices' votes as an indicator of their ideological positions. The set of votes cast by a justice in a Court term provides a reasonable summary measure of where the justice stood ideologically.

As noted, comparisons of voting records across terms might be misleading because of issue change. One means to control for issue change is a procedure in which the average change in the justices' voting patterns over a time period is treated as a measure of issue change (Baum 1988; see Epstein et al. 1998). Adjusted voting scores based on this procedure will be analyzed alongside scores based on raw votes.

A second question is which cases to include. This question has an easy answer. Those who posit the Greenhouse effect concentrate on civil liberties, and most of the issues in other fields are relatively unimportant to the news media and other audiences that might sway the justices.

A third question concerns designation of the "before" and "after" periods to compare in mapping change in a justice's position. The early period should be at the beginning of a justice's tenure, the later period at a point when the justices' audiences would have had sufficient time to exert their influence. The first two terms seem the most appropriate time for the early-tenure period. The most appropriate later period cannot be ascertained for any single justice, and it is likely to vary among justices. Thus any choice is arbitrary. Two periods that seemed the most reasonable were chosen for analysis: the fifth through tenth terms of a justice's tenure and the seventh through tenth terms.[23]

It could be argued that any Greenhouse effect applies to all the justices, but conservative commentaries point to a more focused effect. First, Republican appointees are more susceptible to the influence of liberal audiences. The justices chosen by Democratic presidents, typically liberal in their views, need not adjust their positions to win praise from these audiences.

Further, not all conservative appointees are subject to the Greenhouse effect. Some are sufficiently anchored in their values (or, perhaps, linked with conservative audiences) that they can resist the lure of their liberal environment. One conservative legal commentator contrasted the disappointing Republican appointees with William Rehnquist, Antonin Scalia, and Clarence Thomas. As he saw it, those three justices had proved themselves invulnerable to the Greenhouse effect through their experience in Washington prior to their Supreme Court appointments. If they had not, Republican presidents would not have appointed them. (If this analysis is accurate, John Roberts will make no move to the left during his Court tenure.)

Among the justices who arrive in Washington only after their appointment, however, at least a large share *are* susceptible. "Newcomers to Washington are risks, as Kennedy, O'Connor, and Souter have demonstrated" (Eastland 1993, 34 n. 3; see Wagner 2005). Thus a distinction should be made between Republican appointees who are Washington newcomers ("Republican newcomers") and other justices, both Republicans who are already resident in Washington ("D.C. Republicans") and Democrats.

This leads to the question of how these categories should be defined, but first the appropriate time period for the inquiry should be determined. The year 1953 is a good starting point. The kinds of social influences that conservative commentators describe, to the extent they exist, probably were well established by the end of the New Deal period. The first Republican appointment in more than two decades (Earl Warren) was made in 1953.

Most of the justices appointed since 1953 have had tenures of at least ten terms on the Court. The others (Charles Whittaker, Arthur Goldberg, Abe Fortas) had quite short tenures. Thus only Whittaker, Goldberg, and Fortas are excluded, leaving eighteen justices for analysis.

---

[23] The choice of time periods turned out to make little difference. The results with terms 5–10 and terms 7–10 as the later periods were quite similar. Nor did the results change much when other later periods such as terms 5–8 and terms 7–8 were substituted or when a justice's first term was substituted for terms 1–2.

Those justices need to be placed in the three categories. The distinction between D.C. residents and newcomers is unambiguous. In itself, of course, the distinction between Democratic and Republican appointees is equally clear. It is true that a few justices chosen by Republican presidents (such as Warren) have been perceived as relatively liberal at the time of their appointment, and Kennedy appointee Byron White was perceived as fairly moderate. However, if we measure the justices' initial ideological positions by their civil liberties voting in their first two terms, all the Democratic appointees were more liberal than any Republican appointee—with one exception.

That exception was William Brennan, a Democrat chosen by President Eisenhower without much attention to ideology and one who was perceived at the time to be strongly liberal on civil liberties issues (Bernstein 1956/1984). Brennan's voting record in his first two terms was the second most liberal of any justice in the study. (Lewis Powell, another Democrat appointed by a Republican president, ranked twelfth in liberalism.) Thus Brennan had little room to become more liberal under the influence of Washington, and he is better classified as a Democrat. (The differences among groups change little if Brennan is treated as a Republican.)

As it happens, the D.C. Republicans and Republican newcomers differed in another important respect: the newcomers were more moderate. The average Segal-Cover score (Segal and Cover 1989; Segal et al. 1995) for the Republican newcomers, based on perceptions of Supreme Court nominees by editorial writers, was considerably more liberal than the average for the D.C. Republicans.[24] Moreover, in their first two terms the newcomers cast liberal votes in civil liberties cases a mean of 41 percent of the time, the D.C. Republicans 29 percent of the time. (The proportion for the Democrats was 69 percent.) The scores for different justices are not entirely comparable because of differences in the mix of cases over time, but this appears to be a substantial difference. This difference will be taken into account in interpreting the findings.

Patterns of Voting Change

Tables 5.2 and 5.3 show patterns of voting change for individual justices and groups of justices, first for raw voting scores and then for adjusted voting scores. Each figure represents the change in the proportion of lib-

---

[24] It should be noted that the Segal-Cover scores rank Republican nominees somewhat differently from the classification adopted for this analysis. For instance, conservative Eisenhower appointee John Harlan has a more liberal score than a majority of Democratic appointees. Because of such anomalies, partly a product of the issues on which editorial writers focused, the Segal-Cover scores—valuable for other purposes—are not as useful as the president's party and early-career voting behavior for classification of justices.

eral votes for the justice or group of justices. Thus, the first figure in table 5.2 indicates that there was a mean increase of 10.7 percentage points between the first and second terms and the fifth through tenth terms in the proportion of liberal votes cast by the Republican newcomers.

Adjustment for issue change has considerable effect on the change scores for some individual justices (such as White, Kennedy, and Scalia) and a more limited effect for the Democratic justices as a group. But the basic patterns in the two tables are similar. In each analysis the Republican newcomers as a group showed substantial increases in their support for civil liberties claims between their first two terms and the later periods, about 10 percentage points on all measures. In this respect they differed sharply from the other two groups of justices.

The increases for Warren and Souter were especially large. But Stewart's scores also grew by more than 10 percentage points on all measures, Blackmun's support scores increased markedly (an increase that continued after his tenth term), and Kennedy's raw voting scores increased by more than 10 percentage points.[25] The adjusted scores for Powell and Stevens increased by several percentage points. Harlan was the only justice in this group whose liberalism declined on all measures, and the declines were uniformly small to moderate; O'Connor also showed moderate declines for adjusted voting scores. Among the justices in the other two groups, only Ginsburg's support for civil liberties increased substantially after her first two terms. Thus the Republican newcomers as a group stand out, and the differences between them and other justices are highly significant statistically.

The change processes depicted in tables 5.2 and 5.3 can be explored further with two supplementary analyses. The first is limited to relatively important civil liberties cases. Justices might be most responsive to their audiences in the cases that are most visible to people outside the Court. While case importance can be measured in a variety of ways, the most useful measure for this inquiry is the indicator of "contemporaneous salience" that was devised by Epstein and Segal (2000): "whether the *New York Times* carried a front-page story about the case" (2000, 72). If there is a Greenhouse effect, the prominence given to decisions in Greenhouse's own newspaper would seem to capture their importance to the audiences that create this effect.

The patterns of change in salient cases were similar to the patterns in all civil liberties cases. The declines in civil liberties support among D.C. Republicans were somewhat greater in salient cases, but the other groups showed similar patterns for salient and nonsalient cases, and the Repub-

---

[25] The increases in civil liberties support for these five justices are all significant at the .05 level for both terms 5–10 and terms 7–10.

TABLE 5.2
Changes in Percentages of Pro–Civil Liberties Votes
from Terms 1–2 to Later Periods, Using Raw Voting Scores

Justice	Terms 5–10	Terms 7–10
Republican Newcomers	**+10.7**	**+11.1**
Warren	+34.8	+34.8
Harlan	–2.5	–0.3
Stewart	+13.0	+10.4
Blackmun	+ 6.9	+ 8.9
Powell	+ 2.2	+ 3.3
Stevens	+ 1.6	+ 3.8
O'Connor	+ 1.4	+ 1.4
Kennedy	+13.9	+13.0
Souter	+24.9	+24.4
D.C. Republicans	**–4.3**	**–4.7**
Burger	–4.4	–6.9
Rehnquist	–4.6	–3.7
Scalia	–3.3	–2.3
Thomas	–4.9	–5.9
Democrats	**–0.9**	**–1.5**
Brennan	+ 3.3	+ 2.0
White	–11.2	–11.6
Marshall	+ 1.6	0.0
Ginsburg	+ 5.8	+ 6.9
Breyer	–3.9	–4.6

t-values for differences of means:

Republicans:	3.61	3.96
D.C. vs. newcomers	(.004)	(.002)
Republican newcomers	2.93	3.29
vs. all others	(.007)	(.004)

Note: Within each group, justices are listed in the order of their appointment. Changes are in percentage points. Thus an increase from 20 percent to 30 percent is calculated as 10 percent, not 50 percent. Means for each group are shown in bold. T-tests are for the probability that increases in liberalism are greater for Republican newcomers than for the comparison group; thus, one-tailed tests were used. Equal variances in the two subsamples were not assumed. Significance levels are in parentheses.

TABLE 5.3
Changes in Percentages of Pro–Civil Liberties Votes
from Terms 1–2 to Later Periods, Using Adjusted Voting Scores

Justice	Terms 5–10	Terms 7–10
Republican Newcomers	+10.4	+10.7
Warren	+38.9	+38.6
Harlan	–4.0	–4.0
Stewart	+12.5	+12.4
Blackmun	+ 9.6	+13.4
Powell	+ 7.9	+ 7.5
Stevens	+ 4.4	+ 5.4
O'Connor	–3.0	–4.4
Kennedy	+ 1.6	+ 0.5
Souter	+25.7	+27.0
D.C. Republicans	–6.8	–7.4
Burger	–9.7	–10.0
Rehnquist	+ 2.1	+ 1.5
Scalia	–16.1	–16.3
Thomas	–3.3	–4.8
Democrats	+ 3.2	+ 3.4
Brennan	+ 0.1	–1.3
White	–1.5	–2.1
Marshall	+ 3.9	+ 3.2
Ginsburg	+10.2	+11.6
Breyer	+ 3.2	+ 5.8
t-values for differences of means:		
Republicans:	2.81	2.97
D.C. vs. newcomers	(.010)	(.007)
Republican newcomers	2.19	2.19
vs. all others	(.025)	(.024)

Note: For an explanation of the results shown in this table, see note to table 5.2.

lican newcomers remained a distinctive group. However, the magnitude of voting change for some justices in this group did differ between the two sets of cases. Most notably, Kennedy's raw proportion of liberal votes in salient cases increased by about 35 percentage points between his first two terms and the later two periods. Adjustment for issue content reduced Kennedy's changes to 12–13 percentage points, suggesting that conservative commentators overreacted to his raw voting record in salient cases.

The second supplementary analysis is of economic cases. As discussed earlier, those who have posited a Greenhouse effect focus on the positions of Republican appointees in civil liberties cases. The logic of the Greenhouse hypothesis would not seem to extend to cases involving economic issues, since most of those issues are relatively unimportant to the news media and other audiences that might sway the justices. Thus it is useful to determine whether conservative newcomers also shifted to the left on economic issues.

Voting patterns in economic cases were analyzed in the same way as the patterns in civil liberties cases. The results are simple: none of the groups of justices moved very far in economic cases (though the D.C. Republicans became somewhat more conservative), and the Republican newcomers moved hardly at all. Nor did any individual justice in that group show an increase in economic liberalism of as much as 10 percentage points in either raw or adjusted voting scores. If there was a Greenhouse effect, then, it was limited to civil liberties cases.

Interpreting the Patterns

The evidence on voting change is mixed, but for the most part it is consistent with the claims of a Greenhouse effect. Among the nine Republican justices who moved to Washington to join the Supreme Court, there were clear and substantial increases in liberalism for four and more limited or ambiguous increases for three others. In contrast, only one of the nine justices in the other groups had more than minimal increases in liberalism. But the patterns of voting change for the Republican newcomers might be explained by something other than the impact of the justices' social environment.[26]

One alternative explanation is strategic. Ulmer (1973) and Atkins and Sloope (1986) suggested that the political environment accounted for Justice Black's changing levels of support for civil liberties over his tenure on the Court. We might posit that as conservative justices learned to behave strategically in relation to the public and the other branches, they became more liberal as a result. In one important respect, the political environment could have moved conservative justices to the left: the House was under continuous Democratic control from 1955 through 1994, and the Senate was Democratic for all but six years of that period. But the other branches were not strongly liberal on civil liberties issues throughout that

---

[26] One possible explanation can be set aside. Some scholars posited an "acclimation" effect in which justices initially take moderate positions and then become more extreme (E. Snyder 1958, 237–38; J. Howard 1965). But the Republican newcomers whose voting behavior changed generally shifted toward more moderate positions.

period.[27] Republican presidents served during most of that time, and even Democratic Congresses typically were less liberal on civil liberties issues than on economic issues. In the late 1950s, for instance, Congress pressured the Court to retreat from some of its civil libertarian positions (W. Murphy 1962). Certainly the general public was not highly favorable to most types of civil liberties. Thus strategic considerations could not have moved justices substantially to the left.

A quite different explanation is that the influence of Supreme Court lawyers, the influence of colleagues, or exposure to civil liberties issues had a cumulative impact, gradually giving conservative justices greater appreciation for the value of civil liberties. While this explanation cannot be dismissed out of hand, it is difficult to see why these forces would operate solely in favor of civil liberties, when there are strong advocates and arguments on both sides of the issues that come to the Court.[28] Further, the different patterns for D.C. conservatives and conservative newcomers are more consistent with the Greenhouse hypothesis than with this alternative.

It will be recalled that the Republican newcomers as a group were more moderate than the D.C. Republicans from the start. Perhaps, then, it was relative moderation rather than newcomer status that accounted for the newcomers' collective shift to the left. Their moderation might have given them an incentive to ensure that the Court as a whole did not become strongly conservative. Alternatively, it could have made them more sensitive to civil liberties values that were threatened by the other branches. A final possibility is fully consistent with the Greenhouse effect: moderate conservatives might be more susceptible than strong conservatives to the influence of liberal-leaning audiences.

The impact of Republican justices' pre-Court residency and of their initial ideological positions can be compared through estimates based on the results of regression analyses with those two independent variables and voting change as the dependent variable. Initial ideological positions can be measured by voting scores in the first two terms or, alternatively, by the justices' Segal-Cover scores based on perceptions of their positions at the time of nomination. Because the independent variables were highly correlated, the results are only suggestive, but they are still instructive.

The results do suggest that residency had a greater impact on voting change than initial ideological positions. The difference between the most

---

[27] Civil rights issues are a partial exception, and it is possible that the other branches exerted a leftward pull on the Court in that area during some portions of the period studied (Eskridge 1991a, 1991b).

[28] Some colleagues and commentators have attested to Justice Brennan's persuasive skills (Eisler 1993; Clark 1995). Great though those skills were, it seems unlikely that they could

conservative and least conservative Republican appointee in voting change was not nearly as great as the difference between Washington residents and newcomers, holding the other variable constant. This was true for both measures of justices' initial ideological positions, for both later time periods (terms 5–10 or terms 7–10), and whether raw or adjusted voting scores were used. Thus the patterns of voting change appear to be more consistent with an explanation based on residency than with one based on initial moderation.

By no means does all this establish that the Greenhouse effect exists. The results of the analyses and interpretation of those results do not rule out other explanations altogether. Nor do they rule out the possibility that the patterns of voting change consistent with the Greenhouse effect were essentially a product of chance. This would hardly be the first instance in which a systematic explanation has been grafted onto what is actually a random pattern of political behavior (see Sigelman 1982; Wilcox 1989; Mock and Weisberg 1992).

Even so, the hypothesis of a Greenhouse effect should not be dismissed out of hand. Judges want the approval of individuals and groups that are salient to them, and their interest in approval may affect their judicial behavior. The relative autonomy of Supreme Court justices from concrete pressures leaves a great deal of room for them to respond to their personal audiences. Because of their assumptions about judges' motives, the dominant models of judicial behavior rule out the impact of social environments. But in a more realistic conception of motivation, that impact is assured and the Greenhouse effect could exist.

Harry Blackmun

For Thomas Sowell (1994), quoted earlier, Justice Harry Blackmun epitomized the Greenhouse effect.[29] Examination of Justice Blackmun provides another perspective on the influence that Sowell and others have posited. Blackmun's behavior over time certainly was consistent with the hypothesis of a Greenhouse effect. Tables 5.2 and 5.3 provide evidence of his voting shift in a liberal direction. The shift was even greater than those tables indicate because it continued after his tenth term. While change in a justice's behavior can be difficult to ascertain, in Blackmun's case the evidence of change in a liberal direction is so substantial that there is no doubt about its existence.

---

have produced substantial changes in the positions of several colleagues, including one who replaced him on the Court.

[29] Presumably, Sowell would not have been surprised that Blackmun thought very highly of Linda Greenhouse (H. Blackmun 1994–95, 398–99).

This change is the centerpiece of a well-known story (*Harvard Law Review* 1983; Kobylka 1985, 1992; Wasby 1988; Greenhouse 2005). Appointed in 1970 by a president who sought a reliable conservative, Blackmun fulfilled that expectation early in his tenure on the Court. Gradually his positions changed so that he could be characterized as a moderate liberal. Indeed, with the appointments of the 1980s and early 1990s he became one of the Court's most liberal members. Along with the change in his proportions of liberal and conservative votes, this ideological shift is indicated by the patterns of his voting agreements with colleagues. Over time Blackmun's rate of agreement with conservatives such as Warren Burger declined substantially, while he agreed more frequently with liberals such as William Brennan (*Harvard Law Review* 1983, 717 n. 6; Kobylka 1985, 14–15; Kobylka 1992). Just as striking was Blackmun's increasing support for liberal doctrinal positions (Wasby 1988; Kobylka 1992). Taking into account the length of time during which he adhered to his initial conservatism and the magnitude of his ideological shift, Blackmun's change in behavior has few parallels.

Scholars and other observers have offered several explanations for Blackmun's shift. One straightforward explanation is that the experience of serving on the Supreme Court and exposure to new issues modified his values (Brudney 2005). Liberal colleagues might have helped to reshape his views about legal policy (Greenhouse 1994, A24). Another possibility is that Blackmun's expressed belief in the desirability of a moderate Court (N. Lewis 1986; S. Taylor 1986) led him to counterbalance the effects of Republican appointments that were moving the Court to the right (Wasby 1988, 200; Kobylka 1992, 54). Blackmun himself gave this explanation oblique support in a 1984 speech (Barbash and Kamen 1984).

One explanation concerns Blackmun's relationship with Chief Justice Burger. Like Clarence Thomas, Blackmun was initially viewed as a subordinate partner to a Court colleague. He and Burger were longtime close friends, and as fellow Nixon appointees they were expected to take similar positions. When this did occur in Blackmun's early years they were dubbed the "Minnesota Twins," with "the clear implication that Blackmun was the junior twin" (Greenhouse 1999, A18). Blackmun later indicated his resentment at this depiction (Jenkins 1983, 20, 29; Garrow 1994, 559). In any event, the two gradually became estranged, in part because of Blackmun's perception of how Burger treated him (Greenhouse 2005). Perhaps Blackmun's conflicts with Burger and his desire to establish his independence helped move him to the left (Wasby 1988, 196–97; see Munford 2004; Greenhouse 2004b).

Some commentators see Blackmun's majority opinion in *Roe v. Wade* as critical to his shift in position (*Harvard Law Review* 1983, 724; Kobylka 1992, 51; see Abraham 1999, 260). Certainly *Roe* was a momentous event in Blackmun's career, because of the attention it focused on him and the reactions it evoked. Blackmun sometimes referred to the attacks on him over his role in *Roe* (e.g., *Nightline* 1993b), and in one talk he said that the controversy over that role changed his life (*Harvard Law Review* 1983, 724 n. 47).

This effect is ironic. Blackmun was not the strongest supporter of a pro-choice position in the Court's initial conference on *Roe* and its companion case, and the assignment of the Court's opinions to him probably reflected internal Court strategy (Garrow 1994, 528–34). Moreover, Blackmun's opinion in *Roe* was somewhat idiosyncratic, reflecting the strong identification with the medical profession that he had developed as an attorney at the Mayo Clinic (see H. Blackmun 1980). Yet after the decision was made and became identified with Blackmun, one of his former law clerks said, "Justice Blackmun's own sense of identity became intertwined with his opinion in *Roe*" (Rao 1998, 22). He became a champion of the legal right he had espoused in *Roe*, suspicious of inroads on that right, and emotional in describing threats to its continuation (*Webster v. Reproductive Health Services* 1989, 557; *Planned Parenthood v. Casey* 1992, 922–23; H. Blackmun 1994–95, 273, 361; Greenhouse 2005, 138, 144).

Commentators who suggest that *Roe* had a broader impact on Blackmun's positions almost surely are right. The thinking that he put into the *Roe* opinion and its implications for cases in other fields changed his perspective. Blackmun himself implied that *Roe* had been a catalyst for a broader change in his views (H. Blackmun 1994–95, 207–8).

In conjunction with *Roe* and other sources of change, some portion of what happened can be understood in terms of Blackmun's relationship with his audiences. As noted, early in his Court tenure Blackmun was largely written off as a conservative follower of Burger, and he was not highly respected. His opinion in *Roe* alienated conservatives who had liked his initial ideological stance, and it also received strong criticism from legal scholars (see Garrow 1994, 609–16). At the same time, it drew strong support from people who approved of the result and cared little about the reasoning that underlay it. These divergent reactions helped to orient him toward an audience on the political left.

The perception that Blackmun was moving away from his initial conservatism brought him additional notice and praise in the national news media[30] and from political liberals. He enjoyed both the notice and the praise. He was unusual in the degree of attention that he gave to mail about his work on the Court (Koh 1994, 20; Feldblum 1999; H. Black-

---

[30] The general tone of coverage by the national media is exemplified by the editorials in the *Washington Post* (1999) and the *New York Times* (1999) after Blackmun's death.

mun 1994–95, 204–5, 305, 453–54; Greenhouse 2005, 134, 242). His friendships with some reporters were discussed earlier. More than any of his colleagues, he expressed candid views in public, often through the mass media (Jenkins 1983; Schorr 1984; Barbash and Kamen 1984; *Nightline* 1993a).

Notably, Blackmun made statements on and off the bench that alluded to his personal importance as a defender of liberal values. One example is his musing over his retirement before a group of liberal lawyers, quoted at the beginning of chapter 1. Another came in his appearance before a group of law students in 1986, when he drew a "resounding cheer" with his reference to *Roe*: "If it goes down the drain, I'd still like to regard Roe v. Wade as a landmark in the progress of the emancipation of women" (N. Lewis 1986). Also noteworthy are two passages in opinions issued near the end of his career. While much or most of the language in these passages was written by law clerks (Lane 2004a, A13; Greenhouse 2004a, A16), Blackmun's willingness to include it is striking. In *Planned Parenthood v. Casey* (1992, 943) he made a highly unusual reference to his likely retirement:

> In one sense, the Court's approach is worlds apart from that of the Chief Justice and Justice Scalia. And yet, in another sense, the distance between the two approaches is short—the distance is but a single vote.
>
> I am 83 years old. I cannot remain on this Court forever, and when I do step down, the confirmation process for my successor well may focus on the issue before us today.

The second passage was an announcement of his change of position on the death penalty, a change that liberals would welcome and applaud:

> From this day forward, I no longer shall tinker with the machinery of death. For more than 20 years I have endeavored . . . to develop procedural and substantive rules that would lend more than the mere appearance of fairness to the death penalty endeavor. Rather than continue to coddle the Court's delusion that the desired level of fairness has been achieved and the need for regulation eviscerated, I feel morally and intellectually obligated simply to concede that the death penalty experiment has failed. (*Callins v. Collins* 1994, 1145) (footnote omitted)

Clearly, as Blackmun (1994–95, 469) acknowledged, he enjoyed his reputation as a supporter of civil liberties (see Greenhouse 2005, 223–24).

The impact of liberal audiences on Blackmun's ideological shift is impossible to ascertain. But Blackmun was drawn toward those audiences, which treated him as important, lionized him for the positions he took, and supported him against criticism for *Roe v. Wade*. In this way they offered a subtle but powerful inducement for him to continue moving to the left. If Blackmun's experiences led him to rethink the premises on which his formerly conservative record had been based, the prospect of further praise reinforced that rethinking. Blackmun's statements suggest that liberal audiences ultimately became linked with his personal identity. If so, it is not surprising that he increasingly committed himself to positions that those audiences favored.

CONCLUSIONS

This chapter and the preceding one considered several categories of personal audiences for judges. With the exception of higher courts, one part of the legal community, these audiences receive little attention from students of judicial behavior. That lack of attention results primarily from the models of judicial behavior that dominate research on the bases for judges' choices. To varying degrees those models allow for influence on judges from other individuals and groups, but that influence is based on judges' instrumental motives: judges take other people into account only as a means to achieve goals such as good legal policy. There is no room in these models for influence from personal audiences.

Yet if judges are human beings rather than single-minded seekers of good law or good policy, they care about the regard of people who are important to them. It follows that their interest in that regard can influence their choices on the bench. Among students of judicial behavior, it is widely accepted that the general public influences Supreme Court decisions because justices worry about the erosion of public support for the Court and resulting damage to its efficacy as a policymaker. This is so even though the benefit that the justices could receive from following public opinion is limited, indirect, and uncertain. If that mechanism of influence for the public is nonetheless plausible, the influence of people whose approval or disapproval affects judges' self-esteem is considerably more plausible.

It follows that scholars cannot gain a full comprehension of judicial behavior if they do not consider the roles of judges' personal audiences. Indeed, some implications of those roles for the understanding of judicial behavior have been noted. These implications are considered more systematically in chapter 6.

APPENDIX: PROCEDURES FOR ANALYSIS OF VOTING CHANGE BY SUPREME COURT JUSTICES

Data on justices' votes were obtained from the Supreme Court Database compiled by Harold Spaeth, archived at http://www.as.uky.edu/polisci/

ulmerproject/sctdata.htm. For all analyses, cases were selected from the database with the following specifications: unit of analysis = 0 or 4; decision type = 1, 6, or 7. For analyses of civil liberties votes, it was also specified that value = 1 – 6; for analyses of economics votes, it was specified that value = 7, 8, or 12. Votes were counted as liberal or conservative on the basis of the coding of the Direction variables in the database.

Salient cases, as defined in Epstein and Segal (2000), are those reported on the front page of the *New York Times*. Salient cases through the 2000 terms are listed in *The Supreme Court Compendium* (Epstein et al. 2003, 141–61). Salient cases in the 2001–3 terms were identified with the same criterion through a LEXIS search of the *New York Times*.

Each justice's votes in civil liberties cases, economic cases, or salient civil liberties cases were first aggregated by term. A voting score for a multiterm period (such as a justice's fifth through tenth terms) was calculated as the mean of the proportions of liberal votes for individual terms. Scores for change from the first two terms to later sets of terms were arithmetic differences between the means for the two periods.

Adjusted voting scores were obtained through a modified version of the adjustment procedure presented in Baum (1988). In this procedure, the proportions of liberal and conservative votes for each justice who serves on the Court in two adjoining periods (for this analysis, Court terms) are compared. The results for the justices are aggregated to produce a mean change in the percentage of liberal votes from the first period to the second. This mean change is then used to adjust the voting scores in the second period. Thus, if the justices who served in both year x and year x + 1 have an average increase in liberal voting of 2.5 percentage points, that 2.5 percent is subtracted from the voting scores of all justices in year 2. These corrections for issue change are cumulated across periods.

This procedure incorporates the assumption that the justices' positions do not change, so it is not ideal for the purposes of the inquiry into the Greenhouse effect. To reduce this problem, the justice under consideration was removed from calculations of issue change from term to term so that the justice's own votes do not affect the adjustments of voting scores. Thus in each term each justice has a unique set of adjustments for changes in issue content.

Two other measures of change in justices' positions were not employed despite their considerable merits. Bailey and Chang (2001) used comparison across institutions to estimate preferences for justices. They analyzed change over time for only a limited set of justices, so their scores could not be used in this set of analyses. Martin and Quinn (2002) calculated term-by-term ideal points for the justices through a procedure incorporating Bayesian assumptions, but they cautioned against use of these ideal points as dependent (or independent) variables. More fundamentally, the

Greenhouse hypothesis relates more directly to the justices' voting behavior than to their ideal points.

For the comparison of the effects of newcomer status and justices' initial ideological positions, analyses were limited to Republican appointees. The dependent variables were changes in the proportions of liberal votes in civil liberties cases between terms 1–2 and terms 5–10 or terms 7–10, using raw voting scores or adjusted voting scores. One independent variable was whether the justice was a D.C. Republican or a Washington newcomer. The other was a measure of the justice's initial liberalism, either the justice's Segal-Cover score (obtained from Segal et al. 1995, 816) or the proportion of liberal votes in the first two terms. Thus there were eight analyses. Estimates of the impact of the two independent variables on voting change were based on the Clarify procedure developed by King, Tomz, and Wittenberg (2000). For these estimates, the most conservative and least conservative Republican appointees were compared.

Chapter 6

IMPLICATIONS FOR THE STUDY

OF JUDICIAL BEHAVIOR

I HAVE ARGUED that judging can be understood as self-presentation to a set of audiences. Judges seek the approval of other people, and their interest in approval affects their choices on the bench. As a result, what I have called personal audiences—those whose approval is important to judges for its own sake, not as a means to other ends—shape judicial behavior. Judges' efforts to appeal to their audiences exert an impact even when those efforts are not fully conscious, as is often—indeed usually—the case.

This book is intended to show how a perspective based on the relationships between judges and their audiences can enhance our understanding of judicial behavior. The last section of chapter 1 described several functions that this perspective could serve to that end. This chapter returns to those functions, drawing out the implications of the discussions and analyses in the preceding chapters.

MOTIVATIONAL BASES FOR THE DOMINANT MODELS

The models that dominate the study of judicial behavior in political science share certain assumptions, and each of the competing models adds its own. Some of the most fundamental assumptions have not been given convincing rationales in terms of judges' motivations. As discussed in earlier chapters, an audience-based perspective can supply some of the missing motivational bases for these models while helping to adjudicate disagreements among the models.

The Centrality of Legal Policy

The most important assumption shared by the dominant models is that Supreme Court justices act solely on the goal of achieving good legal policy. Scholars who study other federal courts with versions of the dominant models usually adopt the same assumption.

The scholarship on judicial behavior in political science does not show why judges should focus so much on making good legal policy, and there are reasons to doubt this assumption. For one thing, judges have other goals that are relevant to their choices as decision makers. Further, judges' incentives to act on their interest in good legal policy do not seem so strong that other motives could be left with no room to affect judges' choices. For these reasons the dominant models have a gap in their explanations of judicial behavior.

To a degree, this gap can be filled without reference to judges' audiences. As some scholars outside political science have pointed out, judges gain personal satisfaction from their efforts to make what they regard as good law or good policy. Even a judge who was completely isolated from other people might derive a sense of fulfillment from pursuing these goals.

That fulfillment, however, is enhanced powerfully by the value of approval from judges' personal audiences. When judges adhere to certain policy positions or act on the basis of legal considerations, they do so in part to maintain the esteem of people who care about those goals and who are important to them. They want not just to make good legal policy but to be *perceived* as doing so. Ultimately, it is the judge's own perception of approval by salient reference groups that counts. To take an extreme case, it pleased Justice Felix Frankfurter to think he was taking a path that Oliver Wendell Holmes would have endorsed, even though Holmes had died before Frankfurter joined the Supreme Court (Hirsch 1981, 129–31).

The fulfillment that judges gain from working to make good legal policy does not completely fill the motivation gap in the dominant models. Even when that fulfillment is taken into account, judges' interest in legal policy does not seem strong enough to constitute the only substantial consideration in their choices. Yet it is clear that most judges on higher courts do give considerable weight to achieving what they conceive to be good legal policy. The relationships between judges and their audiences help to explain why this is the case.

Law versus Policy

Among the issues on which models disagree, the most long-standing debate is over the relative weights of legal and policy considerations in judges' decision processes. Especially for the Supreme Court, it is widely thought that policy outweighs law by a large margin. Indeed, depictions of judges who seek to get the law right are often depicted as unrealistic. In part, this view is based on scholars' reading of empirical evidence on judicial behavior. More fundamentally, however, it seems to rest on the implicit premise that judges who seek to make good law give up opportunities to shape public policy for no real benefit.

That premise is questionable, because judges seldom get concrete benefits by acting to make either good law *or* good policy. In pursuing
either goal what they gain is primarily personal satisfaction, satisfaction
that is connected with the anticipated reactions of audiences. Some
audiences applaud what they perceive as good legal interpretation, and
some applaud what they perceive as the right policy choices. For that
reason it is hardly self-evident that judges regularly set law aside in order
to pursue policy.

A case can be made that most judges give a higher priority to good
policy. Advancing what they see as desirable policy may provide more
satisfaction than getting the law right. Further, most audiences that are
salient to judges evaluate court decisions primarily in terms of their content as public policy, not in legal terms.

But this does not necessarily mean that policy considerations over-
whelm legal considerations in judges' thinking. Segments of the legal community, especially judicial colleagues, are important audiences for most
judges. Because those audiences care a good deal about the quality of legal
interpretation, they provide incentives for judges themselves to take the
law seriously. In combination with judges' own training in the law and
participation in the legal system, these incentives operate to make the
pursuit of good law an important element in judicial decision making.
Certainly the relative weights of legal and policy considerations should
be treated as an open question.

Strategic Behavior

The other major debate in the field is over the balance between sincere
and strategic behavior. The view that judges think strategically has won
majority support among students of judicial behavior. In this view, policy-
minded judges regularly calculate the impact of their prospective actions
on the ultimate achievement of their policy goals rather than simply
adopting the positions they most prefer. Scholars strongly disagree about
the consequences of strategic thinking, about the extent to which judges
actually move away from their preferred positions for strategic reasons.
But most agree that judges think about their choices in strategic terms.

This validity of this conclusion is uncertain. Judges differ from people
in some other roles in a key attribute: effective strategic behavior usually
wins them no tangible benefits. They may derive satisfaction from acting
strategically, but they may also gain satisfaction from taking positions
that directly reflect what they regard as good law or good policy. Further,
acting strategically is more difficult and more time-consuming than acting
sincerely. For these reasons strategic behavior is better treated as a possibility rather than a certainty.

On motivational grounds, intracourt strategy in appellate courts should be more common than strategy aimed at a court's political environment.[1] For one thing, the effort required to calculate very good (if not necessarily optimal) intracourt strategies is not overwhelming. Further, audiences that are important to judges encourage some forms of strategic behavior within courts. In particular, judges' colleagues expect them to engage in give-and-take in the decision-making process as a means to reach collective decisions. Moreover, the element of competition involved in building majorities and shaping a court's doctrinal positions motivates judges to act strategically in relation to their colleagues. Judges prefer to perceive themselves and to be perceived by others as winners rather than losers.

This does not mean that appellate judges are completely strategic in the process of reaching collective decisions. The extent of strategy in this arena remains uncertain (see Hettinger, Lindquist, and Martinek 2004), and it is likely that judges engage in a mix of sincere and strategic behavior. But a good deal of strategic behavior does occur within appellate courts. That reality is underlined by research on decision making in the Supreme Court (e.g., Maltzman, Spriggs, and Wahlbeck 2000).

There is a weaker motivational basis for strategic behavior aimed at the other branches of government and the general public. A number of scholars posit what I have called routine adjustment of Supreme Court decisions to the preferences of the other branches, and many posit that the Court shifts the ideological position of its decisions as a whole in response to the public. But calculation of effective strategies aimed at the public and the other branches can be very difficult. More fundamentally, even adoption of the optimal strategy typically does little to advance good legal policy as the justice sees it. In most cases the best strategy coincides with sincere behavior. When they do not coincide, the difference between a statutory decision that is trimmed to avoid a congressional override and the statute that would result from an override may not be very great. Similarly, avoiding an unpopular decision will increase public support for the Court incrementally at most. In turn, that increase could enhance the Court's power as a policymaker only at the margins.

Judges' personal audiences might provide incentives for this type of strategy that are otherwise lacking, but it is doubtful that they do so. Undoubtedly, some judges appreciate effective strategies aimed at legislatures or the public, but seldom would this be a major consideration in

---

[1] Strategy aimed at other courts is probably intermediate in its frequency. The satisfaction gained from trying to shape legal policy within the judicial branch is likely to be greater than that of shaping policy in the other branches of government. In part this is because judges on other courts are a more salient audience. In addition, the chances of exerting a meaningful impact are greater within the judiciary.

their evaluations of colleagues. Audiences outside the courts tend to focus on what judges do rather than on the potential consequences of their actions, and they may not recognize judicial strategy when it occurs. As a result, they are likely to praise sincere behavior rather than strategic behavior.

All this being true, judges do engage in strategic behavior targeted at the public and the other branches. Strategy aimed at the other branches was well documented at least as far back as Walter Murphy's *Elements of Judicial Strategy* (1964). But there is good reason to conclude that externally directed strategy is episodic rather than routine, occurring most often when judges' incentives to engage in it are unusually strong.

This situation can arise when there is a low-cost, straightforward course of action that could advance judges' policy goals.[2] More consequential strategic behavior—reaching decisions that diverge a good deal from judges' conceptions of good legal policy—is likely to take place when two conditions coincide. The first is a high probability that the public or the other branches will respond negatively if judges do not act strategically. The second is an expectation that this predicted response would do damage to a court or its members that judges strongly prefer to avoid. Among elected state judges, these conditions may arise more often with the public as an audience than with the other branches. Among federal judges the opposite surely is true. In the absence of elections the public probably lacks the interest and leverage to elicit much strategic behavior from judges.

DEPARTURES FROM THE DOMINANT MODELS

Thus, reconsideration of the motivational bases for the dominant models of judicial behavior leads to questions about some of their shared and separate assumptions. Thinking about judges' relationships with their audiences also points to ways in which judicial behavior departs from the dominant models. Those departures are of two types.

The Impact of Personal Audiences

The first type of departure follows from the book's perspective in a straightforward way: judges are subject to a significant form of influence

---

[2] One example is inviting Congress to override a statutory decision that accords with judges' reading of the law but conflicts with their policy preferences. Another is deciding a case on statutory grounds in order to avoid negative effects of a constitutional decision on congressional action, as occurred in two instances described in chapter 3.

that lies outside the dominant models. Judges' personal audiences do more than help motivate the interest in good legal policy that is central to those models. Because judges care about the approval of their audiences, their perceptions of what will win that approval shape their choices in other ways as well.

While the most salient reference groups differ from one judge to another, social groups and the legal community are important to at least the great majority of judges. Policy groups are salient to many judges, and the news media may be relevant in themselves or as an intermediary between judges and other audiences. The prevailing models of judicial behavior do not take these audiences into consideration, so any influence that they exert on judges' choices goes unnoticed.

For the most part, these neglected audiences contain elite groups. To the extent that they shape judges' behavior, then, they promote primarily the values held by elites in American society. Those values are more similar to those of the mass public than they are different. When they differ, however, judges' links with their personal audiences will draw them toward the views of elites.

For this reason Justice Scalia's complaints about the impact of elite values on his colleagues and the complaints of some conservatives about a Greenhouse effect should not be dismissed as mere expressions of pique. Their fundamental premise, that judges are influenced by their social environment, is not just credible but clearly valid. The same is true of complaints by liberals in an earlier era about the influence of business elites on judges' thinking.

This does not necessarily mean that these complaints are accurate in their specifics. Elite opinion is far from unanimous, so a judge may be subject to competing influences from the set of groups with which the judge identifies. For the same reason, the net effects of personal audiences can be expected to differ among judges. All this being true, conservatives who are unhappy with what they see as the baleful influence of liberal elite groups on the Supreme Court have called attention to a potentially important mechanism of influence on judges.

Groups that do not serve as personal audiences for judges are at a relative disadvantage in shaping judges' choices unless they connect well with judges' instrumental incentives. The external audiences that receive the greatest attention from scholars are the mass public and the other branches of government. The general public and people in the other branches are significant reference groups for some judges. On the whole, however, the esteem of these audiences is less important to judges than the esteem of other audiences such as their social groups. At least for federal judges, the instrumental value to judges of approval from the public and the other branches is also more limited than often portrayed. As a result, the influence of those two audiences may fall well short of the influence wielded by judges' most salient personal audiences.

Thus the constellation of forces that shape judicial behavior differs from the constellation encompassed by the dominant models of that behavior. Valuable as these models are, their assumptions cause them to leave aside much of what shapes judicial behavior. As a result, their picture of judicial decision making is incomplete.

Variation in the Determinants of Judicial Behavior

The second way in which judicial behavior departs from the dominant models relates to a recurring theme in this book. If judges differ in the audiences that are most salient to them, the considerations that shape their choices also differ. As a result, the best explanations of those choices are certain to vary across judges.

Empirical scholarship on judicial behavior in political science is largely based on disagreements among judges. Indeed, the growing willingness of Supreme Court justices to dissent from decisions was crucial to the field's development. But scholars typically consider only one narrow explanation of differences in judges' responses to the same cases or issues. Because it is implicitly assumed that other considerations are invariant, differences in responses are thought to rest solely on differences in judges' policy preferences, their conceptions of good policy.[3]

Some research does depart from this assumption. Several studies have identified interpersonal variation in motives based on the psychological traits or role orientations of individual judges (e.g., Lasswell 1948; Gibson 1978, 1981; Scheb, Bowen, and Anderson 1991). Other studies have found variation in behavior among Supreme Court justices that may stem from differences in goal orientations (e.g., Mishler and Sheehan 1996; Spaeth and Segal 1999, 290–301). But these findings do not fit comfortably within the dominant models of judicial behavior, and the gap between those models and reality merits scrutiny.

At least within a particular court or set of parallel courts, certain instrumental audiences are likely to be salient to any judge. In a state with highly competitive elections to the supreme court, every justice who seeks

---

[3] The dominant models also incorporate the implicit assumption that, with some limited exceptions, a judge gives the same weight to a particular consideration across all cases. In contrast, some scholars and judges have posited differences in weights across cases based on variation in case characteristics such as salience and the clarity of the law (Wold 1978, 61–62; Satter 1990, 64–78; Edwards 1991, 856–58; Bainbridge and Gulati, 2002; Klarman 2004, 5). A few studies have found strong evidence of that variation (e.g., Maltzman, Spriggs, and Wahlbeck 2000; Bartels 2005). This evidence, like evidence of variation across judges, suggests the need to rethink the structure of the existing models.

another term is concerned with the general public. Probably all Supreme Court justices take Congress into account. But the relative importance of such audiences can still vary considerably among judges. Moreover, a personal audience such as legal academia may be quite salient to some judges and barely relevant to others. And even when judges give equal weight to a particular kind of personal audience, they differ in the specific sets of people whose esteem they seek. To take the most obvious example, individual judges each have their own social groups.

Similarities and differences among judges on the same court are suggested by the formal appearances they make before external audiences. Financial disclosure reports by federal judges list appearances for which judges receive reimbursements, typically events involving travel. Supreme Court justices make many out-of-town appearances, so their reports contain considerable information. This indicator, imperfect though it is, provides a sense of the justices' priorities among potential audiences.

Table 6.1 presents the numbers and types of out-of-town appearances for which the justices received reimbursements in 1998 through 2004. The table shows some similarities among justices. It is noteworthy that most justices make substantial numbers of appearances each year, given the time and energy required for each. (These appearances and the associated travel often require multiple days of a justice's time, and a high proportion occur between October and June.) Clearly, most justices gain considerable satisfaction from direct interactions with these audiences, a fact that is important in itself.

Also of interest is the numerical dominance of appearances before law students and lawyers. For every justice the most common audience at appearances was the legal community. This does not necessarily mean that lawyers are the most salient audience for the justices. At the least, however, the interactions between justices and lawyers enhance the relevance of that audience. Moreover, this indicator is consistent with the pre-Court careers of most justices in the current era, careers focused on the practice of law.

But there were some differences among the justices alongside the similarities. The most striking differences were in the frequency of appearances, with Justice Scalia at one end of the spectrum and Justice Souter at the other. The dearth of out-of-town appearances for Justice Souter reflects a broader pattern. According to one reporter, he "is the justice least likely to be seen on the speaking circuit or at Washington parties" (Biskupic 2004). Turning down an invitation to speak that Justice Blackmun had endorsed, Souter told Blackmun, "I know you get a kick out of these things, but you have to realize that God gave you an element of sociability and I think he gave you the share otherwise reserved for me" (*Morning Edition* 2004). This does not necessarily mean that Souter is

TABLE 6.1
Activities outside Washington, D.C. for Which Supreme Court Justices
Received Reimbursements, 1998–2004

Justice	Total	College	Bar/Bench	Other	Non-U.S.
Breyer	92	48	26	20	18
Ginsburg	89	53	28	9	17
Kennedy	88	43	31	15	24
O'Connor	125	47	51	31	31
Rehnquist	24	22	1	1	4
Scalia	128	70	20	39	25
Souter	3	3	0	0	0
Stevens	14	6	8	0	1
Thomas	57	34	9	14	0

Source: The justices' annual Financial Disclosure Reports, filed with the Administrative Office of the United States Courts.

Note: The total is based on the number of entries in a justice's reports, with appearances in D.C. excluded. The justices sometimes reported multiple appearances on one trip in one entry, sometimes in multiple entries.

The great majority of the appearances at colleges were at law schools. The justices' entries do not always make it possible to determine whether a college appearance was at a law school. "Other" includes all appearances that did not fall into the two preceding categories (e.g., National Women's Hall of Fame, Sun Valley Writers' Conference). These three categories sometimes add to more than a justice's total because some entries included both college and bar/bench activities.

Because justices' labeling of appearances was not fully consistent or complete, the numbers in the table should be treated as approximations.

less interested in the approval of external audiences than colleagues such as Scalia,[4] but the possibility that the justices differ in their personal autonomy is intriguing.

The justices also differed somewhat in the mixes of groups whose invitations they accepted. Most noteworthy were the high proportions of appearances before nonlegal audiences by Justices Breyer, O'Connor, and Scalia. More than other justices, each was willing to spend time inter-

---

[4] Tables 5.2 and 5.3 show that Justice Souter's proportions of liberal votes in civil liberties cases increased sharply during his first decade on the Supreme Court. This finding supports the claims of some conservatives that he was influenced by the Court's social environment. On the other hand, Souter's limited direct contact with segments of that environment raises questions about his susceptibility to something like a Greenhouse effect. However, even a judge who does not interact very much with certain audiences still may be influenced by their anticipated reactions to the judge's choices as a decision maker.

acting with audiences outside the legal system, a fact that suggests the relevance of these audiences to them. This finding is consistent with the evidence that O'Connor cared about her public reputation.

One issue is the frequency with which the justices appear before audiences that can be characterized as policy groups. It is difficult to classify the groups before which the justices appear in those terms, because so many legal groups take positions on policy issues and some groups that do not take positions nonetheless have some ideological coloration. Still, differences among the justices emerged. If organizations of the bar and its specialized segments are excluded, most justices made no appearances before audiences that seem appropriate to label as policy groups.[5] However, by the best count, Justice Breyer made two such appearances and Justices Scalia and Thomas six each. These differences are noteworthy. However, not only are these figures inexact, but most appearances before policy groups would take place in Washington and not be reported.

The frequency of engagements outside the United States for some of the justices may reflect the pleasures of foreign travel more than anything else. Still, it is interesting that some of the justices participated so often in events that brought them into contact with judges from other nations. As suggested in chapter 4, that contact has enhanced the relevance of courts outside the United States for some of these justices (though definitely not for Justice Scalia).

In part, where justices go reflects the invitations they receive. Justice O'Connor had a visibility and a reputation that made her especially attractive as an invitee. But the justices' prestige gives all of them a wide range of potential appearances from which they can choose. The differences in the frequency and types of appearances that the justices make suggest that they also differ in the constellations of audiences that are salient to them.

Whether on the Supreme Court or on other courts, the forces that determine the relevance of various personal audiences to a particular judge are so numerous and complex that they might be considered idiosyncratic. But they surely are not random: judges' life experiences and current circumstances help determine which audiences are most important to them. Some possible effects of those experiences and circumstances were discussed in earlier chapters.

One important aspect of life experiences is judges' career paths. Careers help to determine the sets of reference groups that shape judges'

---

[5] Groups were treated as policy groups if they have explicit positions on public policy issues or a clear ideological orientation related to public policy. Thus the Federalist Society and the American Civil Liberties Union were counted as policy groups. Groups whose ideological orientation is more subtle were not. As noted in the text, nor were groups that represent segments of the bar, even if they have clear policy agendas. Thus the Association of Business Trial Lawyers was not counted.

goals and perspectives.[6] As I have suggested, the mix of law and politics in judges' backgrounds may be especially consequential. For this reason, changes in the kinds of people recruited to the Supreme Court have probably elevated the importance of the legal profession as an audience for the Court and reduced the importance of the public and the other branches of government.

If judges on a particular court differ in their constellations of audiences, the influences that shape their decisions are also likely to vary. The relative importance of legal and policy considerations could be expected to differ among judges. The views of the public or legal academics will carry greater weight with some judges than with others.

Thinking about audiences highlights variation among judges in the considerations that shape their behavior as decision makers, but it is not the only source of that variation. Even judges who were impervious to influence from any audience would differ in the bases for their choices. Thus models of decision making that treat a court's judges as homogeneous in the determinants of their choices inevitably miss some of the realities of judicial behavior. Some of the limitations in our understanding of that behavior stem from insufficient attention to differences among judges.

In contrast with their treatment of judges on the same court, students of judicial behavior have recognized that judges on different types of courts may decide cases on the basis of different considerations. Students of the Supreme Court emphasize the impact of its unique combination of institutional characteristics on the justices' behavior (e.g., Segal and Spaeth 2002, 92–96). Similarly, studies of lower federal courts analyze the impact of appellate review of their decisions, review that distinguishes them from the Supreme Court (e.g., Songer, Segal, and Cameron 1994). Scholars who study state supreme courts adapt the dominant models of judicial behavior to incorporate the effects of insecure tenure in office (e.g., M. Hall and Brace 1992; Langer 2002).

These institutional differences are one important source of variation across courts in the determinants of judges' choices. But courts also differ in the kinds of attention they receive. Those differences affect the composition of judges' audiences, and in turn they can influence the bases for judicial behavior.

In this respect the differences between the Supreme Court and other courts are especially striking. Judges on the federal courts of appeals may attract attention during the confirmation process, and a portion of their

---

[6] Career choices also reflect preexisting values and priorities. Thus the kinds of people who are drawn to careers within the legal system tend to have social identities different from those who are drawn to political careers. This self-selection strengthens the relationship between the justices' career experiences and their priorities among personal audiences.

work is scrutinized by other judges and lawyers. With some exceptions, however, they are essentially unknown outside the legal community. Some federal district judges and state supreme court justices are prominent within their own geographic areas, and a few become famous beyond those areas, but most labor in obscurity.

Supreme Court justices are in a fundamentally different situation. It is true that few justices are household names, and their faces are even less familiar to the general public. But their names are well known in some elite circles, and their votes and opinions receive far greater attention than the decisions of other courts. Contact with the justices is prized by law school faculty, journalists, and Washington hosts. Interest groups praise and denounce them, and legal scholars assess their work in detail. Some of their foibles are chronicled in gossip columns, discussed on late-night television, and depicted in editorial cartoons. Some justices become major historical figures. During and after their lifetimes, all will be given ratings that range from "great" to labels that are distinctly less flattering (Blaustein and Mersky 1972; Bradley 2003).

The scrutiny that the justices receive may heighten their sense of accountability for their choices. Research in social psychology suggests that perceptions of accountability affect decision making in multiple ways (Fiske and Taylor 1991, 158–59; see Bartels 2005). As a result, the bases for the justices' choices might differ systematically from those of judges on lower courts—including themselves, if they had lower-court experience. Appointment to the Court can also modify justices' social identities by giving importance to audiences that had little relevance in the past. One of the possible effects is that justices' self-presentation to a new set of audiences may produce shifts in their policy positions.[7]

Differences among other sets of higher courts also affect judges' constellations of personal audiences. Federal district judges are more closely tied to geographical communities and receive less scrutiny from the legal community than do judges on the courts of appeals, and these differences shape judges' orientations. The impact of electing state supreme court justices is not just on instrumental incentives to heed voters but also on justices' personal identifications with the public, identifications that tend to be weaker for appointed judges.

As much as judges' situations differ across higher courts, the differences between higher and lower courts are considerably greater. Students of

---

[7] Change in the ideological positions of individual justices has presented a challenge to students of judicial behavior. Several studies provide evidence of such changes (e.g., Ulmer 1973; Atkins and Sloope 1986; Epstein et al. 1998; Bailey and Chang 2001). Tables 5.2 and 5.3 offer additional evidence of individual-level change. Only limited progress has been made in explaining these changes, in part because the dominant models of judicial behavior

judicial behavior recognize the importance of lower courts as policymakers, but they continue to concentrate on higher courts. One reason (though hardly the most important one) is the difficulty of knowing how to think about lower-court judges.

Perhaps the key problem concerns what judges are trying to accomplish. So long as judges are thought of as people who are devoted to making good legal policy, their behavior can be placed in familiar frameworks. But judges on state trial courts and intermediate appellate courts do not fit comfortably within those frameworks. Because individual cases are typically narrow and caseload pressures are typically heavy, lower-court judges may care more about disposing of cases than about their outcomes.[8] In any event, the hierarchies of goals that shape their choices seem quite different from those of judges on higher courts (see Baum 1997, 24–25). As a result, the conceptions of judicial behavior that scholars bring to higher courts often do not apply very well to lower courts.

The analytic problems that result from the differences between higher and lower courts can be addressed in multiple ways. Certainly, some concepts and hypotheses from the scholarship on higher courts apply to judges at all levels (Gibson 1978, 1980). Judicial goal orientations provide a broad framework in which to compare courts of different types, so long as restrictive assumptions about judges' goals are relaxed.

An audience-based perspective offers one means to consider and probe the behavior of lower-court judges in comparison with judges on higher courts. Differences in judges' situations among levels of courts affect the relevance of various groups to them, and judges' pre-judicial associations and experiences tend to differ across levels as well. As a result, the sets of audiences that are most salient to judges may vary systematically across courts.

To take one example, on average the other branches of government probably have more direct relevance to state trial judges than they do to judges on higher courts. Judges who serve a city or county are likely to have personal ties with other local officials through schooling, politics, and community activities. They often work in close proximity to people in the other branches and interact with them outside of work. As a result, local government can be a highly salient audience, not because judges fear negative action by the other branches but because they see themselves as part of a team that includes the other branches. This perception helps to explain the frequent willingness of state trial judges to join the initiatives

---

treat judges as social isolates. Setting that assumption aside opens up one way to explain ideological change.

[8] The emphasis on case disposition in state trial courts is well known. On state courts of appeals, see Caldeira and Wold 1978 and Wold 1978.

of other local officials—to reinforce efforts to "clean up" downtown areas, for instance, by meting out severe sentences to defendants accused of certain crimes in those areas (Wolf 2001; see Caruso 2002).

Without question, the determinants of judicial behavior differ very substantially across the range of courts in the United States. Those differences have multiple sources, and no single perspective can fully encompass them. But comparison of audiences across courts is one means to identify the impact of judges' work settings on their choices as decision makers.

PROBING THE IMPACT OF JUDICIAL AUDIENCES

A perspective based on judges' self-presentation to their audiences provides a way to think broadly about patterns of judicial behavior, both those that fit neatly within the dominant models and those that do not. That is the most important benefit of this perspective. But it also leads to more specific expectations that are subject to empirical analysis. A number of expectations have been discussed in the book. Among these are the impact of working arrangements on interpersonal influence in appellate courts, the relationship between judges' experience in electoral politics and the influence of public opinion on their choices, and the relative degrees of strategic behavior directed at court colleagues and other institutions.

Several difficulties confront research into judges' audiences and their impact on judicial behavior. The most obvious difficulty lies in identifying a judge's set of audiences. Many of the expectations that flow from an audience-based perspective do not require direct identification of audiences. Rather, as suggested by the examples just cited, it is possible simply to test for patterns of behavior that would be expected if judges are strongly oriented toward their personal audiences. But such indirect tests have limitations, in that they often cannot rule out alternative explanations that would lead to similar predictions. Ascertaining judges' constellations of audiences would not eliminate this problem altogether, but it would allow for more effective tests of relationships between social identities and judicial behavior.

Constellations of audiences certainly are not easy to measure, but some measurement techniques are available. Political psychologists have developed a number of indicators of individuals' social identities (C. Kaplan and Brady 2004; Neuendorf 2004; Sylvan 2004). These scholars focus on cultural and ethnic identities, which are probably easier to ascertain than identifications with the groups that are most relevant to judges. But some of their indicators could be applied to the task of measuring judges' orientations toward their audiences, especially for judges who can be interviewed or surveyed. Howard's (1981) interviews of federal court of appeals judges, which included questions about audiences, show the feasibility of this approach (see D. Klein 2002).

Archival records are a potentially useful source of information for studies of small numbers of judges about whom a good deal of information is available—a fairly accurate description of the Supreme Court. A good model is Danelski's (1970) use of diaries and correspondence to ascertain the groups with which Justice Harold Burton identified. One type of indicator that may be drawn from archives and other sources is the attention judges give to various audiences. Formal appearances, discussed in the preceding section, are one specific example. Another is judges' extracurricular writing, which can indicate the extent of their interest in audiences such as legal academia and the general public.

A second difficulty in the analysis of audience influence concerns measurement of judicial behavior along some of the relevant dimensions. Research on judicial behavior is dominated by a single dependent variable, the ideological content of votes and decisions. Much of the potential impact of judicial audiences is on a different kind of dependent variable, the mix of considerations that influence judicial behavior. The weights that judges give to particular considerations or the relative weights of different considerations are not as susceptible to measurement as their positions on a liberal-conservative scale.

One example is the impact of legal considerations in judges' choices. Scholars have made progress in measuring the influence of various aspects of the law on judicial behavior (Gates and Phelps 1996; R. Howard and Segal 2002; Scott 2002). They have given particular attention to the impact of a court's own precedents, which are easier to measure than some other legal considerations (Brenner and Stier 1996; Songer and Lindquist 1996; Spaeth and Segal 1999; Richards and Kritzer 2002). But broad measures of the law's impact remain elusive.

The impact of some other influences on decisions, such as public opinion, is easier to gauge. Even so, measurement that is sufficiently precise to allow confident comparisons among judges may be elusive. Thus problems in measuring judicial behavior along some dimensions are an impediment to inquiries into the influence of judicial audiences. But even quite imperfect measures can be sufficient for meaningful analysis, and in any event not all inquiries into audience influence require direct measurement of judicial behavior along these dimensions.

As I have emphasized, variation among judges in the determinants of decisional behavior is one of the key implications of an audience-based perspective. That variation creates another potential difficulty for analysis. It is relatively easy to analyze judges' behavior when it is assumed that all judges at the same court level respond to the same mixes of influences. When that assumption is relaxed, analysis becomes more complicated.

In practice, this difficulty is not very serious. For studies that deal with limited numbers of judges the simplest strategy is to analyze the determinants of decisions separately for each judge, as some scholars already do in Supreme Court studies (e.g., Segal 1986; Marshall 1989, ch. 5; Mishler and Sheehan 1996; Flemming and Wood 1997; Spaeth and Segal 1999, 290–301). A more general strategy is to utilize hierarchical statistical techniques that allow the impact of independent variables to differ among units such as individuals or, more technically, that allow for heterogeneity in the parameters (Glasgow 2001a, 2001b; Raudenbush and Bryk 2002; Western 1998; see Bartels 2005). The advantage of this approach is that it facilitates systematic analysis of the relationship between the characteristics of judges and the weights of particular determinants of behavior.

The difficulties of analyzing judicial audiences should be put in context in two respects. First, the problems involved in ascertaining the impact of judges' social identities are not fundamentally different from the problems of addressing other issues in the study of judicial behavior. For instance, measurement problems are nearly ubiquitous. One example is the strength of the relationship between the policy preferences of Supreme Court justices and the ideological content of their decisional behavior. No other issue in the field has received so much attention for so long. Yet the goal of finding measures of the justices' policy preferences that are independent of their behavior and highly valid has not been achieved despite impressive efforts by scholars in the field (e.g., Segal and Cover 1989; Martin and Quinn 2002; Epstein et al. 2005; see Giles, Hettinger, and Peppers 2001). As a result, our sense of the strength of this relationship is quite imprecise.

Moreover, many of the empirical findings on the determinants of judicial behavior are ambiguous in meaning because they are subject to multiple interpretations. The impact of the ideological mood of the general public on the ideological content of Supreme Court decisions is an example. Findings that the two are meaningfully related might reflect the justices' concern with public legitimacy. But they could also derive from any of several other sources, some of which do not involve any direct influence from the general public. The same is true of patterns of judicial behavior that are consistent with strategic interpretations; these patterns can often be given alternative interpretations as well. In this respect as well, the difficulty of ascertaining the influence of judges' personal audiences is far from unique.[9]

---

[9] This book has been peppered with statements about the impact of judges' audiences that are expressed in indefinite terms (e.g., "may," "might"). In part, this usage reflects the paucity of research on many of the issues considered in the book. But it also reflects the inherent limits in our understanding of the forces that shape behavior such as judicial deci-

Second, some of the difficulties involved in research on judges' audiences result from moving outside standard ways of analyzing judicial behavior. Our understanding of some other issues in the field would be enhanced by making such moves. Thus, confronting these difficulties can be beneficial beyond its value for the analysis of judicial audiences. Use of dependent variables that are not defined in ideological terms is one example.

Another example is interpersonal variation in the determinants of choice. Whatever may be the impact of judges' audiences on their behavior, the assumption that judges on the same court respond to the same influences to the same degree is questionable. The attributes of the Supreme Court reduce the relevance of some potential determinants of choice, but these attributes still leave room for considerable variation in those determinants among judges. The range of possible variation is even greater within other courts. Thus, adopting statistical models that allow for differences among judges in the determinants of choice will facilitate more precise explanations of judicial behavior. Certainly, taking into account the possibility of this type of variation would be a very useful step forward in the study of judicial behavior.

Some Final Thoughts

The scholarship on judicial behavior that currently exists teaches a great deal about the forces that shape judges' choices. Indeed, we are now in a period when our understanding of judicial behavior is growing rapidly. There is no crisis in the field.

Yet the state of this field is not entirely satisfactory, even if we leave aside the difficulties of theory testing.[10] The dominant models of judicial behavior have great value, but they also have significant limitations. Most fundamentally, these models rest on a conception of judges' aims that does not comport well with what we know about human motivations. Models can serve us quite well even if they are not entirely realistic, but a lack of realism limits their explanatory value. A conception of judges as Spocks who lack emotion and eschew self-interest cannot fully comprehend the considerations that shape judicial behavior.

To the extent that the dominant models are unrealistic, they depict a world of judging that is simpler than the real world. That is not entirely a weakness. Simplified models of reality facilitate analysis, and they can

---

sion making. A precise summary of what we know about more conventional issues in judicial behavior would also include a multitude of indefinite statements.

[10] In light of the relatively high level of collective self-criticism among students of judicial politics, it may be worth adding that the state of *no* scholarly field is entirely satisfactory.

have an appealing beauty. Models of strategic policy-oriented judges have gained popularity in part because they are elegant, integrating a wide array of judicial behavior into a simple theoretical conception.

In light of these advantages, it can be argued that we should refrain from adopting more elaborate conceptions of judicial behavior that sacrifice beauty and complicate analysis. "Should the facts be allowed to spoil a good story?" (Lovell 1986, 120; see Conlisk 1996, 669–75) But over time the simplifications of the dominant models in their current forms will become less satisfying, and scholars who subscribe to those models will want to dig deeper. Rather than leaving some judicial motives aside, they will seek to probe the impact of those motives. Rather than assuming that judges are fully strategic, adherents to strategic models will try to determine the conditions that promote or discourage strategic behavior. We might as well start now.

Some of those inquiries might be undertaken within models that are quite different from the existing ones. But the existing models need not be abandoned in order to consider the complexities of judicial behavior. Instead, their assumptions can be relaxed to take those complexities into account. Eventually it will become clearer how well these adaptations work and whether it is preferable to work with different kinds of models. In any event, inquiries into important issues need not be fitted within the framework of a particular model.

This book has described an array of actions by judges that do not easily fit within the usual frameworks for thinking about judicial behavior. Judges write books and articles that do not advance a policy agenda. They talk about pending cases in ways that jeopardize their participation in those cases. They write colorful opinions to attract attention, and they write opinions announcing they are unhappy with the decisions they have reached.

These actions and others like them can be understood in terms of judges' relationships with their audiences. More broadly, that perspective offers a means to consider what we know and still need to learn about judicial behavior. It helps in interpreting patterns of behavior that scholars have identified, such as ideologically structured voting on the Supreme Court. It assists in thinking about issues that lie on the fringes of the current models, such as the sources of temporal change in judges' policy positions. Perhaps most important, it provides a way to reopen issues that particular models close by assumption, such as the balance between legal and policy considerations in judges' choices. In these ways a conception of judging as self-presentation can help in our progress toward a better comprehension of judicial behavior.

REFERENCES

Abraham, Henry J. 1999. *Justices, Presidents, and Senators*. Rev. ed. Lanham, Md.: Rowman & Littlefield.

Abrahamson, Shirley S., Susan M. Fieber, and Gabrielle Lessard. 1993. "Judges on Judging: A Bibliography." *St. Mary's Law Journal* 24:995–1039.

Abramowitz, Alan I., and Kyle L. Saunders. 1998. "Ideological Realignment in the U.S. Electorate." *Journal of Politics* 60:634–52.

Abrams, Dominic, and Michael A. Hogg. 1988. "Comments on the Motivational Status of Self-Esteem in Social Identity and Intergroup Discrimination." *European Journal of Social Psychology* 18:317–34.

———, eds. 1999. *Social Identity and Social Cognition*. Oxford: Blackwell Publishers.

Adams, Cecil. 2001. "What's the Meaning of the Expression, 'That's the Exception That Proves the Rule?'" www.straightdope.com/classics/a3_201.html.

Adams, Henry. 1918. *The Education of Henry Adams: An Autobiography*. Boston: Houghton Mifflin.

Albert, Steve. 1992. "Kozinski and Reinhardt: The Other Big Debate." *Recorder*, October 13, 1.

Akerlof, George A., and Rachel E. Kranton. "Economics and Identity." *Quarterly Journal of Economics* 105:715–53.

All Things Considered. 1994. Transcript of broadcast, National Public Radio, April 6 (#1444–3).

American Bar Association Journal. 1976. "What the Justices are Saying . . . " 62:1454–56.

American Constitution Society. 2005. "About Us," www.acslaw.org/about/index.shtml.

Anderson, Gary M., William F. Shughart II, and Robert D. Tollison. 1989. "On the Incentives of Judges to Enforce Legislative Wealth Transfers." *Journal of Law and Economics* 32:215–28.

Arkin, Robert M. 1980. "Self-Presentation." In *The Self in Social Psychology*, ed. Daniel M. Wegner and Robin R. Vallacher, 158–82. New York: Oxford University Press.

Arnold, R. Douglas. 1990. *The Logic of Congressional Action*. New Haven: Yale University Press.

Asher, Herbert B., and Herbert F. Weisberg. 1978. "Voting Change in Congress: Some Dynamic Perspectives on an Evolutionary Process." *American Journal of Political Science* 22:391–425.

Askin, Frank. 1997. *Defending Rights: A Life in Law and Politics*. Atlantic Highlands, N.J.: Humanities Press.

Aspin, Larry. 1999. "Trends in Judicial Retention Elections, 1946–1998." *Judicature* 83:79–81.

Aspin, Larry T., and William K. Hall. 1994. "Retention Elections and Judicial Behavior." *Judicature* 77:306–15.

Aspin, Larry, T. William K. Hall, Jean Bax, and Celeste Montoya. 2000. "Thirty Years of Judicial Retention Elections: An Update." *Social Science Journal* 37:1–17.

Atkins, Burton, Lenore Alpert, and Robert Ziller. 1980. "Personality Theory and Judging: A Proposed Theory of Self Esteem and Judicial Policy-Making." *Law and Policy Quarterly* 2:189–220.

Atkins, Burton M., and Henry R. Glick. 1974. "Formal Judicial Recruitment and State Supreme Court Decisions." *American Politics Quarterly* 2:427–49.

Atkins, Burton M., and Terry Sloope. 1986. "The 'New' Hugo Black and the Warren Court." *Polity* 18:621–37.

AU News. 2005. "Transcript of Discussion Between U.S. Supreme Court Justices Antonin Scalia and Stephen Breyer—AU Washington College of Law, Jan. 13," http://domino.american.edu/AU/media/mediarel.nsf/.

Auletta, Ken. 2001a. "Maligning the Microsoft Judge." *Washington Post*, March 7, A23.

———. 2001b. *World War 3.0: Microsoft and Its Enemies.* New York: Random House.

Austen-Smith, David. 1992. "Explaining the Vote: Constituency Constraints on Sophisticated Voting." *American Journal of Political Science* 36:68–95.

Badinter, Robert, and Stephen Breyer, eds. 2004. *Judges in Contemporary Democracy: An International Conversation.* New York: New York University Press.

Bailey, Michael, and Kelly H. Chang. 2001. "Comparing Presidents, Senators, and Justices: Interinstitutional Preference Estimation." *Journal of Law, Economics, & Organization* 17:477–506.

Bainbridge, Stephen M., and G. Mitu Gulati. 2002. "How Do Judges Maximize? (The Same Way Everyone Else Does—Boundedly): Rules of Thumb in Securities Fraud Opinions." *Emory Law Journal* 51:83–151.

Baldas, Tresa. 2004. "Law School Turf War Ignites." *National Law Journal*, April 26, 1, 12.

Balkin, Jack M., ed. 2005. *What Roe v. Wade Should Have Said: The Nation's Top Legal Experts Rewrite America's Most Controversial Decision.* New York: New York University Press.

———, ed. 2001. *What Brown v. Board of Education Should Have Said: The Nation's Top Legal Experts Rewrite America's Landmark Civil Rights Decision.* New York: New York University Press.

Barbash, Fred. 1981. "Judge Bazelon's 'Network': The Salon of the Ultimate Liberal." *Washington Post*, March 1, A2.

Barbash, Fred, and Al Kamen. 1984. "Third Justice Speaks Out." *Washington Post*, September 20, A1, A42.

Barber, James David. 1965. *The Lawmakers: Recruitment and Adaptation to Legislative Life.* New Haven, Conn.: Yale University Press.

Barberis, Nicholas, and Richard Thaler. 2003. "A Survey of Behavioral Finance." In *Handbook of the Economics of Finance*, ed. George M. Constantinides, Milton Harris, and Rene M. Stulz, 1053–1123. Amsterdam: Elvesier.

Barnes, Jeb. 2004. *Overruled? Legislative Overrides, Pluralism, and Contemporary Court-Congress Relations.* Stanford, Calif.: Stanford University Press.

Barone, Michael. 2005. "Justices Have Typically Felt Little Compunction About Overturning Laws and Making Public Policy." *Chicago Sun–Times*, July 13, 55.

Barrett, Paul M. 1993. "Thomas is Emerging As Strong Conservative Out to Prove Himself." *Wall Street Journal*, April 27, A1, A6.

Bartels, Brandon L. 2005. "Heterogeneity in Supreme Court Decision-Making: How Case-Level Factors Alter Preference-Based Behavior." Paper presented at the annual conference of the Midwest Political Science Association, Chicago, April 7–10.

Bashman, Howard. 2003. "How Appealing" blog, posts of August 4, http://legalaffairs.org/howappealing/2003_08_01_appellateblog_archive.html.

Bass, Jack. 1981. *Unlikely Heroes.* New York: Simon & Schuster.

———. 1993. *Taming the Storm: The Life and Times of Judge Frank M. Johnson, Jr. and the South's Fight Over Civil Rights.* New York: Doubleday.

Baum, Lawrence. 1983. "The Electoral Fates of Incumbent Judges in the Ohio Court of Common Pleas." *Judicature* 66:420–30.

———. 1988. "Measuring Policy Change in the U.S. Supreme Court." *American Political Science Review* 82:905–12.

———. 1997. *The Puzzle of Judicial Behavior.* Ann Arbor: University of Michigan Press.

———. 1998. *The Supreme Court.* 6th ed. Washington, D.C.: CQ Press.

———. 1999. "Recruitment and the Motivations of Supreme Court Justices." In *Supreme Court Decision-Making: New Institutional Approaches*, ed. Cornell W. Clayton and Howard Gillman, 201–13. Chicago: University of Chicago Press.

Baum, Lawrence, and Bradley C. Canon. 1982. "State Supreme Courts as Activists: New Doctrines in the Law of Torts." In *State Supreme Courts: Policymakers in the Federal System*, ed. Mary Cornelia Porter and G. Alan Tarr, 83–108. Westport, Conn.: Greenwood Press.

Baum, Lawrence, and Lori Hausegger. 2004. "The Supreme Court and Congress: Reconsidering the Relationship." In *Putting the Pieces Together: Lawmaking from an Inter-Branch Perspective*, ed. Mark C. Miller and Jeb Barnes, 107–22. Washington, D.C.: Georgetown University Press.

Baumeister, Roy F. 1982. "A Self-Presentational View of Social Phenomena." *Psychological Bulletin* 91:3–26.

———. 1998. "The Self." In *The Handbook of Social Psychology*, ed. Daniel T. Gilbert, Susan T. Fiske, and Gardner Lindzey, 4th ed., vol. 1, 680–740. Boston: McGraw-Hill.

Bazelon, Emily. 2004. "The Big Kozinski." *Legal Affairs*, January–February, 22–32.

Beck, Paul Allen, and M. Kent Jennings. 1991. "Family Traditions, Political Periods, and the Development of Partisan Orientations." *Journal of Politics* 53:742–63.

Becker, Ernest. 1968. *The Structure of Evil.* New York: George Braziller.

Bergara, Mario, Barak Richman, and Pablo T. Spiller. 2003. "Modeling Supreme Court Strategic Decision Making: The Congressional Constraint." *Legislative Studies Quarterly* 28:247–80.

Bernstein, J. L. 1956/1984. "The Philosophy of Mr. Justice Brennan." *The Reporter* (Passaic County Bar Association), Spring 1984, 30–33. (Reprinted from November 1956 issue.)

Beveridge, Albert J. 1919. *The Life of John Marshall*. Boston: Houghton Mifflin.

Bianco, William T. 1994. *Trust: Representatives and Constituents*. Ann Arbor: University of Michigan Press.

Bilodeau, Otis, and Jonathan Ringel. 2001. "ABA Ouster Sets Stage for Bench Battles." *Legal Times*, March 26, 2001, 1.

Biskupic, Joan. 1994a. "'I Am Not an Uncle Tom,' Thomas Says at Meeting." *Washington Post*, October 28, A1, A24.

———. 1994b. "In Libel Suit U-Turn, Judge Admits Starting in the Wrong Direction." *Washington Post*, May 5, A20.

———. 1994c. "Female Justices Attest to Fraternity on Bench." *Washington Post*, August 21, A24.

———. 1995a. "Has the Court Lost Its Appeal?" *Washington Post*, October 12, A23.

———. 1995b. "High Court's Justice With a Cause." *Washington Post*, April 17, A1, A4.

———. 1998a. "Nine Supreme Individualists: A Guide to the Conversation." *Washington Post*, April 28, A15.

———. 1998b. "Shedding Silence, Justice Thomas Takes on Critics." *Washington Post*, September 23, A1.

———. 2001. "Thomas is Bolder, Confident—Outside Court." *USA Today*, January 31, 6A.

———. 2004. "Attack on Souter Shows Justices' Minimal Security." *USA Today*, May 3, 4A.

Biskupic, Joan, and Elder Witt. 1997. *Guide to the U.S. Supreme Court*. 3d ed. Washington, D.C.: Congressional Quarterly.

Black, Hugo L., and Elizabeth Black. 1986. *Mr. Justice and Mrs. Black: The Memoirs of Hugo L. Black and Elizabeth Black*. New York: Random House.

Blackmun, Harry A. 1980. "Remarks at the Commencement Exercises of Mayo Medical School." *Mayo Clinic Proceedings* 55:573–78.

———. 1994–95. "The Justice Harry A. Blackmun Oral History Project." Interviews conducted by Harold Hongju Koh. Washington, D.C.: Supreme Court Historical Society and Federal Judicial Center.

Blackmun, Sally. 2004. "Introduction." In *The War on Choice*, ed. Gloria Feldt, xv–xxiii. New York: Random House.

Blaustein, Albert P., and Roy M. Mersky. 1972. "Rating Supreme Court Justices." *American Bar Association Journal* 58:1183–89.

Blumberg, Abraham. 1967. *Criminal Justice*. Chicago: Quadrangle Books.

Blume, John, and Theodore Eisenberg. 1999. "Judicial Politics, Death Penalty Appeals, and Case Selection: An Empirical Study." *Southern California Law Review* 72:465–503.

Bond, Jon R., and Richard Fleisher, eds. 2000. *Polarized Politics: Congress and the President in a Partisan Era*. Washington, D.C.: CQ Press.

Boot, Max. 1998. *Out of Order: Arrogance, Corruption, and Incompetence on the Bench*. New York: Basic Books.

Bork, Robert H. 1992. "Again, a Struggle for the Soul of the Court." *New York Times*, July 8, A19.

Bosmajian, Haig. 1992. *Metaphor and Reason in Judicial Opinions*. Carbondale: Southern Illinois University Press.

Bossert, Rex. 1997. "Conservative Forum Is a Quiet Power." *National Law Journal*, September 8, A1, A29, A30.

Brace, Paul, and Melinda Gann Hall. 1990. "Neo-Institutionalism and Dissent in State Supreme Courts." *Journal of Politics* 52:54–70.

———. 1997. "The Interplay of Preferences, Case Facts, Context, and Rules in the Politics of Judicial Choice." *Journal of Politics* 59:1206–31.

Bradley, Robert C. 2003. "Selecting and Ranking Great Justices: Poll Results." In *Leaders of the Pack: Polls and Case Studies of Great Supreme Court Justices*, ed. William D. Pederson and Norman W. Provizer, 1–22. New York: Peter Lang.

Brehm, John, and Scott Gates. 1997. *Working, Shirking, and Sabotage: Bureaucratic Response to a Democratic Public*. Ann Arbor: University of Michigan Press.

Brennan, William J., Jr. 1977. "State Constitutions and the Protection of Individual Rights." *Harvard Law Review* 90:489–504.

Brenner, Saul. 1980. "Fluidity on the United States Supreme Court: A Reassessment." *American Journal of Political Science* 24:526–35.

———. 1982. "Fluidity on the Supreme Court: 1956–1967." *American Journal of Political Science* 26:388–90.

Brenner, Saul, and Marc Stier. 1996. "Retesting Segal and Spaeth's *Stare Decisis* Model." *American Journal of Political Science* 40:1036–48.

Brewer, Marilynn B. 1991. "The Social Self: On Being the Same and Different at the Same Time." *Personality and Social Psychology Bulletin* 17:475–82.

———. 2001. "The Many Faces of Social Identity: Implications for Political Psychology." *Political Psychology* 22:115–25.

———. 2003. "Optimal Distinctiveness, Social Identity, and the Self." In *Handbook of Self and Identity*, ed. Mark R. Leary and June Price Tangney, 480–91. New York: Guilford Press.

Bronars, Stephen G., and John R. Lott, Jr. 1997. "Do Campaign Donations Alter How a Politician Votes? Or, Do Donors Support Candidates Who Value the Same Things That They Do?" *Journal of Law & Economics* 40:317–48.

Brown, Jonathon D. 1998. *The Self*. Boston: McGraw-Hill.

Brudney, James J. 2005. "Foreseeing Greatness? Measurable Performance Criteria and the Selection of Supreme Court Justices." *Florida State University Law Review* 32.

Brudney, James J., and Corey Ditslear. 2001. "Designated Diffidence: District Court Judges on the Courts of Appeals." *Law & Society Review* 35:565–606.

Brudney, James J., Sara Schiavoni, and Deborah J. Merritt. 1999. "Judicial Hostility Toward Labor Unions? Applying the Social Background Model to a Celebrated Concern." *Ohio State Law Journal* 60:1675–1771.

Bryden, David P. 1992. "Is the Rehnquist Court Conservative?" *Public Interest*, fall, 73–88.

Burbank, Stephen B., and Barry Friedman. 2002. "Reconsidering Judicial Independence." In *Judicial Independence at the Crossroads: An Interdisciplinary*

Approach, ed. Stephen B. Burbank and Barry Friedman, 9–42. Thousand Oaks, Calif.: Sage Publications.

Caldeira, Gregory A. 1977. "Judicial Incentives: Some Evidence From Urban Trial Courts." *Iusticia* 4 (2):1–28.

———. 1985. "The Transmission of Legal Precedent: A Study of State Supreme Courts." *American Political Science Review* 79:178–93.

———. 1986. "Neither the Purse Nor the Sword: Dynamics of Public Confidence in the Supreme Court." *American Political Science Review* 80:1209–26.

———. 1987. "Public Opinion and the U.S. Supreme Court: FDR's Court-Packing Plan." *American Political Science Review* 81:1139–53.

———. 1988. "Legal Precedent: Structures of Communication Between State Supreme Courts." *Social Networks* 10:29–55.

Caldeira, Gregory A., and James L. Gibson. 1992. "The Etiology of Public Support for the Supreme Court." *American Journal of Political Science* 36:635–64.

Caldeira, Gregory A., and John T. Wold. 1978. "Routine Decision-Making in Five California Courts of Appeal." Paper presented at the annual conference of the Western Political Science Association, Los Angeles, March 16–18.

Caldeira, Gregory A., and John R. Wright. 1988. "Organized Interests and Agenda Setting in the U. S. Supreme Court." *American Political Science Review* 82:1109–28.

Camerer, Colin F. 1997. "Progress in Behavioral Game Theory." *Journal of Economic Perspectives* 11:167–88.

Camerer, Colin, and Richard H. Thaler. 1995. "Anomalies: Ultimatums, Dictators, and Manners." *Journal of Economic Perspectives* 9:209–19.

Cameron, Charles M. 1997. "Courts and the Two Institutionalisms." Paper presented at the Second Annual Conference on the Scientific Study of Judicial Politics, November 14–15, Atlanta.

———. 2000. *Veto Bargaining: Presidents and the Politics of Negative Power*. New York: Cambridge University Press.

Cameron, Charles M., Jeffrey A. Segal, and Donald Songer. 2000. "Strategic Auditing in a Political Hierarchy: An Informational Model of the Supreme Court's Certiorari Decisions." *American Political Science Review* 94:101–16.

Caminker, Evan H. 1999. "Sincere and Strategic Voting Norms on Multimember Courts." *Michigan Law Review* 97:2297–2380.

Campbell, Angus. 1971. *White Attitudes Toward Black People*. Ann Arbor: Institute for Social Research, University of Michigan.

Canellos, Peter S. 2003. "A Call to Order Sounds for Liberals on Message." *Boston Globe*, August 5, A3.

Canon, Bradley C., and Lawrence Baum. 1981. "Patterns of Adoption of Tort Law Innovations: An Application of Diffusion Theory to Judicial Doctrines." *American Political Science Review* 75:975–87.

Canon, Bradley C., and Charles A. Johnson. 1999. *Judicial Policies: Implementation and Impact*. 2d ed. Washington, D.C.: CQ Press.

Caplan, Lincoln. 1987. *The Tenth Justice: The Solicitor General and the Rule of Law*. New York: Alfred A. Knopf.

Cardozo, Benjamin N. 1921. *The Nature of the Judicial Process*. New Haven, Conn.: Yale University Press.

Carlsen, William. 1996. "Frontier Justice." *San Francisco Chronicle*, October 6, (Sunday section), 1, 5.

Carney, James, and Matthew Cooper. 2005. "Justice Scalia: The Charm Offensive." *Time*, January 31, 18.

Carp, Robert A. 1972. "The Scope and Function of Intra-Circuit Judicial Communication: A Case Study of the Eighth Circuit." *Law & Society Review* 6:405–26.

Carp, Robert A., and Russell Wheeler. 1972. "Sink or Swim: The Socialization of a Federal District Judge." *Journal of Public Law* 21:359–93.

Carrizosa, Philip. 1992. "O'Connor Urges Court to Speed Its Death Cases." *Los Angeles Daily Journal*, August 7, 1, 13.

Carter, Lief H. 1979. *Reason in Law*. Boston: Little, Brown.

Carter, Terry. 1992. "Crossing the Rubicon." *California Lawyer* 12 (October): 39–40, 103–4.

———. 2001. "The In Crowd: Conservatives Who Sought Refuge in the Federalist Society Gain Clout." *ABA Journal* 87 (September): 46–51.

Caruso, David B. 2002. "Crackdown Will Target Illegal Drivers." *Columbus Dispatch*, April 14, A10.

Casey, Gregory. 1976. "Popular Perceptions of Supreme Court Rulings." *American Politics Quarterly* 4:3–39.

Cass, Ronald A. 1995. "Judging: Norms and Incentives of Retrospective Decision-Making." *Boston University Law Review* 75:941–96.

Casto, William R. 1995. *The Supreme Court in the Early Republic: The Chief Justiceships of John Jay and Oliver Ellsworth*. Columbia: University of South Carolina Press.

Charlotte Observer. 2003. "North Carolina Court Upholds Unconstitutionality of State Redistricting Plan." July 18.

Chartrand, Tanya L., and John A. Bargh. 2002. "Nonconscious Motivations: Their Activation, Operation, and Consequences." In *Self and Motivation: Emerging Psychological Perspectives*, ed. Abraham Tesser, Diederik A. Stapel, and Joanne V. Wood, 13–41. Washington, D.C.: American Psychological Association.

Chase, Megan, ed. 2004. *Almanac of the Federal Judiciary*, 2004–2. New York: Aspen Publishers.

Choi, Stephen, and Mitu Gulati. 2004. "Choosing the Next Supreme Court Justice: An Empirical Ranking of Judicial Performance." *Southern California Law Review* 78:23–117.

Chun, Marc. 2002. "Looking Where the Light is Better: A Review of the Literature on Assessing Higher Education Quality." *Peer Review*, Winter–Spring, 16–25.

Cincinnati Enquirer. 1989. "Rose's Woes." August 25, A9.

Citrin, Jack, and Donald Philip Green. 1986. "Presidential Leadership and the Resurgence of Trust in Government." *British Journal of Political Science* 16:431–53.

Clark, Hunter R. 1995. *Justice Brennan: The Great Conciliator.* New York: Birch Lane Press.

Clayton, Cornell W. 1999. "The Supreme Court and Political Jurisprudence: New and Old Institutionalisms." In *Supreme Court Decision-Making: New Institutionalist Approaches*, ed. Cornell W. Clayton and Howard Gillman, 15–41. Chicago: University of Chicago Press.

Cleveland Plain Dealer. 1989. "Paint the Robe Red." June 27, 14B.

Clines, Francis X., and Warren Weaver Jr. 1982. "Briefing." *New York Times*, May 18, A18.

Clymer, Adam. 2003. "Court Allows a New Approach to Redrawing Districts by Race." *New York Times*, June 27, A1, A18.

Cohen, Adam. 2002. "Hell Hath No Fury Like a Conservative Who is Victorious." *New York Times*, November 24, sec. 4, 12.

Cohen, Jonathan Matthew. 2002. *Inside Appellate Courts: The Impact of Court Organization on Judicial Decision Making in the United States Courts of Appeals.* Ann Arbor: University of Michigan Press.

Cohen, Mark A. 1991. "Explaining Judicial Behavior or What's 'Unconstitutional' About the Sentencing Commission?" *Journal of Law, Economics, and Organization* 7:183–99.

———. 1992. "The Motives of Judges: Empirical Evidence From Antitrust Sentencing." *International Review of Law and Economics* 12:13–30.

Combs, James E. 1980. *Dimensions of Political Drama.* Santa Monica, Calif.: Goodyear.

Committee for Economic Development. 2002. *Justice for Hire: Improving Judicial Selection.* New York: Committee for Economic Development.

Conley, John M., and William M. O'Barr. 1987–88. "Fundamentals of Jurisprudence: An Ethnography of Judicial Decision Making in Informal Courts." *North Carolina Law Review* 66:467–507.

Conlisk, John. 1996. "Why Bounded Rationality?" *Journal of Economic Literature* 34:669–700.

Conover, Pamela Johnston. 1984. "The Influence of Group Identifications on Political Perception and Evaluation." *Journal of Politics* 46:760–85.

———. 1988. "The Role of Social Groups in Political Thinking." *British Journal of Political Science* 18:51–76.

Cook, Beverly Blair. 1971. "The Socialization of New Federal Judges: Impact on District Court Business." *Washington University Law Quarterly* 1971:253–79.

Cook, Elizabeth Adell, Ted G. Jelen, and Clyde Wilcox. 1992. *Between Two Absolutes: Public Opinion and the Politics of Abortion.* Boulder, Colo.: Westview Press.

Cook, Timothy D. 1998. *Governing With the News: The News Media as Political Institution.* Chicago: University of Chicago Press.

Cooper, Alan. 2000. "Rivalry on 4th Circuit." *Richmond Times-Dispatch*, August 7.

Cooper, Phillip J. 1995. *Battles on the Bench: Conflict Inside the Supreme Court.* Lawrence: University Press of Kansas.

"Courts, Law, and the New (Historical) Institutionalism." 1999. Symposium. *Law and Courts* 9 (spring): 1–20.

Cox, Gail Diane. 2001. "Thar He Blows—Again and Again." *National Law Journal*, August 6, A26.

Cray, Ed. 1997. *Chief Justice: A Biography of Earl Warren*. New York: Simon & Schuster.

Crocker, Jennifer, and Lora E. Park. 2003. "Seeking Self-Esteem: Construction, Maintenance, and Protection of Self-Worth." In *Handbook of Self and Identity*, ed. Mark R. Leary and June Price Tangney, 291–313. New York: Guilford Press.

Cross, Frank B. 1997. "Political Science and the New Legal Realism: A Case of Unfortunate Interdisciplinary Ignorance." *Northwestern University Law Review* 92:251–326.

———. 1998. "The Justices of Strategy." *Duke Law Journal* 48:511–70.

———. 2003. "Decisionmaking in the U.S. Courts of Appeals." *California Law Review* 91:1457–1515.

———. 2004. Posting to "Lawcourts-l," Law and Courts Discussion List, September 12. (Quoted with permission of Professor Cross.)

———. N.d. "Appellate Court Adherence to Precedent."

Cross, Frank B., and Blake J. Nelson. 2001. "Strategic Institutional Effects on Supreme Court Decisionmaking." *Northwestern University Law Review* 95:1437–93.

Cross, Frank B., and Emerson H. Tiller. 1998. "Judicial Partisanship and Obedience to Legal Doctrine: Whistleblowing on the Federal Courts of Appeal." *Yale Law Journal* 107:2155–76.

Curriden, Mark. 2004. "Supreme Court is on a Foreign Bent." *Dallas Morning News*, May 22.

Curry, Brett W. 2005. "The Courts, Congress, and the Politics of Federal Jurisdiction." Ph.D. dissertation, Ohio State University.

Cushman, Barry. 1998. *Rethinking the New Deal Court: The Structure of a Judicial Revolution*. New York: Oxford University Press.

Cushman, Clare, ed. 2001. *Supreme Court Decisions and Women's Rights*. Washington, D.C.: CQ Press.

Dahl, Robert A. 1957. "Decision-Making in a Democracy: The Supreme Court as a National Policy-Maker." *Journal of Public Law* 6:279–95.

Dalton, Clare. 1985. "An Essay in the Deconstruction of Contract Doctrine." *Yale Law Journal* 94:997–1114.

D'Amato, Anthony. 1989. "Aspects of Deconstruction: The 'Easy Case' of the Under-Aged President." *Northwestern University Law Review* 84:250–56.

Danelski, David J. 1970. "Legislative and Judicial Decision-Making: The Case of Harold H. Burton." In *Political Decision-Making*, ed. S. Sidney Ulmer, 121–46. New York: Van Nostrand.

Danforth, John C. 1994. *Resurrection: The Confirmation of Clarence Thomas*. New York: Viking Press.

Dateline NBC. 2002. Transcript of broadcast of January 25.

Davies, Thomas Y. 1981. "Gresham's Law Revisited: Expedited Processing Techniques and the Allocation of Appellate Resources." *Justice System Journal* 6:372–404.

Davis, Richard. 1994. *Decisions and Images: The Supreme Court and the Press.* Englewood Cliffs, N.J.: Prentice Hall.

Dawes, Robyn M. 1994. *House of Cards: Psychology and Psychotherapy Built on Myth.* New York: Free Press.

Dawson, Michael D. 1994. *Behind the Mule: Race and Class in African-American Politics.* Princeton, N.J.: Princeton University Press.

Dean, John W. 2001. *The Rehnquist Choice.* New York: Free Press.

Deaux, Kay. 1993. "Reconstructing Social Identity." *Personality and Social Psychology Bulletin* 19:4–12.

Denzau, Arthur, William Riker, and Kenneth Shepsle. 1985. "Farquharson and Fenno: Sophisticated Voting and Home Style." *American Political Science Review* 79:1117–34.

DeParle, Jason. 2005. "Nomination Stirs a Debate on Federalists' Sway." *New York Times,* August 1, 2005, A1, A12.

Ditslear, Corey A. 2002. "Office of the Solicitor General Participation Before the United States Supreme Court: Influences on the Decision-Making Process." Ph.D. dissertation, Ohio State University.

Ditslear, Corey A., and Lawrence Baum. 2001. "Selection of Law Clerks and Polarization in the U.S. Supreme Court." *Journal of Politics* 63:869–85.

Domnarski, William. 1996. *In the Opinion of the Court.* Urbana: University of Illinois Press.

Donald, David Herbert. 2004. "Fit to be Tied." *New York Times,* April 11, sec. 7, 19.

Dorff, Robert H., and Saul Brenner. 1992. "Conformity Voting on the United States Supreme Court." *Journal of Politics* 54:762–75.

Douglas, William O. 1980. *The Court Years, 1939–1975: The Autobiography of William O. Douglas.* New York: Random House.

Drahozal, Christopher R. 1998. "Judicial Incentives and the Appeals Process." *SMU Law Review* 51:469–503.

Drechsel, Robert E. 1983. *News Making in the Trial Courts.* New York: Longman.

Dubois, Philip L. 1984. "Voting Cues in Nonpartisan Trial Court Elections: A Multivariate Assessment." *Law & Society Review* 18:395–436.

Durr, Robert H., Andrew D. Martin, and Christina Wolbrecht. 2000. "Ideological Divergence and Public Support for the Supreme Court." *American Journal of Political Science* 44:768–76.

Dworkin, Ronald. 1977. *Taking Rights Seriously.* Cambridge, Mass.: Harvard University Press.

———. 1986. *Law's Empire.* Cambridge, Mass.: Belknap Press.

Eagly, Alice H., and Shelly Chaiken. 1993. *The Psychology of Attitudes.* Fort Worth, Tex.: Harcourt Brace Jovanovich.

Easterbrook, Frank H. 1990. "What's So Special About Judges?" *University of Colorado Law Review* 61:773–82.

———. 1992. "Some Tasks in Understanding Law Through the Lens of Public Choice." *International Review of Law and Economics* 12:284–88.

Eastland, Terry. 1993. "The Tempting of Justice Kennedy." *American Spectator,* February, 32–37.

Easton, David. 1965. *A Systems Analysis of Political Life.* New York: John Wiley & Sons.

Edsall, Thomas B. 2001. "Federalist Society Becomes a Force in Washington." *Washington Post*, April 18, A4.

Edwards, Harry T. 1991. "The Judicial Function and the Elusive Goal of Principled Decisionmaking." *Wisconsin Law Review* 1991:837–65.

———. 2003. "The Effects of Collegiality on Judicial Decision Making." *University of Pennsylvania Law Review* 151:1639–89.

Egler, Daniel. 1984. "Hallowed Chambers." *Chicago Tribune*, March 12, sec. 2, 8.

Eisenstein, James, and Herbert Jacob. 1977. *Felony Justice: An Organizational Analysis of Criminal Courts*. Boston: Little, Brown.

Eisler, Kim Isaac. 1993. *A Justice For All: William J. Brennan, Jr., and the Decisions That Transformed America*. New York: Simon & Schuster.

Epstein, Lee, Valerie Hoekstra, Jeffrey A. Segal, and Harold J. Spaeth. 1998. "Do Political Preferences Change? A Longitudinal Study of U.S. Supreme Court Justices." *Journal of Politics* 60:801–18.

Epstein, Lee, and Jack Knight. 1998. *The Choices Justices Make*. Washington, D.C.: CQ Press.

———. 1999. "Mapping Out the Strategic Terrain: The Informational Role of *Amici Curiae*." In *Supreme Court Decision-Making: New Institutionalist Approaches*, ed. Cornell W. Clayton and Howard Gillman, 215–35. Chicago: University of Chicago Press.

———. 2000. "Toward a Strategic Revolution in Judicial Politics: A Look Back, a Look Ahead." *Political Research Quarterly* 53:625–61.

Epstein, Lee, Jack Knight, and Andrew D. Martin. 2001. "Review Essay: The Supreme Court as a Strategic National Policy-Maker." *Emory Law Journal* 50:583–611.

———. 2003. "The Norm of Prior Judicial Experience and Its Consequences for Career Diversity on the U.S. Supreme Court." *California Law Review* 91:903–66.

Epstein, Lee, Andrew D. Martin, Jeffrey A. Segal, and Chad Westerland. 2005. "The Judicial Common Space." Paper presented at the Law and Positive Political Theory Conference, Evanston, Ill., April 29.

Epstein, Lee, and Jeffrey Segal. 2000. "Measuring Issue Salience." *American Journal of Political Science* 44:66–83.

Epstein, Lee, Jeffrey A. Segal, and Timothy Johnson. 1996. "The Claim of Issue Creation on the U.S. Supreme Court." *American Political Science Review* 90:845–52.

Epstein, Lee, Jeffrey A. Segal, Harold J. Spaeth, and Thomas G. Walker. 2003. *The Supreme Court Compendium: Data, Decisions and Developments*. 3d ed. Washington, D.C.: CQ Press.

Epstein, Lee, and Thomas G. Walker. 1995. "The Role of the Supreme Court in American Society: Playing the Reconstruction Game." In *Contemplating Courts*, ed. Lee Epstein, 315–46. Washington, D.C.: CQ Press.

Erikson, Robert S., and Kent L. Tedin. 2005. *American Public Opinion: Its Origins, Content, and Impact*. 7th ed. New York: Pearson Longman.

Eskridge, William N., Jr. 1991a. "Overriding Supreme Court Statutory Interpretation Decisions." *Yale Law Journal* 101:331–455.

Eskridge, William N., Jr. 1991b. "Reneging on History? Playing the Court/Congress/President Civil Rights Game." *California Law Review* 79:613–84.

Eskridge, William N., Jr., and Philip P. Frickey. 1994. "Foreword: Law as Equilibrium." *Harvard Law Review* 108:26–108.

Federal Judicial Center. 2005. "Federal Judges Biographical Database," http://www.fjc.gov/public/home.nsf/hisj.

Federalist Society. 1998. "A Panel Discussion on: What Are High Crimes and Misdemeanors?" www.fed-soc.org/highcrimes.html (accessed August 4, 1999; specific site now discontinued).

———. 2003. "Frequently Asked Questions," www.fed-soc.org/Press/FAQs.htm.

Fein, Bruce. 1993. "The Year David Souter Earned His Liberal Laurels." *Legal Times*, July 5, 26.

Feldblum, Chai. 1999. "Former Law Clerk Recalls Blackmun's Humility." *National Law Journal*, March 15, A24.

Fels, Anna. 2004. *Necessary Dreams: Ambition in Women's Changing Lives*. New York: Pantheon Books.

Fenno, Richard F., Jr. 1978. *Home Style: House Members in Their Districts*. Boston: Little, Brown.

———. 1996. *Senators on the Campaign Trail: The Politics of Representation*. Norman: University of Oklahoma Press.

Ferejohn, John A., and Barry R. Weingast. 1992. "Limitation of Statutes: Strategic Statutory Interpretation." *Georgetown Law Journal* 80:565–82.

Ferren, John M. 2004. *Salt of the Earth, Conscience of the Court: The Story of Justice Wiley Rutledge*. Chapel Hill: University of North Carolina Press.

Finifter, Ada W. 1974. "The Friendship Group as a Protective Environment for Political Deviants." *American Political Science Review* 68:607–25.

Fiorina, Morris P., with Samuel J. Abrams and Jeremy C. Pope. 2005. *Culture War? The Myth of a Polarized America*. New York: Pearson Longman.

Fish, Peter Graham. 1973. *The Politics of Federal Judicial Administration*. Princeton, N.J.: Princeton University Press.

Fisher, Marc. 1995. "The Private World of Justice Thomas." *Washington Post*, September 11, B1, B4.

Fisher, William W., III, Morton J. Horwitz, and Thomas A. Reed, eds. 1993. *American Legal Realism*. New York: Oxford University Press.

Fiske, Susan T., and Shelley E. Taylor. 1991. *Social Cognition*. 2d ed. New York: McGraw-Hill.

Fleisher, Richard, and Jon R. Bond. 1996. "The President in a More Partisan Legislative Arena." *Political Research Quarterly* 49:729–48.

———. 2004. "The Shrinking Middle in the U.S. Congress." *British Journal of Political Science* 34:429–51.

Flemming, Roy B., Peter F. Nardulli, and James Eisenstein. 1992. *The Craft of Justice: Politics and Work in Criminal Court Communities*. Philadelphia: University of Pennsylvania Press.

Flemming, Roy B., and B. Dan Wood. 1997. "The Public and the Supreme Court: Individual Justice Responsiveness to American Public Moods." *American Journal of Political Science* 41:468–98.

Foskett, Ken. 2001a. "The Clarence Thomas You Don't Know." *Atlanta Journal and Constitution*, July 1, A1, A12–A14.

———. 2001b. "Refusing to Court Favor." *Atlanta Journal and Constitution*, July 3, 2001, A1, A6, A7.

———. 2004. *Judging Thomas: The Life and Times of Clarence Thomas*. New York: William Morrow.

Frank, Jerome. 1930. *Law and the Modern Mind*. New York: Brentano's.

Frank, Michael J. 2003. "Judge Not, Lest Ye be Judged Unworthy of a Pay Raise: An Examination of the Federal Judicial Salary 'Crisis.' " *Marquette Law Review* 87:55–122.

Frankfurter, Felix. 1956. *Of Law and Men: Papers and Addresses of Felix Frankfurter, 1939–1956*. New York: Harcourt, Brace.

Freeman, Jo. 1975. *The Politics of Women's Liberation*. New York: David McKay.

Friedman, Barry. 2003. "Mediated Popular Constitutionalism." *Michigan Law Review* 101:2596–2636.

Friedman, Milton. 1953. *Essays in Positive Economics*. Chicago: University of Chicago Press.

Friendly, Henry J. 1967. *Benchmarks*. Chicago: University of Chicago Press.

Fuetsch, Michele. 1999. "Judicial Fight's Result Still in Doubt." *Cleveland Plain Dealer*, May 29, 1B.

Fuld, Stanley H. 1953. "A Judge Looks at the Law Review." *New York University Law Review* 28:915–21.

Garrow, David J. 1994. *Liberty and Sexuality: The Right to Privacy and the Making of Roe v. Wade*. New York: Macmillan.

Gates, John B., and Glenn A. Phelps. 1996. "Intentionalism in Constitutional Opinions." *Political Research Quarterly* 49:245–61.

Gellman, Barton. 1990. "Barry Judge's Remarks Break Judicial Norms." *Washington Post*, November 2, D1.

Georgakopoulos, Nicholas L. 2000. "Discretion in the Career and Recognition Judiciary." *University of Chicago Law School Roundtable* 7:205–25.

George, Tracey E. 2001. "Court Fixing." *Arizona Law Review* 43:9–62.

Geracimos, Ann. 1998. "D.C. Power Players Ponder Big Deals." *Washington Times*, November 10, A1.

Gerchik, Julie R. F. 2000. "Slouching Toward Extremism: The Federalist Society and the Transformation of American Jurisprudence." *IDS Insights* 1(2): 1–5.

Gerstein, Josh. 2004. "Audience Gasps as Judge Likens Election of Bush to Rise of Il Duce." *New York Sun*, June 21, A1.

Gettleman, Jeffrey. 2003. "Alabama Panel Ousts Judge Over Ten Commandments." *New York Times*, November 14, A12.

Gibson, James L. 1978. "Judges' Role Orientations, Attitudes, and Decisions: An Interactive Model." *American Political Science Review* 72:911–24.

———. 1980. "Environmental Constraints on the Behavior of Judges: A Representational Model of Judicial Decision Making." *Law & Society Review* 14:343–70.

———. 1981. "Personality and Elite Political Behavior: The Influence of Self Esteem on Judicial Decision Making." *Journal of Politics* 43:104–25.

Gibson, James L. 1983. "From Simplicity to Complexity: The Development of Theory in the Study of Judicial Behavior." *Political Behavior* 5:7–49.

Gibson, James L., and Gregory A. Caldeira. 1992. "Blacks and the United States Supreme Court: Models of Diffuse Support." *Journal of Politics* 54:1120–45.

Gibson, James L., Gregory A. Caldeira, and Lester Kenyatta Spence. 2003a. "Measuring Attitudes Toward the United States Supreme Court." *American Journal of Political Science* 47:354–67.

———. 2003b. "The Supreme Court and the U.S. Presidential Election of 2000: Wounds, Self-Inflicted or Otherwise?" *British Journal of Political Science* 33:535–56.

Giles, Micheal W., Virginia A. Hettinger, and Todd Peppers. 2001. "Picking Federal Judges: A Note on Policy and Partisan Selection Agendas." *Political Research Quarterly* 54:623–41.

Gillman, Howard. 1997. "Placing Judicial Motives in Context: A Response to Lee Epstein and Jack Knight." *Law and Courts* 7 (Spring): 10–13.

———. 1999. "The Court as an Idea, Not a Building (or a Game): Interpretive Institutionalism and the Analysis of Supreme Court Decision-Making." In *Supreme Court Decision-Making: New Institutionalist Approaches*, ed. Cornell W. Clayton and Howard Gillman, 65–87. Chicago: University of Chicago Press.

———. 2001a. *The Votes That Counted: How the Court Decided the 2000 Presidential Election*. Chicago: University of Chicago Press.

———. 2001b. "What's Law Got to Do With It? Judicial Behavioralists Test the 'Legal Model' of Judicial Decision Making." *Law & Social Inquiry* 26:465–504.

———. 2004. "Elements of a New 'Regime Politics' Approach to the Study of Judicial Politics." Paper presented at the annual meeting of the American Political Science Association, Chicago, September 2–5.

Ginsburg, Ruth Bader. 1985. "Some Thoughts on Autonomy and Equality in Relation to *Roe v. Wade*." *North Carolina Law Review* 63:375–86.

Glaberson, William. 2000. "Fierce Campaigns Signal a New Era for State Courts." *New York Times*, June 5, A1, A22.

Glasgow, Garrett. 2001a. "Mixed Logit Models for Multiparty Elections." *Political Analysis* 9:116–36.

———. 2001b. "Mixed Logit Models in Political Science." Paper presented at the annual Political Methodology Summer Conference, Atlanta, Ga., July 19–21.

Glendon, Mary Ann. 1994. *A Nation Under Lawyers: How the Crisis in the Legal Profession Is Transforming American Society*. New York: Farrar, Straus and Giroux.

Glennon, Robert Jerome. 1985. *The Iconoclast as Reformer: Jerome Frank's Impact on American Law*. Ithaca, N.Y.: Cornell University Press.

Goffman, Erving. 1959. *The Presentation of Self in Everyday Life*. New York: Doubleday.

Goldberg, Carey. 1999. "Judge W. Arthur Garrity Jr. is Dead at 79." *New York Times*, September 18, A15.

Goldberg, Deborah. 2003. "Public Funding of Judicial Elections: The Roles of Judges and the Rules of Campaign Finance." *Ohio State University Law Journal* 64:95–125.

Goldberg, Deborah, Craig Holman, and Samantha Sanchez. 2002. *The New Politics of Judicial Elections*. Washington, D.C.: Justice at Stake Campaign.

Goldiner, Dave. 2004. "Judge 'Something' Else! Harrison-Case Ruling Diagnoses Doc in Verse." *New York Daily News*, November 25, 3.

Goldman, Sheldon. 1975. "Voting Behavior on the U.S. Courts of Appeals Revisited." *American Political Science Review* 69:491–506.

———. 1997. *Picking Federal Judges: Lower Court Selection From Roosevelt Through Reagan*. New Haven, Conn.: Yale University Press.

Goldman, Sheldon, and Austin Sarat, eds. 1978. *American Court Systems: Readings in Judicial Process and Behavior*. San Francisco: W. H. Freeman.

Goldman, Sheldon, Elliot Slotnick, Gerard Gryski, and Sara Schiavoni. 2005. "W. Bush's Judiciary: The First Term Record." *Judicature* 88: 244–75.

Goldstein, Robert Justin. 1996. *Burning the Flag: The Great 1989–1990 American Flag Desecration Controversy*. Kent, Ohio: Kent State University Press.

Goodsell, Charles T. 1977. "Bureaucratic Manipulation of Physical Symbols: An Empirical Study." *American Journal of Political Science* 21:79–91.

Goodwin, Doris Kearns. 1991. *Lyndon Johnson and the American Dream*. New York: St. Martin's.

Gordon, Sanford C., and Gregory A. Huber. 2005. "Incumbent Incentives and the Informational Role of Challengers." Paper presented at the annual meeting of the Midwest Political Science Association, Chicago, April 7–10.

Goulden, Joseph C. 1974. *The Benchwarmers: The Private World of the Powerful Federal Judges*. New York: Weybright and Talley.

Graber, Doris A. 2002. *Mass Media and American Politics*. 6th ed. Washington, D.C.: CQ Press.

Graber, Mark A. 1998. "Establishing Judicial Review? *Schooner Peggy* and the Early Marshall Court." *Political Research Quarterly* 51:221–39.

———. 2004. "Legal, Strategic, or Legal Strategy: Deciding to Decide During the Civil War and Reconstruction." Typescript.

Grafton, Samuel. 1950. "Lonesomest Man in Town." *Collier's*, April 29, 20–21, 49–50.

Greeley, Andrew M., and Paul B. Sheatsley. 1971. "Attitudes Toward Racial Integration." *Scientific American* 225:13–19.

Green, Donald P., Bradley Palmquist, and Eric Schickler. 2002. *Partisan Hearts and Minds: Political Parties and the Social Identities of Voters*. New Haven, Conn.: Yale University Press.

Green, Donald P., and Ian Shapiro. 1995. "Reflections on Our Critics." *Critical Review* 9:235–76.

Greenberg, Jack. 1994. *Crusaders in the Courts*. New York: Basic Books.

Greenhouse, Linda. 1994. "Justice Harry Blackmun's Journey: From Moderate to a Liberal." *New York Times*, April 7, A1, A24.

———. 1995. "Warren E. Burger Is Dead at 87." *New York Times*, June 26, A1, C10, C11.

———. 1996. "Telling the Court's Story: Justice and Journalism at the Supreme Court." *Yale Law Journal* 105:1537–61.

———. 1999. "Justice Blackmun, Author of Abortion Right, Dies." *New York Times*, March 5, A1, A18, A19.

Greenhouse, Linda. 2004a. "Documents Reveal the Evolution of a Justice." *New York Times*, March 4, A1, A16, A17.

———. 2004b. "Friends for Decades, But Years on Court Left Them Strangers." *New York Times*, March 5, A1, A16.

———. 2005. *Becoming Justice Blackmun: Harry Blackmun's Supreme Court Journey.* New York: Times Books.

Greenwald, Anthony G., and Steven J. Breckler. 1985. "To Whom is the Self Presented?" In *The Self and Social Life*, ed. Barry R. Schlenker, 126–45. New York: McGraw-Hill.

Grey, David L. 1968. *The Supreme Court and the News Media.* Evanston, Ill.: Northwestern University Press.

Groner, Jonathan. 2002a. "Judge Nominees Told to Speak Very Softly." *Legal Times*, April 22, 8.

———. 2002b. "Estrada: Just One Vote Away?" *Legal Times*, September 30, 1.

Grosskopf, Anke, and Jeffrey J. Mondak. 1998. "Do Attitudes Toward Specific Supreme Court Decisions Matter? The Impact of *Webster* and *Texas v. Johnson* on Public Confidence in the Supreme Court." *Political Research Quarterly* 51:633–54.

Grossman, Joel B. 1965. *Lawyers and Judges: The ABA and the Politics of Judicial Selection.* New York: John Wiley and Sons.

Gulati, Mitu, and C.M.A. McCauliff. 1998. "On Not Making Law." *Law & Contemporary Problems* 61 (Summer): 157–227.

Gulati, Mitu, and Veronica Sanchez. 2002. "Giants in a World of Pygmies? Testing the Superstar Hypothesis with Judicial Opinions in Casebooks." *Iowa Law Review* 87:1142–212.

Gunther, Gerald. 1994. *Learned Hand: The Man and the Judge.* New York: Alfred A. Knopf.

Guttieri, Karen, Michael D. Wallace, and Peter Suedfeld. 1995. "The Integrative Complexity of American Decision Makers in the Cuban Missile Crisis." *Journal of Conflict Resolution* 39:595–621.

Haire, Susan Brodie. 2001. "Rating the Ratings of the American Bar Association Standing Committee on Federal Judiciary." *Justice System Journal* 22:1–17.

Halcom, Chad. 2003. "Eminem's Opponent is Dissed; Judge Says Lawsuit Dismissed." *Macomb Daily*, October 18.

Hall, Melinda Gann. 1987. "Constituent Influence in State Supreme Courts: Conceptual Notes and a Case Study." *Journal of Politics* 49:1117–24.

———. 1992. "Electoral Politics and Strategic Voting in State Supreme Courts." *Journal of Politics* 54:427–46.

———. 1995. "Justices as Representatives: Elections and Judicial Politics in the American States." *American Politics Quarterly* 23:485–503.

———. 2001a. "State Supreme Courts in American Democracy: Probing the Myths of Judicial Reform." *American Political Science Review* 95:315–30.

———. 2001b. "Voluntary Retirements from State Supreme Courts: Assessing Democratic Pressures to Relinquish the Bench." *Journal of Politics* 63:1112–40.

Hall, Melinda Gann, and Paul Brace. 1992. "Toward an Integrated Model of Judicial Voting Behavior." *American Politics Quarterly* 20:147–68.

Hall, Richard G., Phillip E. Varca, and Terri D. Fisher. 1986. "The Effect of Reference Groups, Opinion Polls, and Attitude Polarization on Attitude Formation and Change." *Political Psychology* 7:309–21.

Hammond, Thomas H., Chris W. Bonneau, and Reginald S. Sheehan. 2005. *Strategic Behavior and Policy Choice on the U.S. Supreme Court*. Stanford, Calif.: Stanford University Press.

Hannah, Susan B. 1978. "Competition in Michigan's Judicial Elections: Democratic Ideals vs. Judicial Realities." *Wayne Law Review* 24:1267–1306.

Hansford, Thomas G., and David F. Damore. 2000. "Congressional Preferences, Perceptions of Threat, and Supreme Court Decision Making." *American Politics Quarterly* 28:490–510.

Hanssen, F. Andrew. 1999. "The Effect of Judicial Institutions on Uncertainty and the Rate of Litigation: The Election versus Appointment of State Judges." *Journal of Legal Studies* 28:205–32.

Harsanyi, John C. 1969. "Rational-Choice Models of Political Behavior vs. Functionalist and Conformist Theories." *World Politics* 21:513–38.

Harvard Law Review. 1983. "Note: The Changing Social Vision of Justice Blackmun." 96:717–36.

Hausegger, Lori, and Lawrence Baum. 1998. "Behind the Scenes: The Supreme Court and Congress in Statutory Interpretation." In *Great Theatre: The American Congress in the 1990s*, ed. Herbert F. Weisberg and Samuel C. Patterson, 224–47. New York: Cambridge University Press.

———. 1999. "Inviting Congressional Action: A Study of Supreme Court Motivations in Statutory Interpretation." *American Journal of Political Science* 43:162–85.

Heinz, John P., Edward O. Laumann, Robert L. Nelson, and Ethan Michelson. 1998. "The Changing Character of Lawyers' Work: Chicago in 1975 and 1995." *Law & Society Review* 32:751–75.

Heinz, John P., Robert L. Nelson, Rebecca L. Sandefur, and Edward O. Laumann. 2005. *Urban Lawyers: The New Social Structure of the Bar*. Chicago: University of Chicago Press.

Helland, Eric, and Alexander Tabarrok. 2002. "The Effect of Electoral Institutions on Tort Awards." *American Law and Economics Review* 4:341–70.

Hellman, Arthur D. 1990. *Restructuring Justice: The Innovations of the Ninth Circuit and the Future of the Federal Courts*. Ithaca, N.Y.: Cornell University Press.

———. 1996. "The Shrunken Docket of the Rehnquist Court." *The Supreme Court Review* 1996:403–38.

Helmke, Gretchen. 2005. *Courts Under Constraints: Judges, Generals, and Presidents in Argentina*. New York: Cambridge University Press.

Herald, Marybeth. 1998. "Reversed, Vacated and Split: The Supreme Court, the Ninth Circuit, and Congress." *Oregon Law Review* 77:405–96.

Hermann, Margaret G. 1986. "Ingredients of Leadership." In *Political Psychology*, ed. Margaret G. Hermann, 167–92. San Francisco: Jossey-Bass.

Hess, Stephen. 1981. *The Washington Reporters*. Washington, D.C.: Brookings Institution.

Hetherington, Marc J. 2001. "Resurgent Mass Partisanship: The Role of Elite Polarization." *American Political Science Review* 95:619–31.

Hettinger, Virginia A., Stefanie A. Lindquist, and Wendy L. Martinek. 2004. "Comparing Attitudinal and Strategic Accounts of Dissenting Behavior on the U.S. Courts of Appeals." *American Journal of Political Science* 48:123–37.

Hettinger, Virginia A., and Christopher Zorn. 2005. "Explaining the Incidence and Timing of Congressional Responses to the U.S. Supreme Court." *Legislative Studies Quarterly* 30:5–28.

Hewitt, John P. 1998. *The Myth of Self-Esteem: Finding Happiness and Solving Problems in America.* New York: St. Martin's Press.

Heymann, Philip B., and Douglas E. Barzelay. 1973. "The Forest and the Trees: *Roe v. Wade* and Its Critics." *Boston University Law Review* 53:765–84.

Higgins, Richard S., and Paul H. Rubin. 1980. "Judicial Discretion." *Journal of Legal Studies* 9:129–38.

Hines, Crystal Nix. 2001. "Young Liberal Law Group is Expanding." *New York Times*, June 1, A17.

Hirsch, H. N. 1981. *The Enigma of Felix Frankfurter.* New York: Basic Books.

Hoekstra, Valerie J. 2000. "The Supreme Court and Local Public Opinion." *American Political Science Review* 94:89–100.

———. 2003. *Public Reactions to Supreme Court Decisions.* New York: Cambridge University Press.

Holding, Reynolds. 1992. "Blackmun Says Court Direction Disappointing." *San Francisco Chronicle*, June 10, A12.

Howard, J. Woodford. 1965. "Justice Murphy: The Freshman Years." *Vanderbilt Law Review* 18:473–505.

———. 1968a. *Mr. Justice Murphy: A Political Biography.* Princeton, N.J.: Princeton University Press.

———. 1968b. "On the Fluidity of Judicial Choice." *American Political Science Review* 62:43–56.

———. 1981. *Courts of Appeals in the Federal Judicial System.* Princeton, N.J.: Princeton University Press.

Howard, Robert M., and Jeffrey A. Segal. 2002. "An Original Look at Originalism." *Law & Society Review* 36:113–38.

Howe, Mark De Wolfe, ed. 1953. *Holmes-Laski Letters: The Correspondence of Mr. Justice Holmes and Harold J. Laski, 1916–1935.* Cambridge, Mass.: Harvard University Press.

Hoyle, Rick H., Michael H. Kernis, Mark R. Leary, and Mark W. Baldwin. 1999. *Selfhood: Identity, Esteem, Regulation.* Boulder, Colo.: Westview Press.

Huber, Gregory A., and Sanford C. Gordon. 2004. "Accountability and Coercion: Is Justice Blind When it Runs for Office?" *American Journal of Political Science* 48:247–63.

Huckfeldt, Robert, Paul Allen Beck, Russell J. Dalton, and Jeffrey Levine. 1995. "Political Environments, Cohesive Social Groups, and the Communication of Public Opinion." *American Journal of Political Science* 39:1025–54.

Hughes, Charles Evans. 1928. *The Supreme Court of the United States: Its Foundation, Methods and Achievements, an Interpretation.* New York: Columbia University Press.

Hughes, Jim. 2003. "5–2 Ruling on Redistricting Could Ripple Beyond Colorado, Expert Says." *Denver Post*, December 2, A1.

Human Events. 1996. "High Court Performs Arrogant Act of Judicial Tyranny." May 31–June 7, 1, 7.

Hutchinson, Dennis J. 1998. *The Man Who Once Was Whizzer White: A Portrait of Justice Byron R. White*. New York: Free Press.

———. 1999. "Remembering Lewis F. Powell." *Green Bag* 2:163–67.

Jackman, Mary R. 1978. "General and Applied Tolerance: Does Education Increase Commitment to Racial Integration?" *American Journal of Political Science* 22:302–24.

———. 1981. "Education and Policy Commitment to Racial Integration." *American Journal of Political Science* 25:256–69.

Jackson, Robert A., and Thomas M. Carsey. 2002. "Group Effects on Party Identification and Party Coalitions Across the United States." *American Politics Research* 30:66–92.

Jackson, Robert H. 2003. *That Man: An Insider's Portrait of Franklin D. Roosevelt*. Ed. John Q. Barrett. New York: Oxford University Press.

Jacobson, Gary C. 2004. "Partisan and Ideological Polarization in the California Electorate." *State Politics & Policy Quarterly* 4:113–39.

Janofsky, Michael. 2004. "Scalia Refusing to Take Himself Off Cheney Case." *New York Times*, March 19, A1, A15.

Jeffries, John C., Jr. 1994. *Justice Lewis F. Powell, Jr.: A Biography*. New York: Charles Scribner's Sons.

Jenkins, John A. 1983. "A Candid Talk with Justice Blackmun." *New York Times Magazine*, February 20, 20–29, 57–66.

Jennings, M. Kent, and Richard G. Niemi. 1981. *Generations and Politics: A Panel Study of Young Adults and Their Parents*. Princeton, N.J.: Princeton University Press.

Jewell, Malcolm E. 1982. *Representation in State Legislatures*. Lexington: University Press of Kentucky.

Johnson, Charles A. 1977. "The Shapley-Shubik Power Index and the Supreme Court: A Few Empirical Notes." *Jurimetrics Journal* 18:40–45.

———. 1987. "Law, Politics, and Judicial Decision Making: Lower Federal Court Uses of Supreme Court Decisions." *Law & Society Review* 21:325–40.

Johnson, Richard M. 1967. *The Dynamics of Compliance*. Evanston, Ill.: Northwestern University Press.

Johnston, John D., Jr., and Charles Knapp. 1971. "Sex Discrimination by Law: A Study in Judicial Perspective." *NYU Law Review* 46:675–747.

Jones, Andrea. 2003. "Justice to UGA Grads: Be Heroes." *Atlanta Journal-Constitution*, May 18, 1F.

Jones, Edward E. 1964. *Ingratiation: A Social Psychological Analysis*. New York: Appleton-Century-Crofts.

———. 1990. *Interpersonal Perception*. New York: W. H. Freeman.

Jones, Edward E., and Thane S. Pittman. 1982. "Toward a General Theory of Strategic Self-Presentation." In *Psychological Perspectives on the Self*, vol. 1, ed. Jerry Suls, 231–62. Hillsdale, N.J.: Lawrence Erlbaum Associates.

Jordan, Adalberto. 1987. "Imagery, Humor, and the Judicial Opinion." *University of Miami Law Review* 41:693–727.

Judicature. 1996. "What is Judicial Independence? Views from the Public, the Press, the Profession, and the Politicians." 80:73–83.

Judicial Council of California. 2005. "William W. Bedsworth, Associate Justice," http:/www.courtsinfo.ca.gov/courts/courts of appeal/4thDistrictDiv3/justices/bedsworth.htm.

Kahneman, Daniel, and Amos Tversky, eds. 2000. *Choices, Values, and Frames.* New York: Cambridge University Press.

Kalman, Laura. 1990. *Abe Fortas: A Biography.* New Haven, Conn.: Yale University Press.

Kaplan, Cynthia S., and Henry E. Brady. 2004. "Conceptualizing and Measuring Ethnic Identity." Paper presented at the Harvard Identity Conference, Cambridge, Mass., December 9–11.

Kaplan, Sheila. 1987. "Justice for Sale." *Common Cause*, May–June, 29–32.

Kaplan, Sheila, and Zoe Davidson. 1998. "The Buying of the Bench." *The Nation*, January 26, 11–17.

Kasindorf, Martin. 2003. "The Court Conservatives Hate." *USA Today*, February 7, 3A.

Kaye, Judith S. 1986. "My 'Freshman Years' on the Court of Appeals." *Judicature* 70:166–67.

Keeton, Robert E. 1969. *Venturing to Do Justice: Reforming Private Law.* Cambridge, Mass.: Harvard University Press.

Kelley, Stanley, Jr. 1995. "Rational Choice: Its Promises and Limitations." *Critical Review* 9:95–106.

Kemerer, Frank R. 1991. *William Wayne Justice: A Judicial Biography.* Austin: University of Texas Press.

Kendall, Douglas T., and Jason C. Rylander. 2004. "Tainted Justice: How Private Judicial Trips Undermine Public Confidence in the Judiciary." *Georgetown Journal of Legal Ethics* 18:65–134.

Kennedy, Robert F., Jr. 1978. *Judge Frank M. Johnson, Jr.: A Biography.* New York: Putnam.

Kernell, Samuel. 1997. *Going Public: New Strategies of Presidential Leadership.* 3d ed. Washington, D.C.: CQ Press.

King, Gary, Michael Tomz, and Jason Wittenberg. 2000. "Making the Most of Statistical Analyses: Improving Interpretation and Presentation." *American Journal of Political Science* 44:347–61.

Kirkpatrick, David D., and Linda Greenhouse. 2003. "Justice Thomas Reportedly Has $1.5 Million Book Deal." *New York Times*, January 10, A19.

Klain, Ronald. 2002. "Farewell, Camelot." *National Law Journal*, April 22, A21.

Klarman, Michael J. 2004. *From Jim Crow to Civil Rights: The Supreme Court and the Struggle for Racial Equality.* New York: Oxford University Press.

Klein, David E. 2002. *Making Law in the United States Courts of Appeals.* New York: Cambridge University Press.

Klein, David E., and Robert J. Hume. 2003. "Fear of Reversal as an Explanation of Lower Court Compliance." *Law & Society Review* 37:579–606.

Klein, David E., and Darby Morrisroe. 1999. "The Prestige and Influence of Individual Judges on the U.S. Courts of Appeals." *Journal of Legal Studies* 28:371–91.

Klein, Ethel. 1984. *Gender Politics: From Consciousness to Mass Politics*. Cambridge, Mass.: Harvard University Press.

Kleinfeld, Andrew J. 1993–94. "Politicization: From the Law Schools to the Courts." *Academic Questions* 6 (Winter): 9–19.

Klerman, Daniel. 1999. "Nonpromotion and Judicial Independence." *Southern California Law Review* 72:455–63.

Kobylka, Joseph F. 1985. "The Court, Justice Blackmun, and Federalism: A Subtle Movement With Potentially Great Ramifications." *Creighton Law Review* 19:9–49.

———. 1992. "The Judicial Odyssey of Harry Blackmun: The Dynamics of Individual-Level Change on the U.S. Supreme Court." Paper presented at the conference of the Midwest Political Science Association, Chicago, April 9–11.

Koch, Jeffrey W. 1994. "Group Identification in Political Context." *Political Psychology* 15:687–98.

Koh, Harold Hongju. 1994. "A Tribute to Justice Harry A. Blackmun." *Harvard Law Review* 108:20–22.

Koppelman, Andrew. 1990. "Forced Labor: A Thirteenth Amendment Defense of Abortion." *Northwestern University Law Review* 54:480–535.

Kornhauser, Lewis A. 1995. "Adjudication by a Resource-Constrained Team: Hierarchy and Precedent in a Judicial System." *Southern California Law Review* 68:1605–29.

Kornhauser, Lewis A., and Lawrence G. Sager. 1993. "The One and the Many: Adjudication in Collegial Courts." *California Law Review* 81:1–59.

Kozinski, Alex. 1991. "My Pizza with Nino." *Cardozo Law Review* 12:1583–91.

———. 1993a. "Sanhedrin II." *New Republic*, September 13, 16–18.

———. 1993b. "What I Ate for Breakfast and Other Mysteries of Judicial Decision Making." *Loyola of Los Angeles Law Review* 26:993–99.

———. 1994. "Mickey & Me." *University of Miami Entertainment & Sports Law Review* 11:465–70.

———. 1995. "Justice Sutherland, One of Us." *National Review*, February 20, 64–66.

———. 1997a. "In Praise of Moot Court—Not!" *Columbia Law Review* 97:178–97.

———. 1997b. "Teetering on the High Wire." *Colorado Law Review* 68:1217–29.

———. 1997c. "Tinkering with Death." *New Yorker*, February 10, 48–53.

———. 2001. "How I Narrowly Escaped Insanity." *UCLA Law Review* 48:1293–1303.

———. 2004. "The *Real* Issues of Judicial Ethics." *Hofstra Law Review* 32:1095–1106.

Kozinski, Alex, and Sean Gallagher. 1995. "Death: The Ultimate Run-On Sentence." *Case Western Law Review* 46:1–32.

Kozlowski, Mark. 2003. *The Myth of the Imperial Judiciary: Why the Right is Wrong About the Courts*. New York: New York University Press.

Kreps, David M. 1990. *Game Theory and Economic Modelling*. Oxford: Clarendon Press.

Kritzer, Herbert M., and Mark J. Richards. 2003. "Jurisprudential Regimes and Supreme Court Decisionmaking: The *Lemon* Regime and Establishment Clause Cases." *Law & Society Review* 37:827–40.

Kuklinski, James H., ed. 2002. *Thinking About Political Psychology*. New York: Cambridge University Press.

Kuklinski, James H., and John E. Stanga. 1979. "Political Participation and Government Responsiveness: The Behavior of California Superior Courts." *American Political Science Review* 73:1090–99.

Kuran, Timur. 1995. *Private Truths, Public Lies: The Social Consequences of Preference Falsification*. Cambridge, Mass.: Harvard University Press.

Lacovara, Philip Allen. 2003. "Off to Work They Go." *Legal Times*, December 29, 36–38.

Landay, Jerry M. 2000. "The Conservative Cabal That's Transforming American Law." *Washington Monthly* 32 (March): 19–23.

Landes, Elisabeth M., and Richard A. Posner. 1978. "The Economics of the Baby Shortage." *Journal of Legal Studies* 7:323–48.

Landes, William M., Lawrence Lessig, and Michael E. Solimine. 1998. "Judicial Influence: A Citation Analysis of Federal Courts of Appeals Judges." *Journal of Legal Studies* 27:271–332.

Landes, William M., and Richard A. Posner. 1975. "The Independent Judiciary in an Interest-Group Perspective." *Journal of Law and Economics* 18:875–901.

Lane, Charles. 2002. "Justice Kennedy's Future Role Pondered." *Washington Post*, June 17, A1.

———. 2003. "High Court to Consider Pledge in Schools." *Washington Post*, October 15, A1, A9.

———. 2004a. "How Justices Handle a Political Hot Potato: Blackmun Offers Rare View of Abortion Case." *Washington Post*, March 5, A1, A13.

———. 2004b. "Courting O'Connor." *Washington Post Magazine*, July 4, 10–15, 22–27.

———. 2005. "Roberts Listed in Federalist Society '97–98 Directory." *Washington Post*, July 25, A1.

Langer, Laura. 2002. *Judicial Review in State Supreme Courts: A Comparative Study*. Albany: State University of New York Press.

Lash, Joseph P., ed. 1975. *From the Diaries of Felix Frankfurter*. New York: W. W. Norton.

Lasswell, Harold Dwight. 1948. *Power and Personality*. New York: Norton.

Lau, Richard R. 1989. "Individual and Contextual Influences on Group Identification." *Social Psychology Quarterly* 52:220–31.

Lave, Charles A., and James G. March. 1975. *An Introduction to Models in the Social Sciences*. New York: Harper and Row.

Law, Sylvia A. 1984. "Rethinking Sex and the Constitution." *University of Pennsylvania Law Review* 132:955–1040.

Layman, Geoffrey C., and Thomas M. Carsey. 2002. "Party Polarization and 'Conflict Extension' in the American Electorate." *American Journal of Political Science* 46:786–802.

Leary, Mark R. 1996. *Self-Presentation: Impression Management and Interpersonal Behavior.* Boulder, Colo.: Westview Press.

———., ed. 2001. *Interpersonal Rejection.* New York: Oxford University Press.

Leary, Mark R., and Deborah Downs. 1995. "Interpersonal Functions of the Self-Esteem Motive: The Self-Esteem System as a Sociometer." In *Efficacy, Agency, and Self-Esteem,* ed. Michael H. Kernis, 123–44. New York: Plenum Press.

Lee, Emery G., III. 2005. "Policy and Institutional Goals on the United States Courts of Appeals." Paper presented at the annual meeting of the Midwest Political Science Association, April 7–10, Chicago.

Legal Times. 1992. "Attacking Activism, Judge Names Names." June 22, 14–17.

———. 1994. "Thomas Critiques the 'Rights Revolution.' " May 23, 23–25.

———. 1995. "Justice Thomas: On Heroes and Victims." October 16, 10–13.

———. 2000. "Scalia: Article Off Base." October 2, 85.

———. 2003. "Awards." June 2, 6.

Leiby, Richard. 2005. "The Reliable Source." *Washington Post,* April 27, C3.

Leonnig, Carol D. 2004. "Judges Are Urged to Quite Board Positions." *Washington Post,* March 23, A2.

———. 2005a. "Judges to Leave Environmental Group's Board." *Washington Post,* May 7, A9.

———. 2005b. "Ethics Complaint Against Judge is Dismissed." *Washington Post,* June 22, A7.

Levey, Collin. 2004. "One Court-Decided Election is More Than Enough." *Seattle Times,* October 29, B7.

Levin, Mark R. 2005. *Men in Black: How the Supreme Court is Destroying America.* Washington, D.C.: Regnery Publishing.

Levin, Martin A. 1972. "Urban Politics and Judicial Behavior." *Journal of Legal Studies* 1:193–221.

———. 1977. *Urban Politics and the Criminal Courts.* Chicago: University of Chicago Press.

Levine, John M., and Richard L. Moreland. 1991. "Culture and Socialization in Work Groups." In *Perspectives on Socially Shared Cognition,* ed. Lauren B. Resnick, John M. Levine, and Stephanie D. Teasley, 257–79. Washington, D.C.: American Psychological Association.

Levine, Samantha. 2005. "Legislators Diverge on Judicial Issues." *Houston Chronicle,* April 6, A10.

Lewis, Anthony. 1981. "A Public Right to Know About Public Institutions: The First Amendment as Sword." In *The Supreme Court Review 1980,* ed. Philip B. Kurland and Gerhard Casper, 1–25. Chicago: University of Chicago Press.

Lewis, Neil A. 1986. "Blackmun on Search for the Center." *New York Times,* March 8, A7.

———. 1991. "Conservative 'Outsiders' Now at Hub of Power." *New York Times,* March 29, B16.

———. 1993. "2 Years After His Bruising Hearing, Justice Thomas Still Shows the Hurt." *New York Times,* November 27, 6.

———. 1995. "A Supreme Court Justice with a Less-than-Shining Image Begins to Step Out in Public." *New York Times,* January 13, B8.

Lewis, Neil A. 2001a. "A Conservative Legal Group Thrives in Bush's Washington." *New York Times*, April 18, A1, A16.

———. 2001b. "Justice Thomas Raises Issue of Cultural Intimidation." *New York Times*, February 14, A28.

Linde, Hans A. 1980. "First Things First: Rediscovering the States' Bills of Rights." *University of Baltimore Law Review* 9:379–96.

Linder, Douglas O. 1985. "How Judges Judge: A Study of Disagreement on the United States Court of Appeals for the Eighth Circuit." *Arkansas Law Review* 38:479–560.

Link, Michael W. 1995. "Tracking Public Mood in the Supreme Court: Cross-Time Analysis of Criminal Procedure and Civil Rights Cases." *Political Research Quarterly* 48:61–78.

Liptak, Adam. 2003. "Order Lacking on a Court: U.S. Appellate Judges in Cincinnati Spar in Public." *New York Times*, August 12, A10.

Liptak, Adam, and Ralph Blumenthal. 2004. "Death Sentences in Texas Cases Try Supreme Court's Patience." *New York Times*, December 5, 1, 40.

Lithwick, Dahlia. 2002. "Nino's Chain Gang." *Slate* (slate.msn.com), April 17.

———. 2003a. "Fun with *Bush v. Gore*." *Slate* (slate.msn.com), September 17.

———. 2003b. "Scaliapalooza." *Slate* (slate.msn.com), October 30.

Little, Laura E. 1995. "Loyalty, Gratitude, and the Federal Judiciary." *American University Law Review* 44:699–755.

Lloyd, Randall D. 1995. "Separating Partisanship from Party in Judicial Research: Reapportionment in the U.S. District Courts." *American Political Science Review* 89:413–20.

Loewenstein, George, and Jon Elster, eds. 1992. *Choice Over Time*. New York: Russell Sage Foundation.

Loewenstein, George, and Richard H. Thaler. 1989. "Anomalies: Intertemporal Choice." *Journal of Economic Perspectives* 3:181–93.

LoPucki, Lynn M. 2005. *Courting Failure: How Competition for Big Cases is Corrupting the Bankruptcy Courts*. Ann Arbor: University of Michigan Press.

Los Angeles Times. 2004. "GOP Lawmakers Ask Ginsburg to Withdraw from Abortion Cases." March 19, A18.

Lovell, Michael C. 1986. "Tests of the Rational Expectations Hypothesis." *American Economic Review* 76:110–24.

Lukas, J. Anthony. 1976. *Nightmare: The Underside of the Nixon Years*. New York: Viking Press.

Luttbeg, Norman R. 1981. "Introduction." In *Public Opinion and Public Policy: Models of Political Linkage*, 3d ed., ed. Norman R. Luttbeg, 1–10. Itasca, Ill.: F. E. Peacock.

Macey, Jonathan R. 1994. "Judicial Preferences, Public Choice, and the Rules of Procedure." *Journal of Legal Studies* 23:627–46.

MacFarquhar, Larissa. 2001. "The Bench Burner." *New Yorker*, December 10, 78–89.

Madigan, Charles M. 2002. "Name Supremes? Not Diana Ross." *Chicago Tribune*, April 28, sec. 2, 5.

Magagnini, Stephen. 1996. "Nevada's Top Court Hogtied by Feud." *Sacramento Bee*, March 17, A1.

Mahler, Jonathan. 1998. "The Federalist Capers: Inside Ken Starr's Intellectual Auxiliary." *Lingua Franca*, September, 38–47.

Maltzman, Forrest, James F. Spriggs II, and Paul J. Wahlbeck. 2000. *Crafting Law on the Supreme Court: The Collegial Game*. New York: Cambridge University Press.

Maltzman, Forrest, and Paul J. Wahlbeck. 1996. "Strategic Policy Considerations and Voting Fluidity on the Burger Court." *American Political Science Review* 90:581–92.

Mann, Thomas E. 1978. *Unsafe at Any Margin: Interpreting Congressional Elections*. Washington, D.C.: American Enterprise Institute Press.

Mansbridge, Jane J., ed. 1990. *Beyond Self-Interest*. Chicago: University of Chicago Press.

Marcus, Ruth. 1998. "Issues Groups Fund Seminars for Judges." *Washington Post*, April 9, A1, A12.

———. 2005. "Booting the Bench." *Washington Post*, April 11, A19.

Margolick, David. 1992. "Sustained by Dictionaries, a Judge Rules That no Word, or Word Play, is Inadmissible." *New York Times*, March 27, B16.

———. 2003. "Bush's Court Advantage." *Vanity Fair*, December, 144–62.

Markus, Hazel, and Daphna Oyserman. 1989. "Gender and Thought: The Role of the Self-Concept." In *Gender and Thought: Psychological Perspectives*, ed. Mary Crawford and Margaret Gentry, 100–27. New York: Springer-Verlag.

Marschak, Jacob, and Roy Radner. 1972. *Economic Theory of Teams*. New Haven, Conn.: Yale University Press.

Marshall, Thomas R. 1989. *Public Opinion and the Supreme Court*. Boston: Unwin Hyman.

Marshall, Thomas R., and Joseph Ignagni. 1994. "Supreme Court and Public Support for Rights Claims." *Judicature* 78:146–51.

Martin, Andrew D. 1998. "Strategic Decision Making and the Separation of Powers." Ph.D. dissertation, Washington University.

———. 2001. "Statutory Battles and Constitutional Wars: Congress and the Supreme Court." Paper presented at the Conference on Institutional Games and the U.S. Supreme Court, College Station, Texas, November 1–3.

Martin, Andrew D., and Kevin M. Quinn. 2002. "Dynamic Ideal Point Estimation via Markov Chain Monte Carlo for the U.S. Supreme Court, 1953–1999." *Political Analysis* 10:134–53.

Marvell, Thomas B. 1978. *Appellate Courts and Lawyers: Information Gathering in the Adversary System*. Westport, Conn.: Greenwood Press.

Mason, Alpheus Thomas. 1956. *Harlan Fiske Stone: Pillar of the Law*. New York: Viking Press.

Mather, Lynn, and Barbara Yngvesson. 1980–81. "Language, Audience, and the Transformation of Disputes." *Law & Society Review* 15:775–821.

Mauro, Tony. 1992. "Justice Thomas Won't be Reading This." *Legal Times*, March 16, 10–11.

———. 1995. "High Court Highs and Lows." *Legal Times*, December 18–25, 20, 23.

———. 1998a. "Back Into the Spotlight." *Legal Times*, December 21–28, 18–20.

Mauro, Tony. 1998b. "A Journalist's Perspective." In *The Burger Court: Counter-Revolution or Confirmation?* ed. Bernard Schwartz, 216–21. New York: Oxford University Press.

———. 2002. "A Campus Tempest Over Thomas." *National Law Journal,* March 18, A14.

———. 2003. "Supreme Court Opening Up to World Opinion." *Legal Times,* July 7, 1, 8.

———. 2004. "At the High Court: The Chosen Few." *Legal Times,* July 12, 1, 10, 11.

Maveety, Nancy, ed. 2003. *The Pioneers of Judicial Behavior.* Ann Arbor: University of Michigan Press.

Mayer, Jane, and Jill Abramson. 1994. *Strange Justice: The Selling of Clarence Thomas.* Boston: Houghton Mifflin.

Mayer, Thomas. 1996. "The Dark Side of Economic Modeling." In *Foundations of Research in Economics: How Do Economists Do Economics?* ed. Steven G. Medema and Warren J. Samuels, 191–203. Cheltenham, U.K.: Edward Elgar.

Mayhew, David R. 1974. *Congress: The Electoral Connection.* New Haven, Conn.: Yale University Press.

McCall, Madhavi. 2001. "Campaign Contributions and Judicial Decisions: Can Justice be Bought?" *American Review of Politics* 22:349–74.

———. 2003. "The Politics of Judicial Elections: The Influence of Campaign Contributions on the Voting Patterns of Texas Supreme Court Justices, 1994–1997." *Politics & Policy* 31:314–43.

McCarthy, Rebecca. 2002. "Protest Set for Clarence Thomas Visit to UGA." *Atlanta Journal-Constitution,* December 20, 8D.

McCarty, Nolan, Keith T. Poole, and Howard Rosenthal. 1997. *Income Redistribution and the Realignment of American Politics.* Washington, D.C.: AEI Press.

McCloskey, Robert G., and Sanford Levinson. 2000. *The American Supreme Court.* 3d ed. Chicago: University of Chicago Press.

McElroy, Lisa Tucker. 1999. *Meet My Grandmother: She's a Supreme Court Justice.* Brookfield, Conn.: Millbrook Press.

McGarity, Thomas O. 1995. "On Making Judges Do the Right Thing." *Duke Law Journal* 44:1104–9.

McGinnis, John O., and Matthew Schwartz. 2003. "Conservatives Need Not Apply." *Wall Street Journal,* April 1, A14.

McGuire, Kevin T. 1993. *The Supreme Court Bar: Legal Elites in the Washington Community.* Charlottesville: University of Virginia Press.

———. 1995. "Repeat Players in the Supreme Court: The Role of Experienced Lawyers in Litigation Success." *Journal of Politics* 57:187–96.

———. 1998. "Explaining Executive Success in the U.S. Supreme Court." *Political Research Quarterly* 51:505–26.

McGuire, Kevin T., and James A. Stimson. 2004. "The Least Dangerous Branch Revisited: New Evidence on Supreme Court Responsiveness to Public Preferences." *Journal of Politics* 66:1018–35.

McIntosh, Wayne V., and Cynthia L. Cates. 1997. *Judicial Entrepreneurship: The Role of the Judge in the Marketplace of Ideas.* Westport, Conn.: Greenwood Press.

McKenzie, Mark Jonathan. 2004. "The Politics of Judicial Decision-Making and Redistricting: Do Federal Judges Revert to Partisanship When it Comes to Representation?" Paper presented at the annual meeting of the American Political Science Association, September 2–4, Chicago.

Medina, Harold R. 1954. *Judge Medina Speaks*. Albany, N.Y.: Matthew Bender.

———. 1959. *The Anatomy of Freedom*. New York: Henry Holt.

Meernik, James, and Joseph Ignagni. 1997. "Judicial Review and Coordinate Construction of the Constitution." *American Journal of Political Science* 41:447–67.

Meinke, Scott R. 2005. "Long-Term Change and Stability in House Voting Decisions: The Case of the Minimum Wage." *Legislative Studies Quarterly* 30: 103–26.

Melnick, R. Shep. 1994. *Between the Lines: Interpreting Welfare Rights*. Washington, D.C.: Brookings Institution.

Merida, Kevin, and Michael A. Fletcher. 2004a. "Enigmatic on the Bench, Influential in the Halls." *Washington Post*, October 10, A1, A18.

———. 2004b. "Thomas's Across-the-Aisle Aid Puzzles Even the Beneficiaries." *Washington Post*, October 10, A19.

Merrill, Thomas W. 1997. "Institutional Choice and Political Faith." *Law & Social Inquiry* 22:959–98.

———. 2003. "The Making of the Second Rehnquist Court: A Preliminary Analysis." *Saint Louis University Law Review* 47:569–658.

Merritt, Deborah Jones. 1998. "Research and Teaching on Law Faculties: An Empirical Exploration." *Chicago-Kent Law Review* 73:765–820.

Merritt, Deborah Jones, and James J. Brudney. 2001. "Stalking Secret Law: What Predicts Publication in the United States Courts of Appeals." *Vanderbilt Law Review* 54:71–121.

Merryman, John Henry. 1977. "Toward a Theory of Citations: An Empirical Study of the Citation Practice of the California Supreme Court in 1950, 1960, and 1970." *Southern California Law Review* 50:381–428.

Mezey, Susan Gluck. 2003. *Elusive Equality: Women's Rights, Public Policy, and the Law*. Boulder, Colo.: Lynne Rienner.

Miceli, Thomas J., and Metin M. Cosgel. 1994. "Reputation and Judicial Decision-Making." *Journal of Economic Behavior and Organization* 23:31–51.

Miller, Arthur Selwyn, ed. 1984. *On Courts and Democracy: Selected Nonjudicial Writings of J. Skelly Wright*. Westport, Conn.: Greenwood Press.

Miroff, Bruce. 1995. "The Presidency and the Public: Leadership as Spectacle." In *The Presidency and the Political System*, 4th ed., ed. Michael Nelson, 273–96. Washington, D.C.: CQ Press.

Mishler, William, and Reginald S. Sheehan. 1993. "The Supreme Court as a Countermajoritarian Institution? The Impact of Public Opinion on Supreme Court Decisions." *American Political Science Review* 87:87–101.

———. 1996. "Public Opinion, the Attitudinal Model, and Supreme Court Decision Making: A Micro-Analytic Perspective." *Journal of Politics* 58:169–200.

Mitchell, Jerry. 2003. "Bickering among Justices Revealed." *Jackson [Mississippi] Clarion-Ledger*, October 28.

Mock, Carol, and Herbert F. Weisberg. 1992. "Political Innumeracy: Encounters with Coincidence, Improbability, and Chance." *American Journal of Political Science* 36:1023–46.

Moe, Terry M. 1980. *The Organization of Interests: Incentives and the Internal Dynamics of Political Interest Groups.* Chicago: University of Chicago Press.

Mondak, Jeffrey J., and Shannon Ishiyama Smithey. 1997. "The Dynamics of Public Support for the Supreme Court." *Journal of Politics* 59:1114–42.

Monroe, Kristen Renwick. 1996. *The Heart of Altruism: Perceptions of a Common Humanity.* Princeton, N.J.: Princeton University Press.

———. 2002a. "A Paradigm for Political Psychology." In *Political Psychology,* ed. Kristen Renwick Monroe, 399–415. Mahwah, N.J.: Lawrence Erlbaum Associates.

———., ed. 2002b. *Political Psychology.* Mahwah, N.J.: Lawrence Erlbaum Associates.

Moore, Roy, with John Perry. 2005. *So Help Me God: The Ten Commandments, Judicial Tyranny, and the Battle for Religious Freedom.* Nashville, TN.: Broadman & Holman.

Morley, Jefferson. 1999. "Shoreline Path Breaks Law; Ruling Breaks Hearts." *Washington Post,* June 23, B1, B4.

Morning Edition. 2004. Transcript of broadcast, National Public Radio, March 5.

Morriss, Andrew P., Michael Heise, and Gregory C. Sisk. 2005. "Signaling and Precedent in Federal District Court Opinions." *Supreme Court Economic Review* 13:63–97.

Moyer, Thomas J. 2003. "Interpreting Ohio's Sunshine Laws: A Judicial Perspective." *New York University Annual Survey of American Law* 59:247–68.

Muir, William K., Jr. 1967. *Prayer in the Public Schools: Law and Attitude Change.* Chicago: University of Chicago Press.

Munford, Luther T. 2004. "The Parting of the Ways." *National Law Journal,* May 31, 26.

Murphy, Bruce Allen. 2003. *Wild Bill: The Legend and Life of William O. Douglas.* New York: Random House.

Murphy, Walter F. 1962. *Congress and the Court.* Chicago: University of Chicago Press.

———. 1964. *Elements of Judicial Strategy.* Chicago: University of Chicago Press.

Murphy, Walter F., and Joseph Tanenhaus. 1968. "Public Opinion and the United States Supreme Court: A Preliminary Mapping of Some Prerequisites for Court Legitimation of Regime Changes." *Law & Society Review* 2:357–84.

Musmanno, Michael A., ed. Wilmore Brown. 1966. *That's My Opinion.* Charlottesville, Va.: Michie.

Nakamura, Robert T. 1977–78. "Impressions of Ford and Reagan." *Political Science Quarterly* 92:647–54.

Nardulli, Peter F., James Eisenstein, and Roy B. Flemming. 1988. *The Tenor of Justice: Criminal Courts and the Guilty Plea Process.* Urbana: University of Illinois Press.

Nelson, William E. 2004. *In Pursuit of Right and Justice: Edward Weinfeld as Lawyer and Judge.* New York: New York University Press.

Neuendorf, Kimberly A. 2004. "Quantitative Content Analysis Options for the Measurement of Identity." Paper presented at the Harvard Identity Conference, Cambridge, Mass., December 9–11.

New York Times. 1999. "Justice Blackmun's Journey" (editorial). March 5, A20.

Newfield, Jack. 2002. "The Right's Judicial Juggernaut." *The Nation,* October 7, 11–15.

Newman, Roger K. 1997. *Hugo Black: A Biography.* New York: Fordham University Press.

Nicholson, Stephen P., and Robert M. Howard. 2003. "Framing Support for the Supreme Court in the Aftermath of *Bush v. Gore.*" *Journal of Politics* 65: 676–95.

Niemi, Richard G., Roman Hedges, and M. Kent Jennings. 1977. "The Similarity of Husbands' and Wives' Political Views." *American Politics Quarterly* 5:133–48.

Nightline. 1993a. Transcript of broadcast, ABC News, November 18 (#3259).

———. 1993b. Transcript of broadcast, ABC News, December 2 (#3269).

Nimoy, Leonard. 1977. *I Am Not Spock.* New York: Ballantine.

Nisbett, Richard, and Lee Ross. 1980. *Human Inference: Strategies and Shortcomings of Social Judgment.* Englewood Cliffs, N.J.: Prentice-Hall.

Noonan, John T., Jr. 2000. "Judges as Scholars: Are They? Should They Be?" *Judicature* 84:7–9, 47.

———. 2002. *Narrowing the Nation's Power: The Supreme Court Sides with the States.* Berkeley and Los Angeles: University of California Press.

Norpoth, Helmut, and Jeffrey A. Segal. 1994. "Popular Influence on Supreme Court Decisions—Comment." *American Political Science Review* 88:711–16.

O'Brien, David M. 1997. "Join-3 Votes, The Rule of Four, the *Cert.* Pool, and the Supreme Court's Shrinking Plenary Docket." *Journal of Law & Politics* 13:779–808.

———., ed. 2003. *Judges on Judging: Views From the Bench.* 2d ed. New York: Chatham House.

O'Connor, Sandra Day. 2003. *The Majesty of the Law: Reflections of a Supreme Court Justice.* New York: Random House.

O'Connor, Sandra Day, and H. Alan Day. 2002. *Lazy B: Growing Up on a Cattle Ranch in the American Southwest.* New York: Random House.

Owens, Timothy J., Sheldon Stryker, and Norman Goodman. 2001. *Extending Self-Esteem Theory and Research: Sociological and Psychological Currents.* New York: Cambridge University Press.

Pacelle, Richard L., Jr. 2003. *Between Law and Politics: The Solicitor General and the Structuring of Race, Gender, and Reproductive Rights Litigation.* College Station: Texas A & M University Press.

Page, Clarence. 1998. "In Washington, Days of Whine and Poses." *Chicago Tribune,* August 2, sec. 1, 17.

Parker, Glenn R. 1986. *Homeward Bound: Explaining Changes in Congressional Behavior.* Pittsburgh: University of Pittsburgh Press.

Payne, James L., and Oliver H. Woshinsky. 1972. "Incentives for Political Participation." *World Politics* 24:518–46.

Peltason, J. W. 1971. *Fifty-Eight Lonely Men: Southern Federal Judges and School Desegregation.* Urbana: University of Illinois Press.

Peretti, Terri Jennings. 1999. *In Defense of a Political Court*. Princeton, N.J.: Princeton University Press.

Perkins, Frances. 1946. *The Roosevelt I Knew*. New York: Viking Press.

Perry, Barbara A. 1999. *The Priestly Tribe: The Supreme Court's Image in the American Mind*. Westport, Conn.: Praeger.

Perry, H. W., Jr. 1991. *Deciding to Decide: Agenda Setting in the United States Supreme Court*. Cambridge, Mass.: Harvard University Press.

Phelps, Timothy M., and Helen Winternitz. 1992. *Capitol Games: Clarence Thomas, Anita Hill, and the Story of a Supreme Court Nomination*. New York: Hyperion.

Pickerill, J. Mitchell. 2004. *Constitutional Deliberation in Congress: The Impact of Judicial Review in a Separated System*. Durham, N.C.: Duke University Press.

Pinello, Daniel R. 1995. *The Impact of Judicial-Selection Methods on State-Supreme-Court Policy: Innovation, Reaction, and Atrophy*. Westport, Conn.: Greenwood Press.

Polling Company. 2002. "Shocking Poll: More Americans Can Name Rice Krispies Characters than Supreme Court Justices!" http://www.pollingcompany.com/News.asp?FormMode=ViewReleases.

Posner, Richard A. 1987. "Adoption and Market Theory: The Regulation of the Market in Adoptions." *Boston University Law Review* 67:59–72.

———. 1990. *Cardozo: A Study in Reputation*. Chicago: University of Chicago Press.

———. 1995. *Overcoming Law*. Cambridge, Mass.: Harvard University Press.

———. 1996. *The Federal Courts: Challenge and Reform*. Cambridge, Mass.: Harvard University Press.

———. 1999. *An Affair of State: The Investigation, Impeachment, and Trial of President Clinton*. Cambridge, Mass.: Harvard University Press.

———. 2001. *Breaking the Deadlock: The 2000 Election, the Constitution, and the Courts*. Princeton, N.J.: Princeton University Press.

———. 2004. *Catastrophe: Risk and Response*. New York: Oxford University Press.

Post, Robert. 2001. "The Supreme Court Opinion as Institutional Practice: Dissent, Legal Scholarship, and Decisionmaking in the Taft Court." *Minnesota Law Review* 85:1267–1390.

Powe, Lucas A. 2000. *The Warren Court and American Politics*. Cambridge, Mass.: Harvard University Press.

Preston, Julia. 2004. "U.S. Judge Apologizes for Equating Victories of Bush and Hitler." *New York Times*, June 25, B4.

Price, Vincent, and Anca Romantan. 2004. "Confidence in Institutions Before, During, and After 'Indecision 2000.' " *Journal of Politics* 66:939–56.

Pritchett, C. Herman. 1954. *Civil Liberties and the Vinson Court*. Chicago: University of Chicago Press.

———. 1961. *Congress Versus the Supreme Court*. Minneapolis: University of Minnesota Press.

Rabin, Matthew. 2002. "A Perspective on Psychology and Economics." *European Economic Review* 46:657–85.

Radelat, Ana. 2004a. "Many in State Join Federalists." *Montgomery Advertiser*, January 20.

———. 2004b. "Bush Likely to Opt for Court Nominee with Federalist Ties." *Detroit News*, March 28.

Rao, Radhika. 1998. "The Author of Roe." *Hastings Constitutional Law Quarterly* 26:21–40.

Raudenbush, Stephen W., and Anthony S. Bryk. 2002. *Hierarchical Linear Models: Applications and Data Analysis Methods*. Thousand Oaks, Calif.: Sage Publications.

Raymond, Paul, and Peter Paluch. 1994. "The American Voter in a Local, Judicial Election." Paper presented at the annual meeting of the Midwest Political Science Association, April 14–16, Chicago.

Reddick, Malia, and Sara C. Benesh. 2000. "Norm Violation by the Lower Courts in the Treatment of Supreme Court Precedent: A Research Framework." *Justice System Journal* 21:117–42.

Reed, Douglas S. 2001. *On Equal Terms: The Constitutional Politics of Educational Opportunity*. Princeton, N.J.: Princeton University Press.

Reeves, Richard. 2001. *President Nixon: Alone in the White House*. New York: Simon & Schuster.

Rehnquist, William H. 1992. *Grand Inquests: The Historic Impeachments of Justice Samuel Chase and President Andrew Johnson*. New York: William Morrow.

———. 1998. *All the Laws but One: Civil Liberties in Wartime*. New York: Alfred A. Knopf.

———. 2001. *The Supreme Court*. New York: Alfred A. Knopf.

———. 2004. *Centennial Crisis: The Disputed Election of 1876*. New York: Alfred A. Knopf.

Reidinger, Paul. 1987. "The Politics of Judging." *American Bar Association Journal* 73 (April): 52–58.

Reingold, Beth, and Heather Foust. 1998. "Exploring the Determinants of Feminist Consciousness in the United States." *Women & Politics* 19:19–48.

Renshon, Stanley A., ed. 1995. *The Clinton Presidency: Campaigning, Governing, and the Psychology of Leadership*. Boulder, Colo.: Westview Press.

Richards, Mark J., and Herbert M. Kritzer. 2002. "Jurisprudential Regimes in Supreme Court Decision Making." *American Political Science Review* 96:305–20.

Richardson, Frank K. 1983. "Law Reviews and the Courts." *Whittier Law Review* 5:385–93.

Richey, Warren. 2004. "One Justice's Vision of Role of the Courts." *Christian Science Monitor*, November 16, 1, 4.

Riesman, David. 1950. *The Lonely Crowd: A Study of the Changing American Character*. New Haven, Conn.: Yale University Press.

Ring, Kevin A., ed. 2004. *Scalia Dissents: Writings of the Supreme Court's Wittiest, Most Outspoken Justice*. Washington, D.C., Regnery Publishing.

Ringel, Jonathan. 2003. "Supreme Court Clerk Speaks His Mind." *Legal Times*, September 15, 11.

Ripple, Kenneth F. 2000. "The Role of the Law Review in the Tradition of Judicial Scholarship." *New York University Annual Survey of American Law* 57:429–44.

Roccas, Sonia, and Marilynn B. Brewer. 2002. "Social Identity Complexity." *Personality and Social Psychology Review* 6:88–106.

Roderick, Lee. 1994. *Leading the Charge: Orrin Hatch and 20 Years of America.* Carson City, Nev.: Gold Leaf Press.

Rohde, David W. 1972. "Policy Goals and Opinion Coalitions in the Supreme Court." *Midwest Journal of Political Science* 16:208–24.

Rohde, David W., and Harold J. Spaeth. 1976. *Supreme Court Decision Making.* San Francisco: W. H. Freeman.

Rosen, Jeffrey. 1996. "The Agonizer." *New Yorker,* November 11, 82–90.

———. 1997. "The New Look of Liberalism on the Court." *New York Times Magazine,* October 5, 60–65, 86, 90, 96–97.

———. 2001. "The O'Connor Court: America's Most Powerful Jurist." *New York Times Magazine,* June 3, 32, 34–37, 64, 68, 76, 79.

Rosenberg, Gerald N. 1991. *The Hollow Hope: Can Courts Bring About Social Change?* Chicago: University of Chicago Press.

———. 1992. "Judicial Independence and the Reality of Political Power." *Review of Politics* 54:369–98.

———. 2000. "Incentives, Reputation, and the Glorious Determinants of Judicial Behavior." *University of Cincinnati Law Review* 68:637–49.

Ross, William G. 1996. "The Ratings Game: Factors That Influence Judicial Reputation." *Marquette Law Review* 79:401–52.

Rothman, Stanley, and S. Robert Lichter. 1985. "Personality, Ideology and World View: A Comparison of Media and Business Elites." *British Journal of Political Science* 15:29–49.

Rowland, C. K., and Robert A. Carp. 1996. *Politics and Judgment in Federal District Courts.* Lawrence: University Press of Kansas.

Rudolph, Marshall. 1989. "Judicial Humor: A Laughing Matter?" *Hastings Law Journal* 41:175–200.

Ryan, John Paul, Allan Ashman, Bruce D. Sales, and Sandra Shane-DuBow. 1980. *American Trial Judges: Their Work Styles and Performance.* New York: Free Press.

Sala, Brian R., and James F. Spriggs II. 2004. "Designing Tests of the Supreme Court and the Separation of Powers." *Political Research Quarterly* 57: 197–208.

Salmon, Jacqueline L. 2003. "Scalia Defends Public Expression of Faith." *Washington Post,* January 13, B3.

Salokar, Rebecca Mae. 1992. *The Solicitor General: The Politics of Law.* Philadelphia: Temple University Press.

Sanders, Francine. 1995. "*Brown v. Board of Education*: An Empirical Reexamination of Its Effects on Federal District Courts." *Law & Society Review* 29:731–56.

Sapiro, Virginia, and Pamela Johnston Conover. 2001. "Gender Equality in the Public Mind." *Women & Politics* 22:1–35.

Sarat, Austin. 1977. "Judging in Trial Courts: An Exploratory Study." *Journal of Politics* 39:368–98.

Satter, Robert. 1990. *Doing Justice: A Trial Judge at Work.* New York: Simon and Schuster.

Savage, David G. 1992. *Turning Right: The Making of the Rehnquist Supreme Court*. New York: John Wiley & Sons.

Savage, David G., and Richard A. Serrano. 2004. "Scalia was Cheney Hunt Trip Guest." *Los Angeles Times*, February 5, A1, A22.

Scalia, Antonin. 1994. "The Dissenting Opinion." *Journal of Supreme Court History* 1994:33–44.

Schauer, Frederick. 1995. "Opinions as Rules." *University of Chicago Law Review* 62:1455–75.

———. 2000. "Incentives, Reputation, and the Inglorious Determinants of Judicial Behavior." *Cincinnati Law Review* 68:615–36.

Scheb, John M., II, Terry Bowen, and Gary Anderson. 1991. "Ideology, Role Orientations, and Behavior in the State Courts of Last Resort." *American Politics Quarterly* 19:324–35.

Schick, Marvin. 1970. *Learned Hand's Court*. Baltimore: Johns Hopkins Press.

Schlenker, Barry R. 1980. *Impression Management: The Self-Concept, Social Identity, and Interpersonal Relations*. Monterey, Calif.: Brooks/Cole.

Schlenker, Barry R., and Beth A. Pontari. 2000. "The Strategic Control of Information: Impression Management and Self-Presentation in Daily Life." In *Psychological Perspectives on Self and Identity*, ed. Abraham Tesser, Richard B. Felson, and Jerry M. Suls, 199–232. Washington, D.C.: American Psychological Association.

Schlenker, Barry R., and Michael F. Weigold. 1992. "Interpersonal Processes Involving Impression Regulation and Management." *Annual Review of Psychology* 43:133–68.

Schmidhauser, John R. 1959. "The Justices of the Supreme Court: A Collective Portrait." *Midwest Journal of Political Science* 3:1–57.

———. 1979. *Judges and Justices: The Federal Appellate Judiciary*. Boston: Little, Brown.

Schmidhauser, John R., and Larry L. Berg. 1972. *The Supreme Court and Congress: Conflict and Interaction, 1945–1968*. New York: Free Press.

Schorr, Daniel. 1984. "A Justice Speaks Out: A Conversation with Harry A. Blackmun." In *American Government: Readings and Cases*, ed. Peter Woll, 569–83. Boston: Little, Brown.

Schotland, Roy. 1998. "Judicial Campaign Finance Could Work." *National Law Journal*, November 23, A21.

Schubert, Glendon. 1963. "Judicial Attitudes and Voting Behavior: The 1961 Term of the United States Supreme Court." *Law and Contemporary Problems* 28:100–42.

———. 1965. *The Judicial Mind: Attitudes and Ideologies of Supreme Court Justices, 1946–1963*. Evanston, Ill.: Northwestern University Press.

Schuessler, Alexander A. 2000. *A Logic of Expressive Choice*. Princeton, N.J.: Princeton University Press.

Schuman, Howard, Charlotte Steeh, and Lawrence Bobo. 1985. *Racial Attitudes in America: Trends and Interpretations*. Cambridge, Mass.: Harvard University Press.

Schwartz, Bernard. 1983. *Super Chief: Earl Warren and His Supreme Court—A Judicial Biography*. New York: New York University Press.

Schwartz, Bernard. 1998. *The Burger Court: Counter-Revolution or Confirmation?* New York: Oxford University Press.

Schwartz, Edward P., Pablo T. Spiller, and Santiago Urbiztondo. 1994. "A Positive Theory of Legislative Intent." *Law & Contemporary Problems* 57 (Winter–Spring):51–74.

Scigliano, Robert. 1971. *The Supreme Court and the Presidency.* New York: Free Press.

Scott, Kevin Matthew. 2002. "Double Agents: An Exploration of the Motivations of Court of Appeals Judges." Ph.D. dissertation, Ohio State University.

———. 2004. "Time for a Divorce? Splitting the Ninth Circuit Court of Appeals." Paper presented at the annual meeting of the Midwest Political Science Association, April 15–18, Chicago.

Sears, David O., and Harris M. Allen, Jr. 1984. "The Trajectory of Local Desegregation Controversies and Whites' Opposition to Busing." In *Groups in Contact: The Psychology of Desegregation*, ed. Norman Miller and Marillyn B. Brewer, 123–51. Orlando, Fla.: Academic Press.

Sears, David O., Carl P. Hensler, and Leslie K. Speer. 1979. "Whites' Opposition to 'Busing': Self-Interest or Symbolic Politics?" *American Political Science Review* 73:369–84.

Sears, David O., Leonie Huddy, and Robert Jervis, eds. 2003. *Oxford Handbook of Political Psychology.* New York: Oxford University Press.

Segal, Jeffrey A. 1986. "Supreme Court Justices as Human Decision Makers: An Individual-Level Analysis of the Search and Seizure Cases." *Journal of Politics* 48:938–55.

———. 1990. "Supreme Court Support for the Solicitor General: The Effect of Presidential Appointments." *Western Political Quarterly* 43:137–52.

———. 1991. "Courts, Executives, and Legislatures." In *The American Courts: A Critical Assessment*, ed. John B. Gates and Charles A. Johnson, 373–393. Washington, D.C.: CQ Press.

———. 1997. "Separation-of-Powers Games in the Positive Theory of Law and Courts." *American Political Science Review* 91:28–44.

Segal, Jeffrey A., and Albert Cover. 1989. "Ideological Values and the Votes of U.S. Supreme Court Justices." *American Political Science Review* 83:557–65.

Segal, Jeffrey A., Lee Epstein, Charles M. Cameron, and Harold J. Spaeth. 1995. "Ideological Values and the Votes of U.S. Supreme Court Justices Revisited." *Journal of Politics* 57:812–23.

Segal, Jeffrey A., and Harold J. Spaeth. 1993. *The Supreme Court and the Attitudinal Model.* New York: Cambridge University Press.

———. 2002. *The Supreme Court and the Attitudinal Model Revisited.* New York: Cambridge University Press.

Serrano, Richard A., and David G. Savage. 2004. "Ginsburg Has Ties to Activist Group." *Los Angeles Times*, March 11, A1.

Seymour, Liz. 1999. "Good Deed Gets Va. Teen Suspended Over Knife." *Washington Post*, December 8, B1.

Shapiro, Martin. 1970. "Decentralized Decision Making in the Law of Torts." In *Political Decision-Making*, ed. S. Sidney Ulmer, 44–75. New York: Van Nostrand.

———. 1978. "The Supreme Court: From Warren to Burger." In *The New American Political System*, ed. Anthony King, 179–211. Washington, D.C.: American Enterprise Institute.

Shatzkin, Kate. 1997. "Judge Takes His Case to Court of Talk Radio." *Baltimore Sun*, March 12, 1A.

Shestack, Jerome J. 2002. "The Rehnquist Court and the Legal Profession." In *The Rehnquist Court: A Retrospective*, ed. Martin H. Belsky, 167–94. New York: Oxford University Press.

Sickels, Robert J. 1965. "The Illusion of Judicial Consensus: Zoning Decisions in the Maryland Court of Appeals." *American Political Science Review* 59: 100–104.

Sigelman, Lee. 1982. "The Presidential Horoscope: Predicting Performance in the White House." *Presidential Studies Quarterly* 12:434–39.

Silber, Norman I. 2004. *With All Deliberate Speed: The Life of Philip Elman*. Ann Arbor: University of Michigan Press.

Silverstein, Mark. 2003. "Conclusion: Politics and the Rehnquist Court." In *Rehnquist Justice: Understanding the Court Dynamic*, ed. Earl M. Maltz, 277–91. Lawrence: University Press of Kansas.

Simon, James F. 1980. *Independent Journey: The Life of William O. Douglas*. New York: Harper & Row.

———. 1989. *The Antagonists: Hugo Black, Felix Frankfurter and Civil Liberties in Modern America*. New York: Simon & Schuster.

———. 1995. *The Center Holds: The Power Struggle Inside the Rehnquist Court*. New York: Simon & Schuster.

Singer, Eleanor. 1981. "Reference Groups and Social Evaluations." In *Social Psychology: Sociological Perspectives*, ed. Morris Rosenberg and Ralph H. Turner, 66–93. New York: Basic Books.

Sirica, John J. 1979. *To Set the Record Straight: The Break-In, the Tapes, the Conspirators, the Pardon*. New York: Norton.

Sisk, Gregory C., Michael Heise, and Andrew P. Morriss. 1998. "Charting the Influences on the Judicial Mind: An Empirical Study of Judicial Reasoning." *New York University Law Review* 73:1377–1500.

Slaughter, Anne-Marie. 2004. *A New World Order*. Princeton, N.J.: Princeton University Press.

Slind-Flor, Victoria. 1998. "Justices Feud in Wash. State." *National Law Journal*, June 15, A1, A19.

Slovak, Jeffrey S. 1979. "Working for Corporate Actors: Social Change and Elite Attorneys in Chicago." *American Bar Foundation Research Journal* 1979:465–500.

Smith, Adam. 1759/2000. *The Theory of Moral Sentiments*. Amherst, N.Y.: Prometheus Books.

Smith, Alexander B., and Abraham S. Blumberg. 1967. "The Problem of Objectivity in Judicial Decision-Making." *Social Forces* 46:96–105.

Smith, Christopher E., and Joyce A. Baugh. 2000. *The Real Clarence Thomas: Confirmation Veracity Meets Performance Reality*. New York: Peter Lang.

Smith, Rogers M. 1988. "Political Jurisprudence, the 'New Institutionalism,' and the Future of Public Law." *American Political Science Review* 82:89–108.

Smith, Rogers M. 1994. "Symposium: The Supreme Court and the Attitudinal Model." *Law and Courts* 4 (Spring): 8–9.

Snyder, Eloise C. 1958. "The Supreme Court as a Small Group." *Social Forces* 36:232–38.

Snyder, Mark. 1987. *Public Appearances, Private Realities: The Psychology of Self-Monitoring.* New York: W. H. Freeman.

Solimine, Michael E., and James L. Walker. 1992. "The Next Word: Congressional Response to Supreme Court Statutory Decisions." *Temple Law Review* 65:425–58.

Solomon, John. 2004. "FBI Interviews Terror Trial Judge." *The State* (Columbia, S.C.), July 3 (Internet edition, at www.thestate.com).

Songer, Donald R. 1987. "The Impact of the Supreme Court on Trends in Economic Policy Making in the United States Courts of Appeals." *Journal of Politics* 49:830–41.

———. 1990. "Criteria for Publication of Opinions in the U.S. Courts of Appeals: Formal Rules Versus Empirical Reality." *Judicature* 73:307–13.

Songer, Donald R., and Stefanie A. Lindquist. 1996. "Not the Whole Story: The Impact of Justices' Values on Supreme Court Decision Making." *American Journal of Political Science* 40:1049–63.

Songer, Donald R., Jeffrey A. Segal, and Charles M. Cameron. 1994. "The Hierarchy of Justice: Testing a Principal-Agent Model of Supreme Court–Circuit Court Interactions." *American Journal of Political Science* 38:673–96.

Songer, Donald R., and Reginald S. Sheehan. 1990. "Supreme Court Impact on Compliance and Outcomes: *Miranda* and *New York Times* in the United States Courts of Appeals." *Western Political Quarterly* 43:297–316.

Sowell, Thomas. 1994. "Blackmun Plays to the Crowd." *St. Louis Post-Dispatch*, March 4, 7B.

———. 2003. "Justice Kennedy Goes Soft on Crime." *Columbus Dispatch*, August 13, A11.

Spaeth, Harold J. 1964. "The Judicial Restraint of Mr. Justice Frankfurter: Myth or Reality?" *Midwest Journal of Political Science* 8:22–38.

———. 1979. *Supreme Court Policy Making: Explanation and Prediction.* San Francisco: W. H. Freeman.

Spaeth, Harold J., and Michael F. Altfeld. 1985. "Influence Relationships Within the Supreme Court: A Comparison of the Warren and Burger Courts." *Western Political Quarterly* 38:70–83.

Spaeth, Harold J., and Douglas R. Parker. 1969. "Effects of Attitude Toward Situation Upon Attitude Toward Object." *Journal of Psychology* 73:173–82.

Spaeth, Harold J., and Jeffrey A. Segal. 1999. *Majority Rule or Minority Will: Adherence to Precedent on the U.S. Supreme Court.* New York: Cambridge University Press.

Spiller, Pablo T., and Rafael Gely. 1992. "Congressional Control or Judicial Independence: The Determinants of U.S. Supreme Court Labor-Relations Decisions, 1949–1988." *RAND Journal of Economics* 23:463–92.

Spiller, Pablo T., and Matthew L. Spitzer. 1995. "Where is the Sin in Sincere? Sophisticated Manipulation of Sincere Judicial Voters (With Application to Other Environments)." *Journal of Law, Economics, and Organization* 11:32–63.

Spiller, Pablo T., and Emerson H. Tiller. 1996. "Invitations to Override: Congressional Reversals of Supreme Court Decisions." *International Review of Law and Economics* 16:503–21.

Spriggs, James F., II, and Paul J. Wahlbeck. 1997. "Amicus Curiae and the Role of Information at the Supreme Court." *Political Research Quarterly* 50:365–86.

Stanga, John Ellis, Jr. 1971. "The Press and the Criminal Defendant: Newsmen and Criminal Justice in Three Wisconsin Cities." Ph.D. dissertation, University of Wisconsin, Madison.

Stephenson, Donald Grier, Jr. 1999. *Campaigns and the Court: The U.S. Supreme Court in Presidential Elections.* New York: Columbia University Press.

Stets, Jan E., and Peter J. Burke. 2003. "A Sociological Approach to Self and Identity." In *Handbook of Self and Identity,* ed. Mark R. Leary and June Price Tangney, 128–52. New York: Guilford Press.

Stimson, James A. 1992. *Public Opinion in America: Moods, Cycles, and Swings.* Boulder: Westview Press.

Stimson, James A., Michael B. MacKuen, and Robert S. Erikson. 1995. "Dynamic Representation." *American Political Science Review* 89:543–65.

Stinchcombe, Arthur L. 1990. "Reason and Rationality." In *The Limits of Rationality,* ed. Karen Schweers Cook and Margaret Levi, 285–317. Chicago: University of Chicago Press.

Stout, Lynn A. 2002. "Judges as Altruistic Hierarchs." *William & Mary Law Review* 43:1605–27.

Stow, Mary Lou, and Harold J. Spaeth. 1992. "Centralized Research Staff: Is There a Monster in the Judicial Closet?" *Judicature* 75:216–21.

Swenson, Karen. 2004. "Federal District Court Judges and the Decision to Publish." *Justice System Journal* 25:121–42.

Sylvan, Donald A. 2004. "Measuring Identity in the Study of Israeli-Palestinian Relations." Paper presented at the Harvard Identity Conference, Cambridge, Mass., December 9–11.

Sylvan, Donald A., and James F. Voss, eds. 1998. *Problem Representation in Foreign Policy Decision Making.* New York: Cambridge University Press.

"Symposium on Social Identity." 2001. *Political Psychology* 22:111–98.

Tabarrok, Alexander, and Eric Helland. 1999. "Court Politics: The Political Economy of Tort Awards." *Journal of Law and Economics* 42:157–88.

Taha, Ahmed E. 2004. "Publish or Paris? Evidence of How Judges Allocate Their Time." *American Law and Economics Review* 6:1–27.

Tajfel, Henri. 1978. *Differentiation Between Social Groups: Studies in the Social Psychology of Intergroup Relations.* London: Academic Press.

Talbot, Margaret. 2005. "Supreme Confidence: The Jurisprudence of Justice Antonin Scalia." *New Yorker,* March 28, 41–55.

Tarr, G. Alan. 1977. *Judicial Impact and State Supreme Courts.* Lexington, Mass.: D. C. Heath.

Tate, C. Neal. 1981. "Personal Attribute Models of the Voting Behavior of U.S. Supreme Court Justices: Liberalism in Civil Liberties and Economic Decisions, 1946–1978." *American Political Science Review* 75:355–67.

Taylor, Guy, and Marion Baillot. 2004. "Breyer: Caseload Puts Premium on International Law." *Washington Times*, November 14, A7.

Taylor, Michael. 1995. "Battering RAMs." *Critical Review* 9:223–34.

Taylor, Stuart, Jr. 1986. "The Morning Line on the Bench, as Revised." *New York Times*, September 25, B10.

———. 2003. "Leftward Ho! Cry the Justices." *Legal Times*, July 7, 46.

Terry, Deborah J., Michael A. Hogg, and Julie M. Duck. 1999. "Group Membership, Social Identity, and Attitudes." In *Social Identity and Social Cognition*, ed. Dominic Abrams and Michael A. Hogg, 280–314. Oxford: Blackwell Publishers.

Tetlock, Philip E., and A. S. R. Manstead. 1985. "Impression Management Versus Intrapsychic Explanations in Social Psychology: A Useful Dichotomy?" *Psychological Review* 92:59–77.

Texans for Public Justice. 2001. *How Big Money Buys Access to the Texas Supreme Court*. Austin: Texans for Public Justice.

Thaler, Richard H. 1988. "Anomalies: The Ultimatum Game." *Journal of Economic Perspectives* 4:195–206.

———. 1991. *Quasi Rational Economics*. New York: Russell Sage.

———. 1992. *The Winner's Curse: Paradoxes and Anomalies of Economic Life*. New York: Free Press.

———. 1996. "Doing Economics Without *Homo Economicus*." In *Foundations of Research in Economics: How Do Economists Do Economics?* ed. Steven G. Medema and Warren J. Samuels, 227–37. Cheltenham, U.K.: Edward Elgar.

———. 2000. "From Homo Economicus to Homo Sapiens." *Journal of Economic Perspectives* 14:133–41.

Thomas, Andrew Peyton. 2001. *Clarence Thomas: A Biography*. San Francisco: Encounter Books.

Thomas, Clarence. 1999. "On Judicial Independence." Federalist Society, www.fed-soc.org/Publications/Transcripts/justicethomas.htm.

———. 1999–2000. "A Tribute to Justice Clarence Thomas: Personal Responsibility." *Regent University Law Review* 12:317–27.

———. 2001. "Be Not Afraid." American Enterprise Institute, http://www.aei.org/publications/pubID.15211.filter.all/pub_detail.asp.

Thomas, Evan, and Michael Isikoff. 2000–2001. "The Truth Behind the Pillars." *Newsweek*, December 25–January 1, 46–51.

Thomas, Virginia Lamp. 1991. "Breaking Silence." *People*, November 11, 108–16.

Tice, Dianne M., and Harry M. Wallace. 2003. "The Reflected Self: Creating Yourself as (You Think) Others See You." In *Handbook of Self and Identity*, ed. Mark R. Leary and June Price Tangney, 91–105. New York: Guilford Press.

Toma, Eugenia F. 1996. "A Contractual Model of the Voting Behavior of the Supreme Court: The Role of the Chief Justice." *International Review of Law and Economics* 16:433–47.

Toobin, Jeffrey. 1993. "The Burden of Clarence Thomas." *New Yorker*, September 27, 38–51.

———. 2000. "The Judge Hunter." *New Yorker*, June 12, 49–54.

Triandis, Harry C. 1989. "The Self and Social Behavior in Differing Cultural Contexts." *Psychological Bulletin* 96:506–20.

Trice, Harrison Miller. 1993. *Occupational Subcultures in the Workplace*. Ithaca, N.Y.: ILR Press.

Trillin, Calvin. 1977. "Remembrance of Moderates Past." *New Yorker*, March 21, 85–97.

Turley, Jonathan. 2004. "Stop Doubting Thomas." *Los Angeles Times*, December 27, B9.

Turner, John C. 1982. "Toward a Cognitive Redefinition of the Social Group." In *Social Identity and Intergroup Relations*, ed. Henri Tajfel, 17–40. Cambridge: Cambridge University Press.

Tushnet, Mark. 1994. "Style and the Supreme Court's Educational Role in Government." *Constitutional Commentary* 11:215–25.

———. 2005. *A Court Divided: The Rehnquist Court and the Future of Constitutional Law*. New York: W. W. Norton.

Ulmer, S. Sidney. 1971. *Courts as Small and Not So Small Groups*. New York: General Learning Press.

———. 1973. "The Longitudinal Behavior of Hugo Lafayette Black: Parabolic Support for Civil Liberties, 1937–1971." *Florida State University Law Review* 1:131–53.

———. 1986. "Are Social Background Models Time-Bound?" *American Political Science Review* 80:957–67.

Uslaner, Eric M. 1993. *The Decline of Comity in Congress*. Ann Arbor: University of Michigan Press.

Van Maanen, John, and Stephen R. Barley. 1984. "Occupational Communities: Culture and Control in Organizations." *Research in Organizational Behavior* 6:287–365.

Verba, Sidney, Kay Lehman Schlozman, and Henry E. Brady. 1995. *Voice and Equality: Civic Voluntarism in American Politics*. Cambridge, Mass.: Harvard University Press.

Vines, Kenneth N. 1964. "Federal District Judges and Race Relations Cases in the South." *Journal of Politics* 26:337–57.

Wagner, David M. 2005. "Beyond 'Strange New Respect': The Stevens-Ginsburg Billet-Doux to Justice Kennedy." *Weekly Standard*, March 14.

Wahlbeck, Paul J., James F. Spriggs II, and Lee Sigelman. 2002. "Ghostwriters on the Court? A Stylistic Analysis of U.S. Supreme Court Opinion Drafts." *American Politics Research* 30:166–92.

Wald, Patricia M. 1984. "Thoughts on Decisionmaking." *West Virginia Law Review* 87:1–12.

———. 1995. "The Rhetoric of Results and the Results of Rhetoric: Judicial Writings." *University of Chicago Law Review* 62:1371–1419.

Walker, Thomas G. 1976. "Leader Selection and Behavior in Small Political Groups." *Small Group Behavior* 7:363–68.

Walker, Thomas G., and Eleanor C. Main. 1973. "Choice Shifts in Political Decisionmaking: Federal Judges and Civil Liberties Cases." *Journal of Applied Social Psychology* 3:39–48.

Wall Street Journal. 1968. "Justice Stewart Dissents." July 3, 6.

———. 2004. "Recuse to Lose" (editorial). March 9, A16.

Walsh, Katherine Cramer. 2004. *Talking About Politics: Informal Groups and Social Identity in American Life*. Chicago: University of Chicago Press.

Walsh, Laurence E. 1998. "The Future of the Independent Counsel Law." *Wisconsin Law Review* 1998:1379–94.

Waltenburg, Eric, and Charles Lopeman. 2000. "Tort Decisions and Campaign Dollars." *Southeastern Political Review* 28:241–63.

Ware, Stephen J. 1999. "Money, Politics and Judicial Decisions: A Case Study of Arbitration Law in Alabama." *Journal of Law & Politics* 15:645–86.

Wasby, Stephen L. 1988. "Justice Harry Blackmun in the Burger Court." *Hamline Law Review* 11:183–245.

Wasby, Stephen L., ed. 1990. *"He Shall Not Pass This Way Again": The Legacy of Justice William O. Douglas*. Pittsburgh: University of Pittsburgh Press.

Washington Post. 1982. "Personalities." June 11, D2.

——. 1999. "Justice Harry Blackmun" (editorial). March 6, A20.

Weary, Gifford, and Robert M. Arkin. 1981. "Attributional Self-Presentation." In *New Directions in Attribution Research*, ed. John H. Harvey, William John Ickes, and Robert F. Kidd, vol. 3, 223–46. Hillsdale, N.J.: Lawrence Erlbaum Associates.

Weaver, David H., and G. Cleveland Wilhoit. 1991. *The American Journalist: A Portrait of U.S. News People and Their Work*. Bloomington: Indiana University Press.

Weisberg, Herbert F., and Samuel C. Patterson, eds. 1998. *Great Theatre: The American Congress in the 1990s*. New York: Cambridge University Press.

Welsh-Huggins, Andrew. 2005. "Justices Wrote Victims' Families to Explain Ruling." *Columbus Dispatch*, April 12, B3.

Western, Bruce. 1998. "Causal Heterogeneity in Comparative Research: A Bayesian Hierarchical Modelling Approach." *Journal of Politics* 42:1233–59.

Westin, Alan F. 1962. "Out-of-Court Commentary by United States Supreme Court Justices, 1790–1962: Of Free Speech and Judicial Lockjaw." *Columbia Law Review* 62:633–69.

White, G. Edward. 2004. "Justices and 'Electoral College' Elections." *Green Bag* 7:387–96.

White, Theodore H. 1975. *Breach of Faith: The Fall of Richard Nixon*. New York: Atheneum.

Whittington, Keith E. 2000. "Once More Unto the Breach: Post-Behavioralist Approaches to Judicial Politics." *Law & Social Inquiry* 25:601–34.

Wilcox, Clyde. 1989. "As Astrological Realignment?" *Journal of Irreproducible Results* 35:12–13.

Wilkerson, John D. 1990. "Reelection and Representation in Conflict: The Case of Agenda Manipulation." *Legislative Studies Quarterly* 15:263–82.

Williams, Armstrong. 1995. "Two Wrongs Don't Make a Right for Thomas." *Charleston Post and Courier*, August 17, A13.

Williams, Juan. 1998. *Thurgood Marshall: American Revolutionary*. New York: Times Books.

Williams, Kipling. 2001. *Ostracism: The Power of Silence*. New York: Guilford Press.

Winter, David G. 1987. "Leader Appeal, Leader Performance, and the Motive Profiles of Leaders and Followers: A Study of American Presidents and Elections." *Journal of Personality and Social Psychology* 52:196–202.

Winter, Ralph K. 1992. "Coexistence and Co-Dependence: Conservatism and Civil Liberties." *Harvard Journal of Law & Public Policy* 15:1–4.

Wise, Daniel. 2003. "Justices Launch New Campaign to Boost Image." *New York Law Journal*, April 4, 1.

Wittes, Benjamin. 2004. "An Election Won by No One." *Washington Post*, April 14, C1.

Wohl, Alexander. 2003. "Liberalizing the Law." *The Nation*, June 16, 6.

Wold, John T. 1978. "Going Through the Motions: The Monotony of Appellate Court Decisionmaking." *Judicature* 62:58–65.

Wolf, Robert Victor. 2001. "New Strategies for an Old Profession: A Court and a Community Combat a Streetwalking Epidemic." *Justice System Journal* 22:347–59.

Woodward, Bob, and Scott Armstrong. 1979. *The Brethren: Inside the Supreme Court*. New York: Simon and Schuster.

Wright, John R. 1996. *Interest Groups and Congress: Lobbying, Contributions, and Influence*. Boston: Allyn and Bacon.

Wrightsman, Lawrence S. 1999. *Judicial Decision Making: Is Psychology Relevant?* New York: Kluwer Academic.

Yarbrough, Tinsley E. 1981. *Judge Frank Johnson and Human Rights in Alabama*. University: University of Alabama Press.

———. 1987. *A Passion for Justice: J. Waties Waring and Civil Rights*. New York: Oxford University Press.

Yates, Jeff. 2002. *Popular Justice: Presidential Prestige and Executive Success in the Supreme Court*. Albany: State University of New York Press.

Yngvesson, Barbara, and Lynn Mather. 1983. "Courts, Moots, and the Disputing Process." In *Empirical Theories About Courts*, ed. Keith O. Boyum and Lynn Mather, 51–83. New York: Longman.

Young, James Sterling. 1966. *The Washington Community, 1800–1828*. New York: Columbia University Press.

COURT DECISIONS

Adams v. Clinton. 2000. 90 F. Supp. 2d 35. (D.D.C.).

Atkins v. Virginia. 2002. 536 U.S. 304.

Bradshaw v. Unity Marine Corporation, Inc. 2001. 147 F. Supp. 2d 668 (S.D. Texas).

Briggs v. Elliott. 1951. 98 F. Supp. 529 (D.S.C.).

Brown v. Board of Education. 1954. 347 U.S. 483.

Bush v. Gore. 2000. 531 U.S. 98.

Calderon v. Thompson. 1998. 523 U.S. 538.

Callins v. Collins. 1994. 510 U.S. 1141.

Cheney v. United States District Court. 2004a. Motion to Recuse (received February 23).

Cheney v. United States District Court. 2004b. 541 U.S. 913 (Memorandum of Justice Scalia).

Cheney v. United States District Court. 2004c. 542 U.S. 367.

Clinton v. Jones. 1997. 520 U.S. 681.

Department of Commerce v. U.S. House of Representatives. 1999. 525 U.S. 316.

Elk Grove Unified School District v. Newdow. 2004. 542 U.S. 1.

Elmore v. Rice. 1947. 72 F. Supp. 516 (D.S.C.).

Escola v. Coca Cola Bottling Company. 1944. 150 P.2d 436 (Calif.).

Ex parte McCardle. 1869. 7 Wallace 506.

Faragher v. City of Boca Raton. 1998. 524 U.S. 775.

Fitzpatrick v. Cucinotta. 1999. 726 A.2d 1147 (R.I.).

Flowers v. Carville. 2002. 310 F.3d 1118 (9th Cir.).

Gannett v. De Pasquale. 1979. 443 U.S. 368.

Gebser v. Lago Vista Independent School District. 1998. 524 U.S. 274.

Gibbs v. Babbitt. 2000. 214 F.3d 483 (4th Cir.).

Greenman v. Yuba Power Products, Inc. 1963. 377 P.2d 897 (Calif.).

Grutter v. Bollinger. 2002. 288 F.3d 732 (6th Cir.).

Grutter v. Bollinger. 2003. 539 U.S. 306.

Hamdi v. Rumsfeld. 2004. 542 U.S. 507.

Harding v. City of Philadelphia. 2001. 777 A.2d 1249 (Pa. Comm. Ct.).

Hoyt v. Florida. 1961. 368 U.S. 57.

Hudson v. McMillian. 1992. 503 U.S. 1.

Humphries v. Ozmint. 2005. 397 F.3d 206 (4th Cir.).

In re Blodgett. 1992. 502 U.S. 236.

In re Byrd. 2001. 269 F.3d 544 (6th Cir.).

In re Charges of Judicial Misconduct. 2005. Unpublished. (Judicial Council of the Second Circuit, U.S. Courts.)

In re Williams. 2004. 359 F.3d 811 (6th Cir.).

In the Matter of Roy S. Moore. 2003. Unpublished. (Alabama Ct. of the Judiciary.)

Kremen v. Cohen. 2003. 325 F.3d 1035 (9th Cir.).

Lawrence v. Texas. 2003. 539 U.S. 558.

Lofton v. Secretary of the Department of Children and Family Services. 2004. 377 F.3d 1275 (11th Cir.).

MacPherson v. Buick Motor Co. 1916. 111 N.E. 1050 (N.Y.).

Marks v. United States. 1977. 430 U.S. 188.

Mattel, Inc. v. MCA Records, Inc. 2002. 296 F.3d 894 (9th Cir.).

Milliken v. Bradley. 1974. 418 U.S. 717.

Moldea v. New York Times Company. 1994. 22 F.3d 310 (D.C. Cir.).

Newdow v. United States Congress. 2002. 292 F.3d 597 (9th Cir.).

Nguyen v. Immigration and Naturalization Service. 2001. 533 U.S. 53.

Office of the President v. Office of Independent Counsel. 1998. 525 U.S. 996.

Oregon v. Mitchell. 1970. 400 U.S. 112.

Pasadena City Board of Education v. Spangler. 1976. 427 U.S. 424.

Payne v. Tennessee. 1991. 510 U.S. 808.

People ex rel. Salazar v. Davidson. 2003. 79 P.3d 1221 (Colo.).

Planned Parenthood v. Casey. 1992. 505 U.S. 833.

Rasul v. Bush. 2004. 542 U.S. 466.

Ratner v. Loudoun County Public Schools. 2001. 16 Fed. Appx. 140 (4th Cir.).

Regents of the University of California v. Bakke. 1978. 438 U.S. 265.

Republic of Bolivia v. Philip Morris Companies, Inc. 1996. 943 F. Supp. 782 (S.D. Texas).

Richmond Newspapers, Inc. v. Virginia. 1980. 448 U.S. 555.

Robles v. Prince George's County. 2002. 308 F.3d 437 (4th Cir.).

Roe v. Wade. 1973. 410 U.S. 113.

Romer v. Evans. 1996. 517 U.S. 620.

Roper v. Simmons. 2005. 161 L.Ed. 2d 1.

Rosenberg v. United States. 1953. 346 U.S. 273.

Rubin v. United States. 1998. 525 U.S. 990.

Schiavo ex rel. Schindler v. Schiavo. 2005. 403 F.3d 1223 (11th Cir.).

Shaw v. Terhune. 2003. 353 F.3d 697 (9th Cir.).

Smith v. Colonial Penn Insurance Company. 1996. 943 F. Supp. 782 (S.D. Texas).

Southwest Voter Registration Education Project v. Shelley. 2003. 344 F.3d 882, 344 F.3d 914 (9th Cir.).

State ex rel. Schwaben v. School Employees Retirement System. 1996. 667 N.E.2d 398 (Ohio).

State v. Thorp. 2000. 2 P.3d 903 (Oreg. C.A.).

State v. Yarbrough. 2004. 817 N.E.2d 845 (Ohio).

Stephenson v. Bartlett. 2003. 582 S.E.2d 247 (N.C.).

Texas v. Johnson. 1989. 491 U.S. 397.

United States v. Eichman. 1990. 496 U.S. 310.

United States v. Hussein. 2003. 351 F.3d 9 (1st Cir.).

United States v. Jackson. 2004. 390 F.3d 393 (5th Cir.).

United States v. Microsoft Corporation. 1999. 165 F.3d 952 (D.C. Cir.).

United States v. Microsoft Corporation. 2001. 253 F.2d 34 (D.C. Cir.).

United States v. Nixon. 1974. 418 U.S. 683.

United States v. Nofziger. 1989. 878 F.2d 442 (D.C. Cir.).

United States v. North. 1990. 910 F.2d 843 (D.C. Cir.).

United States v. Virginia. 1996. 518 U.S. 515.

Urofsky v. Gilmore. 2000. 216 F.3d 401 (4th Cir.).

Wallace v. Castro. 2003. 65 Fed. Appx. 618 (9th Cir.).

Webster v. Reproductive Health Services. 1989. 492 U.S. 490.

West Virginia Board of Education v. Barnette. 1943. 319 U.S. 624.

Yellow Cab Company of Sacramento v. Yellow Cab of Elk Grove. 2005. 419 F.3d 925 (9th Cir.).

NAME INDEX

SUBJECT AND CASE INDEX